EDUCATION FOR LIFE AND WORK

Developing Transferable Knowledge and Skills in the 21st Century

D0036604

Committee on Defining Deeper Learning and 21st Century Skills

James W. Pellegrino and Margaret L. Hilton, *Editors*

Board on Testing and Assessment
and
Board on Science Education

Division of Behavioral and Social Sciences and Education

NATIONAL RESEARCH COUNCIL
OF THE NATIONAL ACADEMIES

THE NATIONAL ACADEMIES PRESS
Washington, D.C.
www.nap.edu

THE NATIONAL ACADEMIES PRESS   500 Fifth Street, NW   Washington, DC 20001

NOTICE: The project that is the subject of this report was approved by the Governing Board of the National Research Council, whose members are drawn from the councils of the National Academy of Sciences, the National Academy of Engineering, and the Institute of Medicine. The members of the committee responsible for the report were chosen for their special competences and with regard for appropriate balance.

This study was supported by the Carnegie Corporation of New York under Contract No. B8767, the William and Flora Hewlett Foundation under Contract No. 2009-5117, the John D. and Catherine T. MacArthur Foundation under Contract No. 10-97354-000-HCD, the National Science Foundation under Contract No. DRL-0956223, the Nellie Mae Education Foundation, the Pearson Foundation, the Raikes Foundation, the Susan Crown Exchange Fund, and the Stupski Foundation. Any opinions, findings, conclusions, or recommendations expressed in this publication are those of the authors and do not necessarily reflect the views of the organizations or agencies that provided support for the project.

International Standard Book Number-13:   978-0-309-25649-0
International Standard Book Number-10:   0-309-25649-6

Library of Congress Cataloging-in-Publication data are available from the Library of Congress.

Additional copies of this report are available from the National Academies Press, 500 Fifth Street, NW, Keck 360, Washington, DC 20001; (800) 624-6242 or (202) 334-3313; http://www.nap.edu.

Suggested citation: National Research Council. (2012). *Education for Life and Work: Developing Transferable Knowledge and Skills in the 21st Century.* Committee on Defining Deeper Learning and 21st Century Skills, J.W. Pellegrino and M.L. Hilton, Editors. Board on Testing and Assessment and Board on Science Education, Division of Behavioral and Social Sciences and Education. Washington, DC: The National Academies Press.

THE NATIONAL ACADEMIES
Advisers to the Nation on Science, Engineering, and Medicine

The **National Academy of Sciences** is a private, nonprofit, self-perpetuating society of distinguished scholars engaged in scientific and engineering research, dedicated to the furtherance of science and technology and to their use for the general welfare. Upon the authority of the charter granted to it by the Congress in 1863, the Academy has a mandate that requires it to advise the federal government on scientific and technical matters. Dr. Ralph J. Cicerone is president of the National Academy of Sciences.

The **National Academy of Engineering** was established in 1964, under the charter of the National Academy of Sciences, as a parallel organization of outstanding engineers. It is autonomous in its administration and in the selection of its members, sharing with the National Academy of Sciences the responsibility for advising the federal government. The National Academy of Engineering also sponsors engineering programs aimed at meeting national needs, encourages education and research, and recognizes the superior achievements of engineers. Dr. Charles M. Vest is president of the National Academy of Engineering.

The **Institute of Medicine** was established in 1970 by the National Academy of Sciences to secure the services of eminent members of appropriate professions in the examination of policy matters pertaining to the health of the public. The Institute acts under the responsibility given to the National Academy of Sciences by its congressional charter to be an adviser to the federal government and, upon its own initiative, to identify issues of medical care, research, and education. Dr. Harvey V. Fineberg is president of the Institute of Medicine.

The **National Research Council** was organized by the National Academy of Sciences in 1916 to associate the broad community of science and technology with the Academy's purposes of furthering knowledge and advising the federal government. Functioning in accordance with general policies determined by the Academy, the Council has become the principal operating agency of both the National Academy of Sciences and the National Academy of Engineering in providing services to the government, the public, and the scientific and engineering communities. The Council is administered jointly by both Academies and the Institute of Medicine. Dr. Ralph J. Cicerone and Dr. Charles M. Vest are chair and vice chair, respectively, of the National Research Council.

www.national-academies.org

Acknowledgments

The committee and staff thank the many individuals and organizations who assisted us in our work and without whom this study could not have been completed. First we acknowledge the generous support of the Carnegie Corporation of New York, the William and Flora Hewlett Foundation, the John D. and Catherine T. MacArthur Foundation, the National Science Foundation, the Nellie Mae Education Foundation, the Pearson Foundation, the Raikes Foundation, the Susan Crown Exchange Fund, and the Stupski Foundation. We are particularly grateful to Barbara Chow, program director for education, and Kristi Kimball, former program officer, at the William and Flora Hewlett Foundation, who identified the need for a consensus study of deeper learning and 21st century skills and conveyed the importance of the study to other sponsors. We also thank Bruce Fuchs, director of the Office of Science Education at the National Institutes of Health, who initiated and supported a series of previous National Research Council (NRC) workshops on 21st century skills. These previous activities provided an important starting point for this study, illuminating key strands of relevant research.

Thanks are also due to Susan Bales and Nat Kendall-Taylor of the FrameWorks Institute. The guidance they provided in written memos, presentations, and informal conversations helped to frame and communicate the messages contained in this report.

Many individuals at the NRC assisted the committee. Board on Testing and Assessment director Stuart Elliott played a critical role throughout the project, from conceptualizing the study scope to participating in committee discussions and teleconferences. We thank Kirsten Sampson-Snyder, who shepherded the report through the NRC review process; Robert Pool, who edited the draft report; and Yvonne Wise for processing the report through final production. We are grateful to Kelly Iverson, who arranged logistics for all three committee meetings and assisted with editing and preparing the manuscript for review and final publication. We appreciate the assistance of Patricia Morison, director of the communications office of the NRC Division of Behavioral and Social Sciences and Education, and Sara Frueh, communications officer.

This report has been reviewed in draft form by individuals chosen for their diverse perspectives and technical expertise, in accordance with procedures approved by the NRC's Report Review Committee. The purpose of this independent review is to provide candid and critical comments that will assist the institution in making its published report as sound as possible and to ensure that the report meets institutional standards for objectivity, evidence, and responsiveness to the study charge. The review comments and draft manuscript remain confidential to protect the integrity of the deliberative process. We thank the following individuals for their review of this report: Diane F. Halpern, Department of Psychology, Claremont McKenna College; Karen R. Harris, Department of Special Education and Literacy, Peabody College, Vanderbilt University; Kevin Lang, Department of Economics, Boston University; Richard Lehrer, Department of Teaching and Learning, Peabody College of Vanderbilt University; Frank Levy, Department of Urban Economics, Massachusetts Institute of Technology; Lorrie A. Shepard, School of Education, University of Colorado at Boulder; and Nancy T. Tippins, Sr. Vice President and Managing Principal, Valtera Corporation, Greenville, SC.

Although the reviewers listed above provided many constructive comments and suggestions, they were not asked to endorse the content of the report, nor did they see the final draft of the report before its release. Deborah Stipek of the Stanford University School of Education and Elisabeth M. Drake, retired associate director for new energy technology, Energy Laboratory, Massachusetts Institute of Technology, oversaw the review of this report. Appointed by the NRC, they were responsible for making certain that an independent examination of this report was carried out in accordance with institutional procedures and that all review comments were carefully considered. Responsibility for the final content of this report rests entirely with the author and the institution.

Finally, we thank our colleagues on the committee for their enthusiasm, hard work, and collaborative spirit in thinking through the conceptual issues and challenges associated with addressing the charge to the study committee and in writing this report.

James W. Pellegrino, *Chair*
Margaret L. Hilton, *Study Director*
Committee on Defining Deeper Learning and 21st Century Skills

Contents

Summary   1

1   Introduction   15

2   A Preliminary Classification of Skills and Abilities   21

3   Importance of Deeper Learning and 21st Century Skills   37

4   Perspectives on Deeper Learning   69

5   Deeper Learning of English Language Arts,
Mathematics, and Science   101

6   Teaching and Assessing for Transfer   143

7   Systems to Support Deeper Learning   185

References   195

Appendixes

A   21st Century Skills and Competencies Included in the
OECD Survey   219

B   Reports on 21st Century Skills Used in Aligning and Clustering
Competencies   221

C   Biographical Sketches of Committee Members   225

Index   231

Summary

Americans have long recognized that investments in public education contribute to the common good, enhancing national prosperity and supporting stable families, neighborhoods, and communities. Education is even more critical today, in the face of economic, environmental, and social challenges. Today's children can meet future challenges if their schooling and informal learning activities prepare them for adult roles as citizens, employees, managers, parents, volunteers, and entrepreneurs. To achieve their full potential as adults, young people need to develop a range of skills and knowledge that facilitate mastery and application of English, mathematics, and other school subjects. At the same time, business and political leaders are increasingly asking schools to develop skills such as problem solving, critical thinking, communication, collaboration, and self-management—often referred to as "21st century skills."

Private foundations, policy makers, and education organizations use a variety of names for the lists of broad skills seen as valuable. To help the public understand the research related to the teaching and learning of such skills, several foundations charged the National Research Council (NRC) to:

- Define the set of key skills that are referenced by the labels "deeper learning," "21st century skills," "college and career readiness," "student centered learning," "next generation learning," "new basic skills," and "higher order thinking." These labels are typically used to include both cognitive and noncognitive skills—such as critical thinking, problem solving, collaboration, effective communication, motivation,

1

persistence, and learning to learn that can be demonstrated within core academic content areas and that are important to success in education, work, and other areas of adult responsibility. The labels are also sometimes used to include other important capacities—such as creativity, innovation, and ethics—that are important to later success and may also be developed in formal or informal learning environments.

- Describe how these skills relate to each other and to more traditional academic skills and content in the key disciplines of reading, mathematics, and science. In particular, consider these skills in the context of the work of the National Governors Association and the Council of Chief State School Officers in specifying Common Core State Standards for English language arts and mathematics, and the work of the NRC in specifying *A Framework for K-12 Science Education: Practices, Crosscutting Concepts, and Core Ideas* (hereafter referred to as the NRC science framework).
- Summarize the findings of the research that investigates the importance of such skills to success in education, work, and other areas of adult responsibility and that demonstrates the importance of developing these skills in K-16 education.
- Summarize what is known—and what research is needed—about how these skills can be learned, taught, and assessed. This summary should include both the cognitive foundations of these skills in learning theory and research about effective approaches to teaching and learning these skills, including approaches using digital media.
- Identify features of educational interventions that research suggests could be used as indicators that an intervention is likely to develop the key skills in a substantial and meaningful way. In particular, for learning in formal school-based environments, identify features related to learning these skills in educational interventions in (a) teacher professional development, (b) curriculum, and (c) assessment. For learning in informal environments, identify features related to learning these skills in educational interventions in (d) after-school and out-of-school programs and (e) exhibits, museums, and other informal learning centers. For learning in both formal and informal environments, identify features related to learning these skills in education interventions in (f) digital media.

In approaching this charge, the committee drew on a large research base in cognitive, developmental, educational, organizational, and social psychology and economics for purposes of clarifying and organizing concepts and terms. However, we do not claim to provide precise, scientifically credible definitions of all the various terms that have come to populate this arena of concern and debate. This is due partly to the time constraints of the project and partly to the lack of definitive research on the range of skills and behaviors that have come to fall under the headings of "deeper learning" and "21st century skills." That said, the committee took initial steps toward clarifying the meaning of the term "deeper learning" and its relationship to competency clusters that capture various terms associated with the overarching label 21st century skills. In contrast to a view of 21st century skills as general skills that can be applied to a range of different tasks in various academic, civic, workplace, or family contexts, the committee views 21st century skills as dimensions of expertise that are specific to—and intertwined with—knowledge within a particular domain of content and performance. To reflect our view that skills and knowledge are intertwined, we use the term "competencies" rather than "skills."

CLARIFYING AND ORGANIZING CONCEPTS AND TERMS

The committee views the various sets of terms associated with the 21st century skills label as reflecting important dimensions of human competence that have been valuable for many centuries, rather than skills that are suddenly new, unique, and valuable today. The important difference across time may lie in society's desire that all students attain levels of mastery—across multiple areas of skill and knowledge—that were previously unnecessary for individual success in education and the workplace. At the same time, the pervasive spread of digital technologies has increased the pace at which individuals communicate and exchange information, requiring competence in processing multiple forms of information to accomplish tasks that may be distributed across contexts that include home, school, the workplace, and social networks.

As a way to organize the various terms for 21st century skills and provide a starting point for further research as to their meaning and value, the committee identified three broad domains of competence—cognitive, intrapersonal, and interpersonal. The cognitive domain involves reasoning and memory; the intrapersonal domain involves the capacity to manage one's behavior and emotions to achieve one's goals (including learning goals); and the interpersonal domain involves expressing ideas, and interpreting and responding to messages from others. We then conducted a content analysis, aligning several lists of 21st century skills proposed by various groups and individuals with the skills included in existing research-based taxonomies of cognitive, intrapersonal, and interpersonal skills and abilities.[1] Through this process, we assigned the various 21st century skills to clusters of competencies within each domain. Recognizing that there are areas of overlap between and among the individual 21st century skills

---

[1] The committee views the abilities included in these taxonomies as malleable dimensions of human behavior that can change in response to educational interventions and life experiences, in contrast to the common view of them as fixed traits.

and the larger competency clusters, the committee developed the following initial classification scheme (see Chapter 2):

- The Cognitive Domain includes three clusters of competencies: cognitive processes and strategies, knowledge, and creativity. These clusters include competencies, such as critical thinking, information literacy, reasoning and argumentation, and innovation.
- The Intrapersonal Domain includes three clusters of competencies: intellectual openness, work ethic and conscientiousness, and positive core self-evaluation. These clusters include competencies, such as flexibility, initiative, appreciation for diversity, and metacognition (the ability to reflect on one's own learning and make adjustments accordingly).
- The Interpersonal Domain includes two clusters of competencies: teamwork and collaboration and leadership. These clusters include competencies, such as communication, collaboration, responsibility, and conflict resolution.

IMPORTANCE OF 21ST CENTURY COMPETENCIES

The committee examined evidence of the importance of various types of competencies for success in education, work, health, and other life contexts (see Chapter 3) and concluded:

- **Conclusion: The available research evidence is limited and primarily correlational in nature; to date, only a few studies have demonstrated a causal relationship between one or more 21st century competencies and adult outcomes. The research has examined a wide range of different competencies that are not always clearly defined or distinguished from related competencies.**

Despite the limitations of the research evidence, the committee was able to reach three conclusions about the importance of various competencies:

- **Conclusion: Cognitive competencies have been more extensively studied than have intrapersonal and interpersonal competencies, showing consistent, positive correlations (of modest size) with desirable educational, career, and health outcomes. Early academic competencies are also positively correlated with these outcomes.**

- **Conclusion: Among intrapersonal and interpersonal competencies, conscientiousness (staying organized, responsible, and hardworking) is most highly correlated with desirable educational, career,** and health outcomes. Antisocial behavior, which has both intra-personal and interpersonal dimensions, is negatively correlated with these outcomes.

- Conclusion: Educational attainment—the number of years a person spends in school—strongly predicts adult earnings and also predicts health and civic engagement. Moreover, individuals with higher levels of education appear to gain more knowledge and skills on the job than do those with lower levels of education, and to be able, to some extent, to transfer what they learn across occupations. Since it is not known what mixture of cognitive, intrapersonal, and interpersonal competencies accounts for the labor market benefits of additional schooling, promoting educational attainment itself may constitute a useful complementary strategy for developing 21st century competencies.

At a time when educational and business leaders are increasingly interested in promoting deeper learning and development of 21st century skills, and in light of limitations of the available empirical evidence linking such competencies with desirable adult outcomes, we recommend further research:

- Recommendation 1: Foundations and federal agencies should support further research designed to increase our understanding of the relationships between 21st century competencies and successful adult outcomes. To provide stronger causal evidence about such relationships, the programs of research should move beyond simple correlational studies to include more longitudinal studies with controls for differences in individuals' family backgrounds and more studies using statistical methods that are designed to approximate experiments. Such research would benefit from efforts to achieve common definitions of 21st century competencies and an associated set of activities designed to produce valid and reliable assessments of the various individual competencies.

PERSPECTIVES ON DEEPER LEARNING

We define "deeper learning" as the process through which an individual becomes capable of taking what was learned in one situation and applying it to new situations (i.e., transfer). Through deeper learning (which often involves shared learning and interactions with others in a community), the individual develops expertise in a particular domain of knowledge and/ or performance (see Chapters 4 and 5). The product of deeper learning is transferable knowledge, including content knowledge in a domain and knowledge of how, why, and when to apply this knowledge to answer questions and solve problems. We refer to this blend of both knowledge and skills as "21st century competencies." The competencies are structured around fundamental principles of the content area and their relationships rather than disparate, superficial facts or procedures. It is the way in which the individual and community structures and organizes the intertwined knowledge and skills—rather than the separate facts or procedures per se—that supports transfer. While other types of learning may allow an individual to recall facts, concepts, or procedures, deeper learning allows the individual to transfer what was learned to solve new problems.

The new Common Core State Standards in English language arts and mathematics and the NRC science framework are likely to strongly influence educational policy and practice in the coming decades. The committee reviewed these documents and compared them with our definition of deeper learning and with recent lists of 21st century skills, revealing important areas of overlap. The goals included in the new standards and the NRC science framework reflect each discipline's desire to promote deeper learning and develop transferable knowledge and skills within that discipline. For example, both the mathematics standards and the science framework include a "practices" dimension, calling for students to actively use and apply—i.e., to transfer—knowledge, and the English language arts standards call on students to synthesize and apply evidence to create and effectively communicate an argument. Our review leads to three conclusions (see Chapter 5):

- **Conclusion: Goals for deeper learning and some 21st century competencies are found in standards documents, indicating that disciplinary goals have expanded beyond their traditional focus on basic academic content. A cluster of cognitive competencies—including critical thinking, nonroutine problem solving, and constructing and evaluating evidence-based arguments—is strongly supported across all three disciplines.**

- **Conclusion: Coverage of other competencies—particularly those in the intrapersonal and interpersonal domains—is uneven. For example, standards documents across all three disciplines include discourse and argumentation (which includes both cognitive and interpersonal facets), but the disciplines differ in their view of what counts as evidence and the rules of argumentation. This uneven coverage could potentially lead to learning environments for different subjects that vary in their support for development of 21st century competencies.**

- Conclusion: Development of the full range of 21st century competencies within the disciplines will require systematic instruction and sustained practice. It will be necessary to devote additional instructional time and resources to advance these sophisticated disciplinary learning goals over what is common in current practice.

The standards and framework documents demonstrate each discipline's desire to develop skills and knowledge that will transfer beyond the classroom. However, the goals for transfer are specific to each discipline. For example, the NRC science framework aims to prepare high school graduates to engage in public discussions on science-related issues and to be critical consumers of scientific information. Research is lacking on how to help learners transfer competencies learned in one discipline or topic area outside the discipline or topic area:

- Conclusion: Teaching for transfer within each discipline aims to increase transfer within that discipline. Research to date provides little guidance about how to help learners aggregate transferable competencies across disciplines. This may be a shortcoming in the research or a reflection of the domain-specific nature of transfer.

To fill this gap, we recommend further research:

- Recommendation 2: Foundations and federal agencies should support programs of research designed to illuminate whether, and to what extent, teaching for transfer within an academic discipline can facilitate transfer across disciplines.

Deeper learning can be supported through teaching practices that create a positive learning community in which students gain content knowledge and also develop intrapersonal and interpersonal competencies. For example, an integrated science-literacy curriculum was tested in 94 fourth-grade classrooms in one southern state. The curriculum combined collaborative, hands-on science inquiry activities with reading text, writing notes and reports, and small group discussions. When teachers were randomly assigned to either implement the integrated curriculum or to teach science and literacy separately (using their regular materials), students exposed to the integrated curriculum demonstrated significantly greater gains on measures of science understanding, science vocabulary, and science writing. At the same time, the students developed the intrapersonal competencies of oral communication and discourse, as well as the interpersonal competencies of metacognition and positive dispositions toward learning (see Chapter 5). Other research also illuminates how intrapersonal and interpersonal competencies support deeper learning of school subjects. For example, the process of deeper learning to develop expertise in a domain of knowledge and performance requires months, or even years, of sustained, deliberate practice; such sustained effort is supported by the intrapersonal competency of conscientiousness. Development of expertise also requires feedback to guide and optimize practice activities and an individual with strong interpersonal skills will best understand and apply such feedback. Metacognition—the ability to reflect on one's own learning and make adjustments accordingly—also enhances deeper learning. We conclude (see Chapter 4):

- **Conclusion: The process of deeper learning is essential for the development of transferable 21st century competencies (including both knowledge and skills), and the application of 21st century competencies in turn supports the process of deeper learning, in a recursive, mutually reinforcing cycle.**

INSTRUCTIONAL FEATURES FOR DEEPER LEARNING

The committee's review of the evidence on teaching and learning of cognitive, intrapersonal, and interpersonal competencies supported the following conclusion (see Chapter 6):

- **Conclusion: Although the absence of common definitions and quality measures poses a challenge to research, emerging evidence indicates that cognitive, intrapersonal, and interpersonal competencies can be taught and learned in ways that promote transfer.**

The most extensive and rigorous research related to deeper learning comes from the learning sciences. Although this research has focused on acquisition of cognitive knowledge and skills, it indicates that deeper learning and complex problem solving involves the interplay of cognitive, intrapersonal, and interpersonal competencies. Over a century of research on transfer has yielded little evidence that teaching can develop general cognitive competencies that are transferable to any new discipline, problem, or context, in or out of school. Nevertheless, it has identified features of instruction that are likely to substantially support deeper learning and development of 21st century competencies within a topic area or discipline. For example, we now know that transfer is supported when learners understand the general principles underlying their original learning and the transfer situation or problem involves the same general principles—a finding reflected in the new Common Core State Standards and the NRC science framework, which highlight learning of general principles. Similarly, in solving problems, transfer is facilitated by instruction that helps learners develop deep understanding of the structure of a problem domain and applicable solution methods, but is not supported by rote learning of solutions to specific problems or problem-solving procedures. This kind of deep, well-integrated learning develops gradually and takes time, but it can be started early: recent evidence indicates that even preschool and early elementary students can make meaningful progress in conceptual organization, reasoning, problem solving, representation, and communication in well-chosen topic areas in science, mathematics, and language arts. In addition, teaching that emphasizes the conditions for applying a body of factual or procedural knowledge also facilitates transfer.

For instruction focused on development of cognitive competencies, whether delivered within or outside of school, and irrespective of support by digital media, the committee recommends (see Chapter 6):

- **Recommendation 3: Designers and developers of instruction targeted at deeper learning and development of transferable 21st century competencies should begin with clearly delineated learning goals and a model of how learning is expected to develop, along with assessments to measure student progress toward and attainment of the goals. Such instruction can and should begin with the earliest grades and be sustained throughout students' K-12 careers.**

- **Recommendation 4: Funding agencies should support the development of curriculum and instructional programs that include research-based teaching methods, such as:**

    o **Using multiple and varied representations of concepts and tasks,** such as diagrams, numerical and mathematical representations, and simulations, combined with activities and guidance that support mapping across the varied representations.
    o **Encouraging elaboration, questioning, and explanation**—for example, prompting students who are reading a history text to think about the author's intent and/or to explain specific information and arguments as they read—either silently to themselves or to others.
    o **Engaging learners in challenging tasks,** while also supporting them with guidance, feedback, and encouragement to reflect on their own learning processes and the status of their understanding.
    o **Teaching with examples and cases,** such as modeling step-by-step how students can carry out a procedure to solve a problem and using sets of worked examples.

o **Priming student motivation** by connecting topics to students'
   personal lives and interests, engaging students in collaborative
   problem solving, and drawing attention to the knowledge and
   skills students are developing, rather than grades or scores.
o **Using formative assessment** to: (a) make learning goals clear
   to students; (b) continuously monitor, provide feedback, and
   respond to students' learning progress; and (c) involve students
   in self- and peer assessment.

For instruction focused on development of problem-solving and metacognitive competencies, the committee recommends (see Chapter 6):

- **Recommendation 5: Designers and developers of curriculum, instruction, and assessment in problem solving and metacognition
  should use modeling and feedback techniques that highlight the
  processes of thinking rather than focusing exclusively on the products of thinking. Problem-solving and metacognitive competencies
  should be taught and assessed within a specific discipline or topic
  area rather than as a stand-alone course. Teaching and learning of
  problem-solving and metacognitive competencies need not wait until all of the related component competencies have achieved fluency.
  Finally, sustained instruction and effort are necessary to develop
  expertise in problem solving and metacognition; there is no simple
  way to achieve competence without time, effort, motivation, and
  informative feedback.**

Research on teaching and learning of competencies in the intrapersonal
and interpersonal domains is less extensive and less rigorous than the research on deeper learning of cognitive knowledge and skills. Our review
of the emerging research on these domains, as well as the more extensive
cognitive research, suggests that the instructional features supporting development of transferable competencies in the cognitive domain may also
support transfer in these domains (see Chapter 6):

- **Conclusion: The instructional features listed above, shown by research to support the acquisition of cognitive competencies that
  transfer, could plausibly be applied to the design and implementation of instruction that would support the acquisition of transferable intrapersonal and interpersonal competencies.**

To test this hypothesis, the committee recommends further research:

* **Recommendation 6: Foundations and federal agencies should support research programs designed to fill gaps in the evidence base on teaching and assessment for deeper learning and transfer.** One important target for future research is how to design instruction and assessment for transfer in the intrapersonal and interpersonal domains. Investigators should examine whether, and to what extent, instructional design principles and methods shown to increase transfer in the cognitive domain, are applicable to instruction targeted to the development of intrapersonal and interpersonal competencies. Such programs of research would benefit from efforts to specify more uniform, clearly defined constructs and produce associated measures of cognitive, intrapersonal, and interpersonal competencies.

OPPORTUNITIES AND CHALLENGES

Current educational policies and associated accountability systems rely on assessments that focus primarily on recall of facts and procedures, posing a challenge to wider teaching and learning of transferable 21st century competencies. However, recent policy developments offer opportunities to address this challenge (see Chapter 7). In particular, as noted above, the Common Core State Standards and the NRC science framework provide a deeper conceptualization of the knowledge and skills to be mastered in each discipline, including various facets of 21st century competencies.

While new national goals that encompass 21st century competencies have been articulated in the standards and the NRC science framework, the extent to which these goals are realized in educational settings will be strongly influenced by the nature of their inclusion in district, state, and national assessments. Because educational policy emphasizes the results of summative assessments within accountability systems, teachers and administrators will focus instruction on what is included in state assessments. Thus, as new assessment systems are developed to reflect the new standards in English language arts, mathematics, and science, significant attention will need to be given to the design of tasks and situations that call on students to apply a range of 21st century competencies that are relevant to each discipline.

Although improved assessments would facilitate wider uptake of interventions that support the process of deeper learning, developing such assessments faces several challenges. First, research to date has focused on a plethora of different constructs in the cognitive, intrapersonal, and interpersonal domains. Our taxonomy offers a useful starting point, but further research is needed to more carefully organize, align, and define these constructs. Second, there are psychometric challenges. Progress has been made in assessing a range of simple and complex cognitive competencies, yet much further research is needed to develop assessments of intrapersonal and interpersonal competencies. Such research should initially focus on developing assessments for research purposes, and later on assessments for formative purposes. If these efforts are successful, then summative assessments of intrapersonal and interpersonal competencies could possibly be developed for later use in educational settings. Experiences during the 1980s and 1990s in the development and implementation of performance assessments and assessments with open-ended tasks offer valuable insights, but assessments must be reliable, valid, and fair if they are to be widely used in formal and informal learning environments.

A third challenge is posed by political and economic forces that influence assessment development and use. Policy makers have favored standardized, on-demand, end-of-year tests that are easily scored and quantified for accountability purposes. Composed largely of selected response items, these tests are relatively cheap to implement but are not optimal for assessing 21st century competencies (see Chapter 7). In the face of current fiscal constraints at the federal and state levels, assessment systems may seek to minimize costs by using these types of tests, rather than incorporating the richer, performance- and curriculum-based assessments that can better support the development and assessment of 21st century competencies.

The fourth challenge is teacher capacity. The principles of instruction we outline above are rarely reflected in the knowledge and practices of teachers, students, and school administrators and in administrators' expectations of teachers and teacher evaluation rubrics. Teacher preparation programs will need to help teacher candidates develop specific visions of teaching and learning for transfer and also the knowledge and skills to put these visions into practice. Both novice and experienced teachers will need time to develop new understandings of the subjects they teach as well as understanding of how to assess 21st century competencies in these subjects, making ongoing professional learning opportunities a central facet of every teacher's job. Certainly, teachers will need support from administrators as they struggle with the complexity and uncertainty of revising their teaching practice within the larger effort to institutionalize a focus on deeper learning and effective transfer.

- **Recommendation 7: Foundations and federal agencies should support research to more clearly define and develop assessments of 21st century competencies. In particular, they should provide sustained** support for the development of valid, reliable, and fair assessments of intrapersonal and interpersonal competencies, initially for research purposes, and later for formative assessment. Pending the results of these efforts, foundations and agencies should consider support for development of summative assessments of these competencies.

Two large consortia of states, with support from the U.S. Department of Education, are currently developing new assessment frameworks and methods aligned with the Common Core State Standards in English language arts and mathematics. If these assessment frameworks include the facets of 21st century competencies represented in the Common Core State Standards, they will provide a strong incentive for states, districts, schools, and teachers to emphasize these competencies as part of disciplinary instruction. Next Generation Science Standards based on the NRC science framework are under development, and assessments aligned with these standards have not yet been created. When new science assessments are developed, inclusion of facets of 21st century competencies will provide a similarly strong incentive for states, districts, schools, and teachers to emphasize those facets in classroom science instruction (see Chapter 7).

- **Recommendation 8: As the state consortia develop new assessment systems to reflect the Common Core State Standards in English language arts and mathematics, they should devote significant attention to the design of tasks and situations that call upon a range of important 21st century competencies as applied in each of the major content areas.**

- **Recommendation 9: As states and test developers begin to create new assessment systems aligned with new science standards, they should devote significant attention to designing measures of 21st century competencies properly reflecting a blend of science practices, crosscutting concepts, and core ideas.**

Because 21st century competencies support deeper learning of school subjects, their widespread acquisition could potentially reduce disparities in educational attainment, preparing a broader swathe of young people for successful adult outcomes at work and in other life arenas. However, important challenges remain. For educational interventions focused on developing transferable competencies to move beyond isolated promising examples and flourish more widely in K-12 schooling, larger systemic issues and policies involving curriculum, instruction, assessment, and professional development will need to be addressed. In particular, new types of assessment systems, capable of accurately measuring and supporting acquisition of these competencies, will be needed. A sustained program of research and development will be required to create assessments that are capable of measuring cognitive, intrapersonal, and interpersonal competencies. In addition, it will be important for researchers and publishers to develop new curricula that incorporate the research-based design principles and instructional methods we describe above. Finally, new approaches to teacher preparation and professional development will be needed to help current and prospective teachers understand these instructional principles and methods, as well as the role of deeper learning and 21st century competencies in mastering core academic content. If teachers are to not only understand these ideas but also translate them into their daily instructional practice, they will need support from school and district administrators, including time for learning, shared lesson planning and review, and reflection (see Chapter 7).

- **Recommendation 10: The states and the federal government should establish policies and programs—in the areas of assessment, accountability, curriculum and materials, and teacher education—to support students' acquisition of transferable 21st century competencies. For example, when reauthorizing the Elementary and Secondary Education Act, the Congress should facilitate the systemic development, implementation, and evaluation of educational interventions targeting deeper learning processes and the development of transferable competencies.**

1

Introduction

Americans have long recognized that investments in public education can contribute to the common good, enhance national prosperity, and support stable families, neighborhoods, and communities. In the face of economic, environmental, and social challenges, education is even more critical today than it has been in the past. Today's children can meet future challenges if they have opportunities to prepare for their future roles as citizens, employees, managers, parents, volunteers, and entrepreneurs. To achieve their full potential as adults, young people will need to learn a full range of skills and knowledge that facilitate mastery of English, mathematics, and other school subjects. They will need to learn in ways that support not only retention but also the use and application of skills and knowledge—a process called "transfer" in cognitive psychology.

Today's educational policies and practices will need updating to help all children develop transferable knowledge and skills. American students' performance is not impressive when they are tested through the Programme for International Student Assessment (PISA) for their ability to not only understand but also apply their knowledge. PISA tests are designed to measure students' capacity to apply knowledge and skills in key subject areas as well as their ability to analyze, reason, and communicate effectively as they pose, interpret, and solve problems. On the 2009 PISA reading and science tests, the scores of U.S. 15-year-olds were only average when compared to students from the other industrialized nations making up the OECD; in mathematics, the scores of U.S. 15-year-olds were below the OECD average.[1] Part of the reason for the weak average performance of American students is uneven learning and achievement among different groups of students. Disparities in the relative educational attainment of children from high-income versus low-income families have grown enormously since the 1970s (Duncan and Murnane, 2011). In a related trend, the gap between average incomes of the wealthiest and poorest families has grown.

Business leaders, educational organizations, and researchers have begun to call for new education policies that target the development of broad, transferable skills and knowledge, often referred to as "21st century skills." For example, the Partnership for 21st Century Skills[2] argues that student success in college and careers requires four essential skills: critical thinking and problem solving, communication, collaboration, and creativity and innovation (Partnership for 21st Century Skills, 2010, p. 2).

Although these skills have long been valuable (for example, Thomas Alva Edison observed in 1903 that "Genius is 1 percent inspiration, 99 percent perspiration"), they are particularly salient today, and education officials are beginning to focus on them. Sixteen states have joined the Partnership for 21st Century Skills, based on a commitment to fuse 21st century skills with academic content (Partnership for 21st Century Skills, 2011) in their standards, assessments, curriculum, and teacher professional development. Some state and local high school reform efforts have begun to focus on a four-dimensional framework of college and career readiness that includes not only academic content but also cognitive strategies, academic behaviors, and contextual skills and awareness (Conley, 2011). At the international level, the U.S. secretary of education participates on the executive board of the Assessment and Teaching of 21st Century Skills (ATC21S) project, along with the education ministers of five other nations and the vice presidents of Cisco, Intel, and Microsoft. This project aims to expand the teaching and learning of 21st century skills globally, especially by improving assessment of these skills. In a separate effort, a large majority of 16 OECD nations surveyed in 2009 reported that they are incorporating 21st century skills in their education policies, such as regulations and guidelines (Aniandou and Claro, 2009).

COMMITTEE CHARGE

To increase understanding of the research related to deeper learning, 21st century skills, and related educational goals, the Carnegie Corporation of New York, the William and Flora Hewlett Foundation, the John D. and

---

[1]OECD (2010).

[2]This nonprofit organization includes business, education, community, and governmental groups.

Catherine T. MacArthur Foundation, the National Science Foundation, the Nellie Mae Education Foundation, the Pearson Foundation, the Raikes Foundation, the Susan Crown Enchange Fund, and the Stupski Foundation charged the National Research Council (NRC) as follows:

> An ad hoc committee will review and synthesize current research on the nature of deeper learning and 21st century skills and will address the following:
>
> - Define the set of key skills that are referenced by the labels "deeper learning," "21st century skills," "college and career readiness," "student centered learning," "next generation learning," "new basic skills," and "higher order thinking." These labels are typically used to include both cognitive and noncognitive skills—such as critical thinking, problem solving, collaboration, effective communication, motivation, persistence, and learning to learn that can be demonstrated within core academic content areas and that are important to success in education, work, and other areas of adult responsibility. The labels are also sometimes used to include other important capacities—such as creativity, innovation, and ethics—that are important to later success and may also be developed in formal or informal learning environments.
> - Describe how these skills relate to each other and to more traditional academic skills and content in the key disciplines of reading, mathematics, and science. In particular, consider these skills in the context of the work of the National Governors Association and the Council of Chief State School Officers in specifying Common Core State Standards for English language arts and mathematics, and the work of the NRC in specifying a *A Framework for K-12 Science Education: Practices, Crosscutting Concepts, and Core Ideas* (hereafter referred to as the NRC science framework).
> - Summarize the findings of the research that investigates the importance of such skills to success in education, work, and other areas of adult responsibility and that demonstrates the importance of developing these skills in K-16 education.
> - Summarize what is known—and what research is needed—about how these skills can be learned, taught, and assessed. This summary should include both the cognitive foundations of these skills in learning theory and research about effective approaches to teaching and learning these skills, including approaches using digital media.
> - Identify features of educational interventions that research suggests could be used as indicators that an intervention is likely to develop the key skills in a substantial and meaningful way. In particular, for learning in formal school-based environments, identify features related to learning these skills in educational interventions in (a) teacher professional development, (b) curriculum, and (c) assessment. For learning in informal environments, identify features related to learning these skills in educational interventions in (d) after-school and out-of-school

programs and (e) exhibits, museums, and other informal learning centers. For learning in both formal and informal environments, identify features related to learning these skills in education interventions in (f) digital media.

HOW THE COMMITTEE APPROACHED THE CHARGE

To address these five areas of concern, the committee reviewed research literature across several disciplines, including cognitive science, educational and social psychology, economics, child and adolescent development, literacy, mathematics and science education, psychometrics, educational technology, and human resource development. The committee drew on recent NRC workshops focusing on demand for 21st century skills, the intersection of science education and 21st century skills, and the assessment of 21st century skills, as well as on papers commissioned for an NRC planning process on behalf of the Hewlett Foundation. It considered the work of the ATC21S project and emerging research on the relationship between cognitive and noncognitive skills and abilities and adult outcomes (see Chapter 3).

The committee met three times. The first meeting included an open session with representatives of the FrameWorks Institute, which focused on how the public thinks about education and early childhood development. In the closed session of the first meeting, teams of committee members focusing on each topic in the study charge delivered brief presentations summarizing relevant research findings. These presentations and discussions provided the basis for a preliminary draft of this report. At its second meeting, the committee deliberated on the preliminary draft and decided to focus the report on learning for transfer. Following the second meeting, the committee and staff revised the preliminary draft extensively, and this new draft was discussed at the committee's third meeting. At the third meeting, the committee also developed preliminary conclusions and recommendations based on the draft. Following this meeting, the committee and staff again revised the report. In a final teleconference, the committee discussed and reached consensus on the conclusions and recommendations. The draft report entered the NRC review process in February 2012. Following receipt of review comments it was revised and publicly released in July 2012.

ORGANIZATION OF THE REPORT

Following this introductory chapter, Chapter 2 begins to address the question of how to define deeper learning and 21st century skills, proposing a preliminary taxonomy with clusters of competencies. Chapter 3 summarizes several different strands of research on the importance of these competencies to success in education, work, and other areas of adult responsibility. Chapter 4 focuses on deeper learning, which the committee views as learning for transfer. Chapter 5 discusses deeper learning and 21st century competencies in the disciplines of English language arts, science, and mathematics. Chapter 6 discusses teaching and assessing transferable knowledge and skills, in both formal and informal learning environments, and identifies research-based methods and instructional design principles for effectively developing the desired knowledge and skills. Chapter 7 considers key elements within the larger educational system that may help or hinder wider implementation of educational interventions to support the process of deeper learning and the development of 21st century competencies. Chapters 3 through 7 end with conclusions and recommendations, and all of the conclusions and recommendations are included in the Summary.

2

A Preliminary Classification of Skills and Abilities

This chapter presents an initial classification of skills and abilities, including various terms used to describe "21st century skills." The committee found this preliminary classification scheme useful in addressing each question in the study charge, and the scheme is used to varying degrees throughout the report. At the same time, the committee hopes that the preliminary scheme proves useful for further research to develop shared definitions of these skills.

THREE DOMAINS OF COMPETENCE

As a first step toward describing 21st century skills, the committee identified three domains of competence: cognitive, intrapersonal, and interpersonal. These three domains represent distinct facets of human thinking and build on previous efforts to identify and organize dimensions of human behavior. For example, Bloom's 1956 taxonomy of learning objectives included three broad domains: cognitive, affective, and psychomotor. Following Bloom, we view the cognitive domain as involving thinking and related abilities, such as reasoning, problem solving, and memory.[1] Our intrapersonal domain, like Bloom's affective domain, involves emotions and feelings and includes self-regulation—the ability to set and achieve one's

---

[1]In Bloom's taxonomy of the cognitive domain, knowledge is at the lowest level (or "order"), with comprehension and application of information above. The higher orders include analysis and synthesis, and the highest level is evaluation (Bloom, 1956). The influence of the taxonomy is seen in current calls for schools to teach "higher-order skills."

goals (Hoyle and Davisson, 2011). The interpersonal domain we propose is not included in Bloom's taxonomy but rather is based partly on a recent National Research Council (NRC) workshop that clustered various 21st century skills into the cognitive, intrapersonal, and interpersonal domains (National Research Council, 2011a). In that workshop, Bedwell, Fiore, and Salas (2011) proposed that interpersonal competencies are those used both to express information to others and to interpret others' messages (both verbal and nonverbal) and respond appropriately.

Distinctions among the three domains are reflected in how they are delineated, studied, and measured. In the cognitive domain, knowledge and skills are typically measured with tests of general cognitive ability (also referred to as g or IQ) or with more specific tests focusing on school subjects or work-related content. Research on intrapersonal and interpersonal competencies often uses measures of broad personality traits (discussed further below) or of child temperament (general behavioral tendencies, such as attention or shyness). Psychiatrists and clinical psychologists studying mental disorders use various measures to understand the negative dimensions of the intrapersonal and interpersonal domains (Almlund et al., 2011).

Although we differentiate the three domains for the purpose of understanding and organizing 21st century skills, we recognize that they are intertwined in human development and learning. Research on teaching and learning has begun to illuminate how intrapersonal and intrapersonal skills support learning of academic content (e.g., National Research Council, 1999) and how to develop these valuable supporting skills (e.g., Yeager and Walton, 2011). For example, we now know that learning is enhanced by the intrapersonal skills used to reflect on one's learning and adjust learning strategies accordingly—a process called "metacognition" (National Research Council, 2001; Hoyle and Davisson, 2011). At the same time research has shown that the development of cognitive skills, such as the ability to stop and think objectively about a disagreement with another person, can increase positive interpersonal skills and reduce antisocial behavior (Durlak et al., 2011). And the interpersonal skill of effective communication is supported by the cognitive skills used to process and interpret complex verbal and nonverbal messages and formulate and express appropriate responses (Bedwell, Fiore, and Salas, 2011).

A DIFFERENTIAL PERSPECTIVE ON 21st CENTURY SKILLS

To address our charge to define 21st century skills and describe how they relate to each other, we turn to the research in differential psychology. This research has focused on understanding human behavior by examining systematic ways in which individuals vary and by using relatively stable patterns of individual differences as the basis for structural theories of cognition and personality. Much of this work is rooted in efforts to identify and define skills and competencies through a process of measurement, with inferences drawn about the significance and breadth of a construct by analyzing patterns of correlations.

We view 21st century skills as knowledge that can be transferred or applied in new situations. This transferable knowledge includes both content knowledge in a domain and also procedural knowledge of how, why, and when to apply this knowledge to answer questions and solve problems. The latter dimensions of transferable knowledge (how, why, and when to apply content knowledge) are often called "skills." We refer to this blend of content knowledge and related skills as "21st century competencies." In Chapter 4, we propose that deeper learning is the process through which such transferable knowledge (i.e., 21st century competencies) develops.

Our use of "competencies" reflects the terminology used by the OECD in its extensive project to identify key competencies required for life and work in the current era. According to the OECD (2005), a competency is

> more than just knowledge and skills. It involves the ability to meet complex demands, by drawing on and mobilizing psychosocial resources (including skills and attitudes) in a particular context. For example, the ability to communicate effectively is a competency that may draw on an individual's knowledge of language, practical IT skills, and attitudes towards those with whom he or she is communicating. (OECD, 2005, p. 4)

Differential psychology has traditionally focused on identifying characteristics of individuals, including general cognitive ability and personality traits, that are thought to persist throughout an individual's life. In contrast, the committee views cognitive, intrapersonal, and interpersonal competencies as malleable and subject to change in response to life experience, education, and interventions. In the cognitive domain, for example, the view of intelligence as a single, unitary ability that changes little over a lifetime has been superseded by research indicating that intelligence includes multiple dimensions (Carroll, 1993) and that these dimensions change over time. Horn (1970) found that fluid intelligence (a construct that includes verbal and quantitative reasoning abilities) decreases from adolescence to middle age, while crystallized intelligence (accumulated skills, such as verbal comprehension and listening ability) increases over the same period. McArdle et al. (2000) observed similar patterns of change, finding that fluid intelligence tended to peak in very early adulthood and then to decline, while crystallized intelligence tended to increase over the life cycle. Findings from a series of studies conducted over four decades, summarized by Almlund et al. (2011), indicate that how well individuals perform on intelligence tests is influenced not only by cognitive abilities but also by how much effort they exert, reflecting their motivation and related intrapersonal competencies.

This growing body of evidence showing that dimensions of intelligence are malleable has important implications for teaching and learning. Recent research on interventions designed to increase motivation has found that a learner who views intelligence as changeable through effort is more likely to exert effort in studying (Yaeger and Walton, 2011; see further discussion in Chapter 4).

In the intrapersonal and interpersonal domains, Roberts, Walton, and Viechtbauer (2006) found that both the intrapersonal competency of conscientiousness (sometimes called self-direction or self-management in lists of 21st century skills) and the interpersonal competency of social assertiveness increase with age. Srivastava et al. (2003) analyzed data from the "big five" personality inventories completed by a large sample of over 130,000 adults, finding that both conscientiousness and the interpersonal skill of agreeableness increased throughout early and middle adulthood. The authors also found that neuroticism declined with age among women, but not among men. Reflecting on these various patterns of change, Srivastava et al. (2003) concluded that personality traits are complex and subject to a variety of developmental influences.

In contrast to the prevailing view of personality traits as fixed, some researchers have argued that individual human behavior demonstrates no consistent patterns and instead changes continually in response to various situations (e.g., Mischel, 1968). Based on a review of the research related to both points of view, Almlund and colleagues concluded that "although personality traits are not merely situation-driven ephemera, they are also not set in stone," and suggested that these traits can be altered by experience, education, parental investments, and targeted interventions (Almlund et al., 2011, p. 9). They proposed that interventions to change personality are promising avenues for reducing poverty and educational disadvantage.

With this view of malleability in mind, the committee reviewed lists of 21st century skills included in eight recent reports and papers (see Appendix B). We selected reports and papers for review if they built on, synthesized, or analyzed previous work on 21st century skills. For example, we included a report that reviewed 59 international papers on 21st century skills and found that the skills most frequently referred to were collaboration, communication, information and communications technology (ICT) literacy, and social or cultural competencies (Voogt and Pareja Roblin, 2010). We selected a white paper commissioned by the Assessment and Teaching of 21st Century Skills project that synthesized many previous lists of 21st century skills and organized them into a taxonomy of skills (Binkley et al., 2010). We also included a document from the Hewlett Foundation that lists 15 skills based on previous research by the OECD (Ananiadou and Claro, 2009). In addition, we included papers commissioned by the NRC to more clearly define 21st century skills (e.g., Finegold and Notabartolo,

2010; Hoyle and Davisson, 2011) and a list of college outcomes developed by Oswald and colleagues (2004) based on an analysis of college mission statements.

The reports and papers on 21st century skills used different language to describe the same construct, an instance of the "jangle fallacy" (Coleman and Cureton, 1954). Early in the history of mental measurement, Kelly (1927) observed that investigators sometimes used different measures—and the names associated with these measures—to study and describe a single psychological construct or competency. This problem, which he referred to as the "jangle fallacy," caused waste of scientific resources, as multiple tests were used to study the same construct, and investigators who used one measure to study the construct sometimes ignored the research results of other investigators who used other measures to study the same construct. Today measurement experts continue to struggle with the question of whether various constructs represent different names for the same underlying psychological phenomenon or are truly different dimensions of human competence. A 2002 paper, for example, addressed the question of whether separate measures of self-esteem, neuroticism, locus of control, and generalized self-efficacy were in fact focusing on a single core construct (Judge et al., 2002). The committee identified the "jangle fallacy" in reports that listed, for example, both teamwork and collaboration and both flexibility and adaptability as individual 21st century skills (see Appendix A).

To address this problem, the committee clustered various terms for 21st century skills around a small number of constructs, creating a preliminary taxonomy that may be useful in future research. To identify this small number of constructs, we turned to extant taxonomies of human abilities that have a solid basis in the differential psychology research. Research-based taxonomies are available covering both cognitive (Carroll, 1993) and noncognitive (Goldberg, 1992) competencies. Based on a content analysis, we assigned different 21st century skills from the recent reports into domains within those taxonomies. In addition, we compared the recent reports with earlier reports on workplace skill demands, including the Secretary's Commission on Achieving Necessary Skills (SCANS) report (1991) and the Occupational Information Network (O*NET) report (Peterson et al., 1997).

Skills as Latent Variables and Two Kinds of Latent Variables

It is useful to differentiate between a construct, such as a competency, and its measurement. Social scientists and human resource managers routinely measure a competency, such as leadership, in a variety of ways, ranging from a self-report Likert scale to a workplace performance appraisal or an inbox test. Separating the construct from its measurement is valuable conceptually because a construct may be important even if its measurement is poor. In psychometric modeling, constructs viewed as separate from their measures are referred to as latent (as opposed to observed or measured) variables. There are two types of latent variables: reflective latent variables and formative latent variables (see Figure 2-1).

Following a concept proposed by Spearman (1904, 1927), a reflective latent variable is identified based on correlations among scores from a set of tasks. Differential psychologists discover reflective latent variables using factor analysis and related methods to identify the patterns of correlations among a set of "indicator variables"—scores on tests and rating instruments used to measure cognitive and noncognitive competencies. A reflective latent variable—such as general cognitive ability or one of the "big five" personality factors (McCrae and Costa, 1987)—is thought to reflect the essence of, or the commonality among, the various competencies measured. In psychometric modeling, a reflective latent variable (also called a *factor* because it is discovered through factor analysis) is said to cause the relationships among the set of indicator variables (see Figure 2-1). For example, extraversion, a personality factor, is thought to cause relatively high scores on instruments measuring warmth, gregariousness, and assertiveness. Within a reflective latent variable, the importance or weighting of an individual indicator variable is a function of how highly that particular indicator variable correlates with other indicator variables for the reflective latent variable (Bollen and Lennox, 1991).

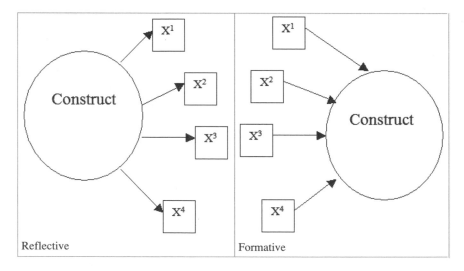

FIGURE 2-1 Casual structures in reflective and formative latent variables.
SOURCE: Stenner, Burdick, and Stone (2008). Reprinted with permission.

A formative latent variable is very different from a reflective latent variable in that the direction of causality runs from the observed indicator variable to the formative latent variable. The indicator variables may be positively correlated, uncorrelated, or even negatively correlated, and patterns of correlations among them are not used to identify formative latent variables. Instead, experts identify formative latent variables through a variety of other means, such as through consensus opinion or traditions in a field. Formative latent variables can be thought of as a "stew"—a mixture of elements that might or might not be related. The various lists of 21st century skills that have been proposed to date are formative variables, identified by consensus opinion and through reviews of earlier reports and standards documents (e.g., Secretary's Commission on Achieving Necessary Skills, 1991; American Association of School Libararians and Association for Educational Communications and Technology, 1998).

Reflective Latent Variables: Taxonomies of Cognitive and Noncognitive Competencies

Because reflective latent variables (factors) are based on empirical research, they provide a strong framework for organizing the formative variables included in lists of 21st century skills. Taxonomies of reflective latent variables are available for both cognitive (Carroll, 1993) and noncognitive (Goldberg, 1992) competencies.

Cognitive Abilities Taxonomy

Carroll (1993) conducted a secondary analysis of over 450 correlation matrices of cognitive test scores that had been produced between 1900 and 1990. He sought to identify a common structure to characterize the pattern of correlations among tests and thereby to identify the factors of human cognition. He found that the data were consistent with a "three stratum" hierarchical model with a general cognitive ability factor at the top, eight second-order abilities (factors) at the middle level, and 45 primary abilities at the bottom of the taxonomy. The second-order factors identified were as follows (with the corresponding primary abilities shown in parentheses):

- Fluid intelligence (reasoning, induction, quantitative reasoning, and Piagetian reasoning, a collection of abstract reasoning abilities described in Piaget's 1963 theory of cognitive development, such as the ability to organize materials that possess similar characteristics into categories and an awareness that physical quantities do not change in amount when altered in appearance)

- Crystallized intelligence (verbal comprehension, foreign language aptitude, communication ability, listening ability, and the ability to provide missing words in a portion of text)
- Retrieval ability (originality/creativity, the ability to generate ideas, and fluency of expression in writing and drawing)
- Memory and learning (memory span, recall by association, free recall, visual memory, and learning ability)
- Broad visual perception (visualization, spatial relations, speed in perceiving and comparing images, and mental processing of images)
- Broad auditory perception (hearing and speech, sound discrimination, and memory for sound patterns)
- Broad cognitive speediness (rate of test taking [tempo] and facility with numbers)
- Reaction time (computer) (simple reaction time to respond to a stimulus, reaction time to choose and make an appropriate response to a stimulus, and semantic retrieval of general knowledge)

We focused the content analysis on the first three factors—fluid intelligence, crystallized intelligence, and retrieval ability—because the primary abilities they included were most closely related to the 21st century skills discussed in the reports and documents. It is important to note that our content analysis did not address how valuable any of the 21st century skills may be for influencing later success in employment, education, or other life arenas. To carry out the content analysis we simply took lists of competencies that other individuals and groups have proposed are valuable and aligned them with research-based taxonomies of cognitive and noncognitive competencies. In the following chapter, we discuss research on the relationship between various competencies and later education and employment outcomes.

Personality Taxonomy

For the past two decades, the "big five" model of personality has been widely accepted as a way to characterize competencies in the interpersonal and intrapersonal domains (McCrae and Costa, 1987; Goldberg, 1993). It is based on the *lexical hypothesis*, which suggests that language evolves to characterize the most salient dimensions of human behavior, and so by analyzing language and the way we use it to describe ourselves or others it is possible to identify the fundamental ways in which people differ from one another (Allport and Odbert, 1936). Based on a review of English dictionaries, psychologists identified personality-describing adjectives and developed many instruments to measure these characteristics. Multiple, independent factor–analytic studies of scores on these instruments, using different samples, converged on five personality factors (Almlund et al., 2011).

This taxonomy has been replicated in many languages, yielding approximately the same five dimensions,[2] defined as follows (American Psychological Association, 2007):

- Openness to experience: the tendency to be open to new aesthetic, cultural, or intellectual experiences
- Conscientiousness: the tendency to be organized, responsible, and hardworking
- Extroversion: an orientation of one's interests and energies toward the outer world of people and things rather than toward the inner world of subjective experience
- Agreeableness: the tendency to act in a cooperative, unselfish manner
- Neuroticism: a chronic level of emotional instability and proneness to psychological distress. The opposite of neuroticism is emotional stability, defined as predictability and consistency in emotional reactions, with absence of rapid mood changes.

Reflecting the fact that they were derived from factor analysis, the five factors are intended to be orthogonal, or uncorrelated with one another. Each can be broken down further into personality facets, which are sets of intercorrelated factors. Facets are not as stable across cultures as the major five dimensions are, but they nevertheless prove useful ways to characterize individual differences more precisely (Paunonen and Ashton, 2001). When various proposals for facets are combined with the five factors, the result is a hierarchical taxonomy. Although no clear consensus has emerged on exactly which facets should be used to further characterize the five personality dimensions, the facets suggested by Costa and McCrae (1992) are widely used and are presented here to illustrate the range of individual characteristics encompassed by each of the five factors:

- Conscientiousness (competence, order, dutifulness, achievement striving, self-discipline, deliberation)
- Agreeableness (trust, straightforwardness, altruism, compliance, modesty, tender-mindedness)
- Neuroticism (anxiety, angry hostility, depression, self-consciousness, impulsiveness, vulnerability)

---

[2]Some languages identify a sixth factor related to honesty (e.g., Ashton, Lee, and Son, 2000).

- Extroversion (warmth, gregariousness, assertiveness, activity, excitement seeking, positive emotions)
- Openness to experience (fantasy, aesthetics, feelings, actions, ideas, values)

To the facets of the neuroticism/emotional stability factor proposed by Costa and McCrae (1992) we added "core self-evaluation," based on a proposal by Judge and Bono (2001). This additional proposed construct is based on empirical findings of correlations between measures of self-esteem, generalized self-efficacy, locus of control,[3] and emotional stability. Almlund et al. (2011) also found that self-esteem and locus of control are related to emotional stability.

The five major factors provided a small number of research-based constructs onto which various terms for 21st century skills could be mapped. The facets helped to define the range of skills and behaviors encompassed within each major factor to serve as a point of comparison with the various 21st century skills.

Formative Latent Variables: Occupational Skills and Other Examples

Unlike reflective latent variables that are discovered, formative latent variables are constructed. Relationships between variables do not constrain the development of formative latent variables; rather, formative latent variables can be whatever a person or community defines them to be. Classic examples appear in economics, such as the consumer price index; in health, such as the stress index; and in business research, such as leadership or positive experience with a product (Jarvis, Mackenzie, and Podsakoff, 2003).

One set of formative latent variables that may be particularly relevant for defining 21st century competencies was identified through expert consensus in the O*NET project (Peterson et al., 1999). O*NET is a large database of information on 965 occupations that is organized around a "content model," which describes occupations along several dimensions, including worker characteristics (abilities, interests, work values, and work styles) and requirements (skills, knowledge, and education). The skills included in the O*NET content model are similar to those in current lists of 21st century lists, as shown in Table 2-1.

---

[3]In differential psychology, *locus of control* refers to the extent to which individuals believe that they can control their own lives (an internal locus of control) or that outside influences control what happens (an external locus of control), as measured by the Rotter scale (Rotter, 1990). The "locus of control" construct has been criticized as being too general, and most researchers currently differentiate beliefs about causality as delineated in attribution theory.

TABLE 2-1 Skills in the O*NET Content Model

Basic Skills	
Content Skills	**Process Skills**
Active listening	Active learning
Reading comprehension	Learning strategies
Writing	Monitoring
Speaking	Critical thinking
Mathematics	
Science	

Cross-Functional Skills	
Complex Problem Solving	**Social Skills**
Complex problem solving	Social perceptiveness
	Coordination
	Persuasion
	Negotiation
	Instruction
	Service orientation
Technical Skills	**Systems Skills**
Operations analysis	Systems analysis
Technology design	Judgment and decision
Equipment selection	making
Installation	Systems evaluation
Programming	
Quality control analysis	
Operation monitoring	
Equipment maintenance	
Troubleshooting	
Repairing	
Resource Management Skills	
Time management	
Management of financial resources	
Managing material resources	
Managing personnel resources	

SOURCE: Adapted from Peterson et al. (1997). Copyright 1999 by the American Psychological Association. Reproduced with permission. The use of APA information does not imply endorsement by APA.

Aligning Lists of 21st Century Skills with Ability and Personality Factors

As a first step toward aligning various lists of competencies included in the reports and documents on 21st century skills with ability and personality factors, the committee compared the eight reports and documents mentioned above, identifying areas of overlap and differences. Another useful step was to divide the various competencies into the three domains

TABLE 2-2 Clusters of 21st Century Competencies

Cluster	Terms Used for 21st Century Skills	O*NET Skills	Main Ability/ Personality Factor
Cognitive Processes and Strategies	Critical thinking, problem solving, analysis, reasoning/argumentation, interpretation, decision making, adaptive learning, executive function	System skills, process skills, complex problem-solving skills	Main ability factor: fluid intelligence (Gf)
Knowledge	Information literacy (research using evidence and recognizing bias in sources); information and communications technology literacy; oral and written communication; active listening	Content skills	Main ability factor: crystallized intelligence (Gc)
Creativity	Creativity, innovation	Complex problem-solving skills (idea generation)	Main ability factor: general retrieval ability (Gr)

COGNITIVE COMPETENCIES

INTRA-PERSONAL COMPETENCIES			
Intellectual Openness	Flexibility, adaptability, artistic and cultural appreciation, personal and social responsibility (including cultural awareness and competence), appreciation for diversity, adaptability, continuous learning, intellectual interest and curiosity	[none]	Main personality factor: openness
Work Ethic/ Conscientious-ness	Initiative, self-direction, responsibility, perseverance, productivity, grit, Type 1 self-regulation (metacognitive skills, including forethought, performance, and self-reflection), professionalism/ethics, integrity, citizenship, career orientation	[none]	Main personality factor: conscientiousness
Positive Core Self-Evaluation	Type 2 self-regulation (self-monitoring, self-evaluation, self-reinforcement), physical and psychological health	[none]	Main personality factor: emotional stability (opposite end of the continuum from neuroticism)

continued

TABLE 2-2 Continued

	Cluster	Terms Used for 21st Century Skills	O*NET Skills	Main Ability/ Personality Factor
INTER-PERSONAL COMPETENCIES	*Teamwork and Collaboration*	Communication, collaboration, teamwork, cooperation, coordination, interpersonal skills, empathy/perspective taking, trust, service orientation, conflict resolution, negotiation	Social skills	Main personality factor: agreeableness
	Leadership	Leadership, responsibility, assertive communication, self-presentation, social influence with others	Social skills (persuasion)	Main personality factor: extroversion

SOURCE: Created by committee.

of cognitive, intrapersonal, and interpersonal competence. Using this approach we found that some of the documents that dealt with 21st century skills focused primarily on one category. For example, Conley's 2007 list of college readiness skills deals mainly with cognitive competencies, while Hoyle and Davisson's 2011 analysis of self-regulation focuses on intrapersonal competencies.

Next, the committee conducted a content analysis, comparing the various competencies included in the eight documents with the reflective latent variables at the top of the cognitive abilities and personality taxonomies. Based on the comparative content analysis, we aligned the various 21st century skills with each other and with the two taxonomies. In addition, we also aligned O*NET skills and additional noncognitive competencies with the two taxonomies. Through these steps we created clusters of closely related competencies within each of the three broad domains (see Table 2-2). Each competency cluster contains the main factor (personality or ability) and the associated 21st century skills and O*NET skills. The result is a preliminary taxonomy of 21st century competencies, which we offer as a starting point for further research.

Based on the committee's content analysis, some of the competencies that appeared in the eight documents and reports were not included in any of the clusters. These included life and career skills (Binkley et al., 2010), social and cultural competencies (Voogt and Pareja Roblin, 2010), study skills and contextual skills (Conley, 2007), and nonverbal communication and intercultural sensitivity (Bedwell, Fiore, and Salas, 2011). These particular competencies were excluded because they did not align well with any of the clusters, rather than because of any judgment that they were less valuable for later life outcomes. In the following chapter, we discuss the question of whether various competencies predict success in education, the workplace, or other areas of adult life.

We offer the proposed taxonomy of competency clusters as an initial step toward addressing the "jangle fallacy." It provides a starting point for further research that may more clearly define each construct and establish its relationship with the other constructs. However, research to date on the importance of 21st century competencies uses a variety of terms for these skills, coined by investigators in the different disciplines. Our review of this research in the following chapter reflects this variety of terms.

SUMMARY

Although many lists of 21st century skills have been proposed, there is considerable overlap among them. Many of the constructs included in such lists trace back to the original SCANS report (Secretary's Commission on Achieving Necessary Skills, 1991), and some now appear in the O*NET database. Aligning the various competencies with extant, research-based personality and ability taxonomies illuminates the relationships between them and suggests a preliminary new taxonomy of 21st century competencies. Much further research is needed to more clearly define the competencies at each level of the proposed taxonomy, to understand the extent to which various competencies and competency clusters may be malleable, to elucidate the relationships among the competencies, and to identify the most effective ways to teach and learn these competencies.

3

Importance of Deeper Learning and 21st Century Skills

This chapter summarizes research on the importance of deeper learning and "21st century skills" to success in education, work, and other areas of adult responsibility. The first section focuses on educational achievement and attainment, the second section on work, the third on health and relationship skills, and the fourth on civic participation. Overall, the research reviewed in these sections finds statistically significant, positive relationships of modest size between various cognitive, intrapersonal, and interpersonal competencies and desirable adult outcomes. However, these relationships are based on correlational research methods.

We also reviewed evidence on the role of formal schooling in adult success, which we include in the sections on work and health. We found statistically significant, positive relationships between years of educational attainment and labor market success, not only in research using correlational methods, but also in studies using stronger research methods (see discussion below). Measured cognitive, intrapersonal, or interpersonal competencies appeared to account for surprisingly little of these relationships between years of educational attainment and labor market success. In the fifth section, we show that the benefits of additional years of formal schooling for individuals include not only higher wages but also somewhat greater adaptability to changes in workplace technology and in jobs.

The literature discussed in this chapter comes from a variety of disciplines, including industrial-organizational psychology, developmental psychology, human resource development, and economics. Researchers in these disciplines have investigated the relationship between a range of different skills and abilities and later outcomes, using a variety of methods and data sets. Some of the evidence we present is correlational in nature, and we call these "simple correlations." Other evidence is longitudinal, in which competencies and other capacities measured at one point are related to outcomes measured years later, often after adjusting for individuals' differences in family backgrounds. We call these "adjusted correlations" and view this evidence as more suggestive of causal connections than the evidence from simple correlations, but still prone to biases from a variety of sources. The strongest causal evidence, particularly the evidence of the impacts of years of completed schooling on adult outcomes, comes from statistical methods that are designed to approximate experiments.

IMPORTANCE TO EDUCATIONAL SUCCESS

Many more studies of school success have focused on the role of general cognitive ability (IQ) than specific interpersonal and intrapersonal competencies (see Table 3-1). Economists tend to lump all competencies other than IQ into the category of "noncognitive skills." Personality and developmental psychologists have developed a much more refined taxonomy of them.

Most personality psychologists have centered their work on the "big five" personality traits—conscientiousness, openness, agreeableness, emotional stability, and extroversion—plus general cognitive ability. Although these traits have traditionally been viewed as relatively stable across the life span, a growing body of evidence indicates that that personality traits change in response to general life experiences (e.g., Roberts, Walton, and Viechtbauer, 2006; Almlund et al., 2011) and to structured interventions (see Chapters 4 and 5).

Developmental psychologists have a dynamic view of competence and behavioral development, with children's competencies and behaviors determined by the interplay between their innate abilities and dispositions and the quality of their early experiences (National Research Council, 2000). Both groups have investigated associations among cognitive, intrapersonal, and interpersonal competencies and children's success in school.

Personality Factors and School Success

The comprehensive Almlund et al. (2011) study of personality and attainment offers the following summary of "prediction" evidence on correlations and, in some cases, adjusted correlations between personality traits and educational attainment (see also Table 3-1):

> Measures of personality predict a range of educational outcomes. Of the
> Big Five, Conscientiousness best predicts overall attainment and achieve-

ment. Other traits, such as Openness to Experience, predict finer measures of educational attainment, such as attendance and course difficulty. Traits related to Neuroticism also affect educational attainment, but the relationship is not always monotonic. Conscientiousness predicts college grades to the same degree that SAT scores do. Personality measures predict performance on achievement tests and, to a lesser degree, performance on intelligence tests. (p. 127)

It is important to note that while these associations are large enough to pass conventional thresholds of statistical significance, they almost never account for more than a nominal amount of the variation in the educational attainment outcomes under study.

The most noteworthy meta-analysis of these kinds of data is by Poropat (2009), who examined studies of the simple correlations between personality factors and school grades in primary, secondary, and higher education.[1] He found a significant positive association between conscientiousness and grades in primary school through college (see top half of Table 3-2). The simple correlations between conscientiousness and grades in high school and college were in the 0.20-0.25 range, about as high as the correlations between measures of general cognitive ability and grades in high school and college.[2] In comparison with other correlates of grades identified in previous studies, these two correlations are at approximately the same level as socioeconomic status (Sirin, 2005) and slightly lower than the correlations found for conscientiousness in industry training programs (Arthur et al., 2003).

In elementary school, general cognitive ability is the strongest correlate of grades, although all five personality factors are positively correlated with grades. Correlations between personality factors and grades generally fall over the course of high school and college. In higher education, among the five personality factors, only conscientiousness is correlated with grades.

Three studies of the correlations between "big five" personality traits and completed schooling have included at least some regression controls (Goldberg et al., 1998; van Eijck and de Graaf, 2004; Almlund et al., 2011). All find positive adjusted associations for concientiousness that range from 0.05 to 0.18, and all find modest negative adjusted associations for extroversion, agreeableness, and neuroticism.

---

[1]The Poropat (2009) analysis included many more studies focused on grades in secondary (24-35 studies) and higher education (75-92 studies) than in elementary school (8 studies).

[2]In social science research, such correlations are generally interpreted following rules of thumb developed by Cohen (1988), in which a correlation of 0.20 is considered small, a correlation of 0.50 is considered medium, and a correlation of 0.80 is considered large.

TABLE 3-1 Key Studies Cited in Chapter 3: The Importance of Deeper Learning and 21st Century Skills

Reference	Key Findings/Conclusions	Research Methods	Measures of Skills
Studies of Personality Factors			
Almlund et al. (2011)	Conscientiousness has strong correlations with outcomes from a number of adult domains.	Research synthesis	"Big five" personality traits measured using a variety of direct and indirect methods
Studies of the Relationship Between Skills and Educational Attainment			
Duncan et al. (2007)	Reading, math, and attention skills at school entry predict subsequent reading and math achievement. Neither behavior problems nor mental health problems were associated with later achievement, holding constant achievement as well as child and family characteristics.	Formal meta-analysis of standardized regression coefficients emerging from the 236 individual study regressions analyzing the relationship between school-entry reading and math achievement and noncognitive skills and later reading and math achievement. Controls for general cognitive ability, behavior and temperament and parent education and income were included in the regressions.	Cognitive Skills: Measures of school-entry reading and math achievement Interpersonal and Intrapersonal Skills: The six longitudinal data sets included measures of attention (intrapersonal), antisocial behavior (both intrapersonal and interpersonal), and mental health (intrapersonal).
Duncan and Magnuson (2011)	Although school-entry reading and math achievement skills predicted later school achievement, single point-in-time assessments of primary school skills were relatively weakly predictive of later outcomes. Children with persistent math or behavior problems were much less likely to graduate from high school or attend college and those with	Review of theory and empirical studies of the relationship between young children's skills and behaviors and their later attainments. The studies included measures of individual students' skills at multiple points in time to identify persistent patterns.	Cognitive Skills: Measures of school-entry reading and math achievement Interpersonal and Intrapersonal Skills: The studies included measures of attention (intrapersonal), antisocial behavior (both intrapersonal and interpersonal), and mental health (intrapersonal).

continued

	persistent behavior problems were much more likely to be arrested or jailed.	
Poropat (2009)	At the elementary school level, cognitive ability is the strongest predictor of grades. At the high school and college levels, cognitive ability is a weaker predictor of grades and conscientiousness is the only personality factor that predicts grades. Where tested, correlations between conscientiousness and academic performance were largely independent of measures of cognitive ability. Studies controlling for secondary academic performance found conscientiousness predicted college grades at about the same level as measures of cognitive ability.	Meta-analysis of studies of the correlation between personality traits and academic performance. Most of the studies came from higher education, with a smaller sample from primary education.	Cognitive Skills: Some of the studies included tests of general cognitive ability.

Interpersonal Skills: Measures of agreeableness and extroversion

Intrapersonal Skills: Measures of conscientiousness, emotional stability, and openness |

TABLE 3-1 Continued

Reference	Key Findings/Conclusions	Research Methods	Measures of Skills
Studies of the Relationship Between Skills and Income/Earnings/Job Performance			
Autor, Levy, and Murnane (2003)	From 1970 to 1988, across the U.S. economy, computerization reduced routine cognitive and manual tasks and increased nonroutine cognitive and interactive tasks. This model explains 60% of the growth in college-educated labor from 1970-1988. Conclusion: Demand is growing for nonroutine problem-solving and complex communication skills.	Paired representative data on job task requirements from the Dictionary of Occupational Titles (DOT) with samples of employed workers from the Census and CPS to create a consistent panel of industry and occupational task input from 1960 to 1998.	Cognitive: DOT measures of: nonroutine cognitive tasks: (1) level of direction, control, and planning of activities; and (2) quantitative reasoning Manual Tasks: DOT measures of routine manual tasks: finger dexterity and nonroutine tasks: eye-hand-foot coordination Interpersonal and Intrapersonal: No direct measures
Barrick, Mount, and Judge (2001) (job performance)	Conscientiousness is a valid predictor of job performance across all performance measures in all occupations studied, with average correlations ranging from the mid .20s to low .30s.	Second-order meta-analysis of the results of 11 prior meta-analyses of the relationship between Five Factor Model personality traits and job performance.	Cognitive: No measures Interpersonal: Measures of extroversion, agreeableness Intrapersonal: Measures of emotional stability, conscientiousness, and openness to experience
Cunha and Heckman (2008) (earnings and high school graduation)	Increased parental investments in their children's skills impact adult earnings and high school graduation rates through effects on both cognitive and noncognitive	Dynamic factor model used to address endogeneity of inputs and multiplicity of parental inputs relative to instruments. Estimated the scale of the factors by estimating	Cognitive Skills: Tests of mathematics and reading recognition Interpersonal and Intrapersonal: Several subscores of the Behavioral Problems

	skills. Improvements in noncognitive skills raised both cognitive and noncognitive skills.	their effects on high school graduation and earnings at age 23. Data: Sample of 1,053 white males from the CNLSY79 data set	Index were combined into a single measure of noncognitive skills. Measures of Parental Investments: Number of books, number of musical instruments, newspaper subscriptions, special lessons, trips to the museum, trips to the theater
Lindqvist and Vestman (2011)	Conclusion: Noncognitive ability is considerably more important than cognitive ability for success in the labor market.	Multiple regression analysis. Authors used ordinary least squares to estimate the effect of cognitive and noncognitive skills on wages, earnings, and unemployment. They matched a dataset on socioeconomic outcomes for a representative sample of the Swedish population with data from the military enlistment.	Cognitive Skills: Test of general intelligence Intrapersonal and Interpersonal Skills: Authors used the overall score and the sum of the subscores assigned by a certified psychologist on the basis of a semi-structured, 25-minute interview. The interview is designed to measure the ability to function during armed combat. A high score reflects both intrapersonal and interpersonal skills

Studies of the Relationship Between Skills and Health

Cutler and Lleras-Muney (2010a)	The effect of education on health increases with increasing years of education and appears to be related to critical thinking and decision-making patterns.	1990, 1991, and 2000 waves of the National Health Interview Survey, National Death Index	Completed years of schooling

SOURCE: Created by the committee.

TABLE 3-2 Correlations and Regression-Adjusted Associations Among Skills, Behaviors, and School Performance

Personality Factors — Outcome is school grades.

Personality Factors	Concurrent (simple) Correlations			Longitudinal (simple) Correlations	Regression-Adjusted Correlations
	Primary school	Secondary	Tertiary	Primary	Primary
Conscientiousness	.28	.21	.23		
Openness	.24	.12	.07		
Agreeableness	.30	.05	.06		
Emotional stability	.20	.01	-.01		
Extroversion	.18	-.01	-.03		
Cognitive ability	.58	.24	.23		

Skills and Behaviors — Concurrent: Outcome is reading achievement. Longitudinal: Outcomes are later reading and math achievement.

Skills and Behaviors	Concurrent (simple) Correlations		Longitudinal (simple) Correlations	Regression-Adjusted Correlations
	Kindergarten	5th grade	Kindergarten	Kindergarten
Reading achievement	—		.44	.13
Math achievement	—		.47	.33
Attention	.29	.38	.25	.07
Antisocial behavior	-.07	-.25	-.14	-.01
Mental health	-.12	-.20	-.10	.00

NOTE: Concurrent correlations for personality factors and cognitive ability come from Poropat (2009). Concurrent correlations for skills and behaviors in kindergarten and fifth grade come from Duncan and Magnuson (2011). Longitudinal and regression-adjusted correlations are from Duncan et al. (2007). Regression controls in the final column include family background, child temperament, and IQ.
SOURCE: Created by the committee.

Skills, Behaviors, and School Success

There are many ways that developmental psychologists classify competencies in the cognitive, intrapersonal, and interpersonal domains, and some of their categories correspond to some of the "big five" personality traits. One recent review classified important competencies into four groups: achievement, attention, behavior problems, and mental health (Duncan and Magnuson, 2011).

Achievement, in the cognitive domain, refers to concrete academic competencies such as literacy (e.g., for kindergarteners, decoding skills such as beginning to associate sounds with letters at the beginning and end of words) and basic mathematics (e.g., ability to recognize numbers and shapes and to compare relative sizes). Although scores on tests of cognitive ability and achievement tend to have substantial correlations, there is an important conceptual difference between cognitive ability as a relatively stable trait and the concrete achievement competencies that develop in response to schooling and other environmental inputs.

Attention, in the intrapersonal domain, refers to the ability to control impulses and focus on tasks (e.g., Raver, 2004). Developmental psychologists often distinguish between two broad dimensions of behavior problems that reflect the domains of interpersonal and intrapersonal competencies—externalizing and internalizing. Externalizing behavior refers to a cluster of related behaviors, including antisocial behavior, conduct disorders, and more general aggression (Moffitt, 1993; Campbell, Shaw, and Gilliom, 2000). Internalizing behavior refers to a similarly broad set of mental health constructs, including anxiety and depression as well as somatic complaints and withdrawn behavior (Bongers et al. ,2003).[3]

Many studies have established simple and, in some cases, adjusted correlations between this set of intrapersonal and interpersonal competencies and academic outcomes in the early grades (e.g., Vitaro et al., 2005, and Currie and Stabile, 2007, for attention; Pianta and Stuhlman, 2004, for antisocial behavior; and Fantuzzo et al., 2003, for depressive symptoms). Duncan and Magnuson (2011) use nationally representative data on kindergarteners and fifth graders to compute the simple correlations shown in the bottom left panel of Table 3-2. Since letter grades are rarely recorded in the early grades, the table shows correlations between reading achievement and measures of attention, antisocial behavior and mental health. All are substantial by fifth grade, with the expected positive achievement

---

[3]Cutting across the attention and externalizing categories is the idea of self-regulation, which current theory and research often subdivides into separate cognitive (cool) and emotional components (hot) (Raver, 2004; Eisenberg et al., 2005; Raver et al., 2005). Cognitive self-regulation fits into our "attention" category while emotional self-regulation fits into our "behavior problems" category.

associations for attention and negative associations for antisocial behavior and mental health problems. All of these associations are smaller in kindergarten, which, in contrast with the research on personality factors (Poropat, 2009), suggests increasing correlations as children grow older.

Averaging across six longitudinal data sets, Duncan et al. (2007) calculate the bivariate correlations shown in the "longitudinal correlations" column of Table 3-2. Shown here are simple correlations among kindergarten entry achievement, attention and behavioral competencies, and math and reading test scores measured 2-8 years later. Correlations between later achievement and the three measures of attention, antisocial behavior, and mental health problems are similar to what was found for corresponding correlations with kindergarten achievement shown in the first column. As might be expected, correlations between math and reading competencies at school entry and later in the elementary school years are quite high.

To more accurately assess the importance of any one of these competencies and behaviors for school and career success, some studies have gone beyond these simple correlations to account for the fact that children with different levels of a given competency or behavior are likely to differ in many other ways as well. Children with, say, higher math scores may also have higher IQs, be better readers, exhibit less antisocial behavior, or come from more advantaged families. When adjustments for differences in these other conditions are made, the size of the relationship between early competencies and behaviors and later outcomes tends to shrink. This is shown in the fifth and sixth columns of numbers in Table 3-2. A clear conclusion from these columns of numbers is that only three of the five school-entry competencies have noteworthy adjusted correlations with subsequent reading and math achievement: reading, math, and attention. Neither behavior problems nor mental health problems demonstrated a statistically significant positive correlation with later achievement, once achievement and child and family characteristics are held constant.[4]

Studies estimating bivariate correlations between high school completion and measures of early competencies and behaviors—including achievement, attention, behavior problems, and mental health—find them to be quite modest (.05 to .10; Entwisle, Alexander, and Olson, 2005; Duncan and Magnuson, 2011, Appendix Table 3.A9). Even when these competencies and behaviors are measured at age 14, none of the correlations with high school completion is stronger than .20.

Much larger correlations are observed for early indications that children have *persistent* deficits in some of these competencies and behaviors. In particular, children with persistently low mathematics achievement and

---

[4]A replication and extension analysis by Grissmer et al. (2010) also found predictive power for measures of fine motor skills.

persistently high levels of antisocial behavior across elementary school were 10-13 percentage points less likely to graduate high school and about 25 percentage points less likely to attend college than children who never have these problems (Duncan and Magnuson, 2011). In contrast, persistent reading and attention problems had very low adjusted correlations with these attainment outcomes.[5]

IMPORTANCE TO WORKPLACE SUCCESS

Technological advances, globalization, and other changes have fueled demand for more highly educated workers over the past four decades. Across much of the 1980s, the inflation-adjusted earnings of high school graduates plunged by 16 percent, while the earnings of college-educated workers rose by nearly 10 percent. In the following two decades, low-skill worker earnings continued to fall, while the earnings of college-educated workers continued their modest rise.[6]

How these occupation and education-related changes in the labor market affect the demand for cognitive, intrapersonal, and interpersonal competencies is the subject of this section. We begin with a brief review of the large literature on the economic payoff to years of formal education, and of the remarkably modest extent to which prior cognitive, intrapersonal, and interpersonal skills account for that payoff. We then turn to a more detailed discussion of trends in demand for 21st century competencies.

Educational Attainment and Employment Outcomes

From the pioneering work in the 1960s and 1970s of Schultz (1961), Becker (1964), and Mincer (1974) to the present, studies have shown that investments in education produce rates of monetary return that are comparable or higher than market rates on investment in physical capital. Remarkable in this literature is that the estimates have changed little as increasingly sophisticated studies have eliminated likely sources of bias in the estimation of the economic payoff to education, the most prominent of which is the self-selection of more able or motivated into higher levels of completed schooling.[7]

---

[5]These results come from an analysis in which the predictive power of any given skill or behavior was assessed after adjusting for the others and for family background characteristics.

[6]Autor, Katz, and Kearney (2008, Table 1). Data are based on weekly earnings for full-time workers with 5 years of experience. Earnings of high school dropouts fell even more than the earnings of high school graduates (see also Levy and Murnane, 2004).

[7]An overview of the efforts to address these bias issues is provided in Card (1999). One strategy for reducing bias from genetic factors is to use siblings or even identical twins to relate earnings and employment differences to schooling differences pairs of otherwise "similar"

In most studies, the so-called private rate of return to added years of schooling (which relates the after-tax earnings benefits enjoyed by workers to the portion of the education costs they have borne) for the United States has varied between 7 and 11 percent, with even higher rates in many other countries (Psacharoupoulos and Patrinos, 2004). The social rate of return tends to be lower than the private rate of return because it includes the full resource costs of schooling provision, much of which is paid through government subsidies rather than the students themselves.

Barrow and Rouse (2005) have concluded that each additional year of schooling generates additional income of about 10 percent, a return that is about the same across the races. And Autor, Katz, and Kearney (2008, Figure 2A) estimate that the earnings advantage for college as opposed to high school graduates rose from about 50 percent higher in the mid-1970s to close to twice as high in 2005. In their summary of evidence on education curriculum, Altonji, Blom, and Maghir (2012) find greater labor market returns to more advanced high school courses and to engineering, business, and science majors in college.

Looking beyond earnings, Oreopoulos and Salvanes (2011) find that workers with higher educational attainment enjoy more nonmonetary employment advantages, including a higher sense of achievement, work in more prestigious occupations, and greater job satisfaction than comparable workers with lower levels of education. Those with more formal education are more likely to be selected for jobs that require further training and that merit training investment. Presumably, the rationale for basing selection decisions on the candidate's level of education is that the costs of training for reaching job proficiency are reduced when more educated persons are chosen for training programs (Thurow, 1975; Lynch, 1994). Finally, evidence suggests that one person's added years of schooling benefits others by raising the productivity of other workers at all levels of education (Moretti, 2004).[8]

In short, the economic importance of a highly educated workforce is impressive and, if anything, increasing. Since the schooling process

---

individuals. For example, using Norwegian data, Oreopoulos and Salvanes (2011) find that, in comparison with their siblings, siblings with 1 additional year of education have annual incomes that are about 5 percent higher and lower probabilities of being unemployed or on welfare. Another is to use instrumental variable strategies based on, for example, compulsory schooling laws, where the obligatory age of school attendance determines the number of years and the permissible date at which students can leave. Since years of schooling under the compulsory attendance requirements are not subject to voluntary choice, differences in education are exogenous to other influences that might affect the amount of education obtained. None of these strategies is free from all potential biases, however.

[8]Using a different estimation strategy that focuses only on the returns to secondary schooling for individuals subject to compulsory school attendance laws, Acemoglu and Angrist produce a smaller, but still positive, estimate of external returns than Moretti (2004).

presumably imparts the competencies and behaviors that are responsible for these productivity advantages, it is important to know how cognitive, intrapersonal, and interpersonal competencies are connected to education's high rates of return.

Test Scores, Education, and Employment Outcomes

Cognitive competencies (as measured by standardized test scores) have the potential to play an important role in accounting for the links between schooling and earnings. First, since smarter people are more likely to acquire more schooling, failure to control for differences in prior cognitive competencies may bias estimates of the role of education *per se*. But second, even if two graduating high school seniors with identical cognitive competencies make different decisions about whether to attend college, the college experience itself might develop capabilities that command higher earnings from employers.

Surprisingly, empirical studies show that cognitive competencies are able to account for only a small fraction of the association between education and earning. Bowles, Gintis, and Osborne (2001) summarized 25 studies conducted over four decades, which yielded 58 estimates of earnings functions that incorporated test scores. They found that the estimated effect of schooling on earnings retained about 82 percent of its value, on average, after accounting for prior test scores, suggesting that most of the impact of years of educational attainment on earnings was attributable to determinants other than the cognitive competencies.

A second, more direct, approach to investigating the role of cognitive competencies on labor market outcomes does not involve the intervening role played by schooling. An extensive literature, including meta-analyses (e.g., Schmidt and Hunter, 1998, 2004) has examined the simple, unadjusted correlations between cognitive ability, personality factors, and job performance. Schmidt and Hunter (2004) reviewed several studies and meta-analyses, finding that measures of general cognitive ability were strongly correlated (the magnitude of these correlations was higher than 0.53) with occupational level, income, job performance, and job training performance. Comparing these correlations with those found in studies of the association between personality traits and job outcomes, they concluded that general cognitive ability was more important for later job success than conscientiousness or any other intrapersonal or interpersonal competency.

It is worth noting that an NRC committee (1989) reanalyzed the data from over 700 criterion-related studies of the concurrent correlations between scores on a test of general cognitive ability and measures of job performance (typically supervisor ratings, but in some cases, grades in a training course) in about 500 jobs. They found that, despite claims of much higher predictive validities (i.e., correlations) in the literature (U.S. Department of Labor, 1983), the average correlation in studies that had been conducted since 1972 was about .25 after correction for sampling error. Cognitive test scores explained about 6 percent of the variance in performance, leaving 94 percent to be explained by other factors. Estimates of predictive validities in one subsequent review of the empirical literature also reflected this modest range (Sackett et al., 2001).

Economists have favored prospective longitudinal studies of the relationship between cognitive competencies and earnings (Hanushek and Woessman, 2008). In their examination of the associations between earnings and the cognitive skills of 15-18-year-olds as measured by the Armed Forces Qualifying Test, Neal and Johnson (1996) found that, with no controls for family background, a one-standard deviation increase in test scores was associated with roughly a 20 percent increase in earnings for both men and women. Using data from the National Child Development Survey (NCDS), which has followed a cohort of British children born in 1958 through midlife, Currie and Thomas (1999) related scores on reading and math tests administered at age 7 to wages and employment at age 33. Even in the presence of extensive family background controls, their models show 10-20 percent earnings differentials when comparing both males and females in the top and bottom quartiles of the two test score distributions. Murnane, Willett, and Levy (1995) show links between the mathematics tests scores of two cohorts of high school seniors and their wages at age 24.

Intrapersonal and Interpersonal Competencies and Employment Outcomes

In an effort to understand the large amount of variation in earnings and other employment outcomes that cannot be attributed to cognitive competencies, researchers have begun to examine the role of a variety of intrapersonal and interpersonal competencies. As with our earlier review of the determinants of achievement and attainment, research divides into a focus on personality factors and on other competencies and behaviors.

Personality Factors

Almlund et al. (2011) summarize their review of correlational evidence on the role of "big five" personality traits for labor market outcomes as follows:

> Personality measures also predict a variety of labor market outcomes. Of the Big Five traits, Conscientiousness best predicts overall job performance but is less predictive than measures of intelligence. Conscientiousness,

however, predicts performance and wages across a broad range of occupational categories, whereas the predictive power of measures of intelligence decreases with job complexity. Additionally, traits related to Neuroticism (e.g. locus of control and self-esteem) predict a variety of labor market outcomes, including job search effort. Many traits predict sorting into occupations, consistent with the economic models of comparative advantage. . . . Personality traits are valued differentially across occupations. (p. 127)

A key study in this literature is Barrick, Mount, and Judge (2001), which conducts a second-order meta-analysis of the results of 11 prior meta-analyses of the simple associations between Five Factor Model personality traits and job performance. They find that conscientiousness is a valid correlate of job performance across all performance measures studied, with average correlations ranging from the mid .20s to low .30s. Emotional stability was correlated with overall work performance although not with all of the work performance criteria examined. The remaining factors—extroversion, openness and agreeableness—failed to correlate consistently with overall work performance.

Skills, Behaviors, and Earnings

The literature on links between earnings and specific achievement and behavioral skills has employed prospective longitudinal data and well-controlled regression models, yielding stronger evidence than that provided by studies of simple correlations. For example, Heckman, Stixrud, and Urzua (2006), using data from the National Longitudinal Study of Youth (NLSY) estimate substantial adjusted correlations between earnings and a scale combining adolescent self-esteem and sense of personal effectiveness.

Carneiro, Crawford, and Goodman (2007) use data from the British NCDS to relate a wide variety of achievement and behavioral measures assessed when the sample children were 11 years old to later earnings. The diversity of their behavioral measures is reflected in their names: "anxiety for acceptance," "hostility toward adults," "withdrawal," and "restlessness." When summed into a single index, a standard deviation increase in this collection of antisocial skills and behaviors is found to be associated (net of parental background) with a 3.3 percent decrease in age-42 earnings, about one-fifth of the estimated positive association for a one standard-deviation increase in achievement tests scores. Ironically, an examination of the social and behavioral subscales found the greatest explanatory power for "inconsequential behavior"—a heterogeneous mixture of items related to inattention ("too restless to remember for long"), antisocial behavior ("in informal play starts off with others in scrapping and rough play"), and inconsistency ("sometimes eager, sometimes doesn't bother").

In more recent work, Cunha and Heckman (2008) used longitudinal data to study cognitive and noncognitive development over time as it affects high school completion and earnings. They developed a battery of noncognitive scores focused on an antisocial construct using student anxiety, headstrongness, hyperactivity, and peer conflict to go along with cognitive test scores in this analysis. Based upon the psychological, neurological, social, and other aspects of child development, they modeled the developmental path and estimated the impact of investments in cognitive and noncognitive competencies on high school graduation and earnings (at age 23) at three different periods during the age span from 6 to 13. The parental investments studied included purchases of books and musical instruments, newspaper subscriptions, special lessons, trips to the museum, and trips to the theater.

The authors found that the impact of investment returns shifts markedly as the child ages, from cognitive competencies at the earlier ages (6 and 7 to 8 and 9) to noncognitive competencies during the later period (9-13). They also found evidence that noncognitive outcomes contribute to cognitive test results, but little evidence that test scores affect noncognitive outcomes. This finding suggests that investments in noncognitive competencies may contribute to economic productivity not only directly but also by increasing cognitive achievement.

One difficulty in research evaluating and comparing the relative associations between labor market outcomes and both cognitive and noncognitive competencies is the lack of strong measures of noncognitive competencies. Cognitive competencies are measured using well-established and validated standardized testing methods. By contrast, noncognitive competencies are almost always measured by ratings rather than tests—either self-ratings or ratings by observers who are not experts.

Better measurement methods, for example, by trained psychologist observers, might result in more valid measurement and therefore an increase in the estimated importance of noncognitive competencies. This apparently is the finding of a study by Lindqvist and Vestman (2011), which analyzed data on military enlistees in Sweden, where enlistment is compulsory for male 18-year-olds. These individuals complete a cognitive ability test and an extensive questionnaire. A trained psychologist combined the latter with results from a 30-minute clinical interview to assess the individual's noncognitive competencies, particularly, responsibility, independence, outgoingness, persistence, emotional stability, and initiative. The researchers examined a Swedish database and were able to match labor market outcomes of 14,703 32- to 41-year-olds who had earlier been tested through the enlistment. Comparing the impact of cognitive and noncognitive measures on wages, unemployment, and annual earnings, they found that, in general, the adjusted correlations between these outcomes and their noncognitive variable were larger than the correlations of earnings with their cognitive variable. Men who did poorly in the labor market were especially likely to lack noncognitive abilities. In contrast, cognitive ability was a stronger correlate of wages and earnings for workers with earnings above the median.

But while this body of research on intrapersonal and interpersonal competencies is growing rapidly, there is little consensus emerging from it. The prospective studies reviewed above capitalize on the haphazard availability of measures in their data sets. Much further investment is needed to specify such competencies and measure them in a streamlined way. Such specification will be useful in understanding how best to teach noncognitive skills to students (Durlak and Weissberg 2011; see Chapter 6) and how mastery of such competencies may, in turn, affect employment, earnings, and other adult outcomes. The European Commission has begun to examine how noncognitive competencies and personality traits contribute to workplace success (Brunello and Schlotter, 2010).

Trends in Demand for 21st Century Competencies

Clearly, labor market demand for increased years of schooling has risen over the past four decades. There is also some evidence that employers currently value and reward a poorly identified mix of cognitive, intrapersonal and interpersonal competencies. As noted in previous chapters, the committee views 21st century skills as dimensions of human competence that have been valuable for many centuries, rather than skills that are suddenly new, unique, and valuable today. One change from the past may lie in society's desire that all students now attain levels of mastery—across multiple areas of skill and knowledge—that were previously unnecessary for individual success in education and the workplace. Another change may lie in the pervasive spread of digital technologies to communicate and share information. Although the underlying communications and information-processing competencies have not changed, they are applied at an increasing pace to accomplish tasks across various life contexts, including the home, school, workplace, and social networks. According to recent press reports, over half of the estimated 845 million Facebook users around the globe log on daily; among those aged 18 to 34, nearly half check Facebook within minutes of waking up and 28 percent do so before getting out of bed (Marche, 2012). An estimated 400 million people use Twitter to send or receive brief messages. Even in the world of print media, the pace of communication has quickened, as newspapers adopt a "digital first" strategy and publish fresh information online as news stories break (Zuckerman, 2012). Here, we review research addressing the question of whether such changes are increasing demand for cognitive, intrapersonal, and interpersonal competencies, and, if so, whether this will continue in the future.

The economy's need for different kinds of worker competencies has shifted over time due to a variety of factors, including shifts in the distribution of occupations. Blue collar jobs have shrunk dramatically over the past 40 years, declining from nearly one-third of all jobs in 1979 to only one-fifth of all jobs in 2009. Over the same time period, white collar administrative support jobs, such as filing clerks and secretaries, also declined. This rapid decline in middle-skill, middle-wage jobs has been accompanied by rapid growth at the top and bottom of the labor market, with a trend toward increasing polarization in wages and educational requirements (Autor, Katz, and Kearney, 2008).

The growth jobs at the top and bottom of the labor market is illustrated by Bureau of Labor Statistics (BLS) data, which organizes all occupations in 10 large clusters, three of which—professional/related, service, and sales—constitute fully half of the labor force. The two largest clusters—professional/related (e.g., computer science, education, healthcare professions) and service (e.g., janitorial, food service, nursing aids, home healthcare workers)—are at the opposite ends of the spectrum in terms of education and wages. These two clusters are projected to create more new jobs than all of the other 8 occupational clusters combined over the period 2008 to 2018 (Lacey and Wright, 2009).

Autor, Levy, and Murnane (2003) conducted a study that analyzed not only the mix of occupations but also the competencies demanded within occupations. Drawing on the *Dictionary of Occupational Titles* (a large catalogue of occupations and their characteristics), they developed measures of the routine and nonroutine cognitive tasks and routine and nonroutine manual tasks required by various occupations. Comparing tasks over time, from 1960 to 1998, they concluded that beginning in 1970 computers reduced routine cognitive and manual tasks and increased nonroutine cognitive and interactive tasks. Their model explained 60 percent of the growth in demand for college-educated labor over the period from 1970-1988. The authors concluded that computers substitute for workers in performing routine tasks and complement workers in performing nonroutine tasks.

Building on this study, Levy and Murnane (2004) argued that demand is growing for expert thinking (nonroutine problem solving) and complex communication competencies (nonroutine interactive skills). Levy and Murnane (2004) also proposed, that demand is growing for verbal and quantitative literacy. They view reading, writing, and mathematics as essential enabling competencies that supported individuals in mastering tasks that require expert thinking and complex communication production processes. Predicting that jobs requiring low or moderate levels of competence will continue to decline in the future, the authors recommended that schools teach complex communication and nonroutine problem-solving competencies, along with verbal and quantitative literacy, to all students.

More recently, Autor, Katz, and Kearney (2008) analyzed data on wages and education levels from 1962 to 2005. The analysis supports the argument that computers complement workers in performing abstract tasks (nonroutine cognitive tasks) and substitute for workers performing routine tasks. However, it also suggests that the continued growth of low-wage service jobs can be explained by computers' lack of impact on nonroutine manual tasks. Noting that these tasks, performed in service jobs such as health aides, security guards, cleaners, and restaurant servers, require interpersonal and environmental adaptability that has proven difficult to computerize, Autor, Katz, and Kearney (2008) suggest that low-wage service work may grow as a share of the labor market.

Goos, Manning, and Salomons (2009) reached a similar conclusion, based on an analysis of occupational and wage data in Europe. They concluded that technology was the primary cause of polarization in European labor markets, eliminating routine tasks concentrated in mid-level manufacturing and clerical work while complementing nonroutine tasks in both high-wage professional jobs and low-wage service jobs.

These two studies both suggest that low-wage service work involves nonroutine tasks that cannot be readily replaced by computers. There is debate in the literature about the level of cognitive, intrapersonal, and interpersonal competencies required to perform such work. Some case studies and surveys suggest that successful performance in low-wage service jobs requires complex communications skills and nonroutine problem solving (Gatta, Boushey, and Appelbaum, 2007). However, the low levels of education required to enter these jobs, together with their low wages and a plentiful supply of unskilled labor, suggests that their competency demands are—and will remain—low (Autor, 2007). Yet another view is that the competencies required by these and other jobs depend largely on management decisions about how the job is structured and the level and type of training provided (National Research Council, 2008).

Borghans, ter Weel, and Weinberg (2008) studied the role of interpersonal competencies in the labor market and concluded that "people skills" are an important determinant of occupations and wages. They argue that interpersonal competencies vary both with personality and across occupations, and that individuals are most productive in jobs that match their personality. They also found evidence that youth sociability affects job assignment in adulthood, and that interpersonal interactions are consistent with the assignment model. This study built on earlier, unpublished work which suggested that technological and organizational changes have increased the importance of interpersonal competencies in the workplace (Borghans, ter Weel, and Weinberg, 2005).

While these studies propose that demand for cognitive, intrapersonal, and interpersonal competencies has grown in recent decades and will continue to grow in the future, some experts disagree. For example, Bowles, Gintis, and Osborne (2001) analyzed longitudinal studies that presented 65 different correlational estimates of the relationship between cognitive test scores and earnings over a 30-year period. The authors found no increase in the estimates over time, indicating that labor market demand for cognitive competencies had not grown. Based on responses to a new national survey of skills, technology, and management practices, Handel (2010) argues that, for most jobs in the U.S. economy, education and academic skill demands are low to moderate, noting that large numbers of workers report educational attainments that exceed the requirements of their jobs.

All efforts to predict future competency demands are, of necessity, based on past trends. For example, BLS has often been criticized for using past trends to project detailed occupational requirements and competency needs a decade into the future (National Research Council, 2000). Similarly, Levy and Murnane (2004) call for schools to teach complex communications skills and nonroutine problem solving based on the assumption that the trends identified by Autor, Levy, and Murnane (2003) will continue for decades.

IMPORTANCE TO HEALTH AND RELATIONSHIP SKILLS

Education, Competencies, and Health Outcomes

There is a long history of research on the associations between education and health. Researchers statistically analyze data from self-reports on health status, behavior, and challenges in terms of explanatory variables, including gender, race, age, education, and income. Based on these analyses, they construct a health gradient demonstrating the conditional relation between education and health status. The overwhelming finding is that general health status, specific health outcomes, and healthy behaviors are strongly and positively correlated with educational attainment.

Cutler and Lleras-Muney (2010a) summarized the literature in which educational attainment is linked both statistically and substantively to health outcomes and behaviors. They found higher levels of educational attainment were associated with an array of reductions in adverse health events and increases in healthy eating and exercise. For example, the age-adjusted mortality rate of high school dropouts was found to be about twice that of those with some college in the 25-64-year-old age group in 1999.

Although these findings are widely accepted, two important questions dominate the literature. The first is to what degree is this relation causal as opposed to the explanation that those with better health are more likely to succeed educationally? That is, to what degree is the coefficient or gradient for health by level of educational attainment biased upward by reverse causation or omitted determinants of both education and health. The second question refers to the mechanism by which education improves health results. While the simplest explanation is that more educated persons are more knowledgeable about how to improve and maintain their health status and are better able to respond to health problems, there are other explanations. These include the effects of education on access to the health-care system (for example, through higher income) or effects of education on increasing consideration for the long-run consequences of present behavior and taking preventative measures.

To answer the first question, health economists have relied increasingly on the use of instrumental variables techniques to isolate the exogenous effects of education on health outcomes. Following the studies on education and labor market outcomes, they have used externally imposed differences in compulsory schooling such as changes in compulsory attendance requirements that affect the amount of education attained. To control for genetic factors and family backgrounds, they have also compared the health of siblings who have different educational attainments. Lochner (2011) provides a recent review of the latest set of studies employing these sophisticated methodologies. His preferred set of 39 estimates shows a wide range of estimates of education effects on mortality, self-reported health, and disability, as well as two health-related behaviors—smoking and obesity. Not all of the estimates are statistically significant, and some have the wrong signs. By and large, the links tend to be stronger in U.S. than European studies.

With respect to trying to isolate the mechanisms by which education influences health outcomes and behavior, the relations are less clear. There is some evidence that both the general cognitive capabilities of more educated persons as well as specific knowledge contributes to this relation. Cutler and Lleras-Muney (2010b) have also attempted to decompose the education-health nexus into major components including differences associated with education, socioeconomic status and income, and access to social networks. They find that about 30 percent of the education-health gradient is due to a combination of the advantages of income, health insurance, and family background associated with more education; 10 percent is due to the advantages of social networks; and about 30 percent is due directly to education. They also explore the educational mechanisms that might account for the relationship. They conclude that it may not be the specific health knowledge conferred by education as much as greater interest and trust of science and general skills such as critical thinking and decision-making abilities, analytic abilities, and information processing skills that enable educated individuals to make better health-related decisions. Such mechanisms as risk aversion and longer-range time considerations (low time discount rate) do not seem to have substantial support in explaining the health gradients.

A few studies have attempted to estimate links between health and cognitive, intrapersonal, and interpersonal competencies. The Almlund et al. (2011) review reaches the following conclusions regarding personality traits:

> All Big Five traits predict some health outcomes. Conscientiousness, however, is the most predictive and can better predict longevity than does intelligence or background. Personality measures predict health both through the channel of education and by improving health-related behavior, such as smoking. (pp. 127-128)

Many of these conclusions are based on the meta-analysis of Roberts et al. (2007), who review evidence from 34 different studies on links between longevity and the "big five" personality traits. They find that conscientiousness was the strongest predictor among the "big five" traits and a stronger predictor than either IQ or socioeconomic status. openness to experience and agreeableness were also associated with longevity, while neuroticism was associated with shorter life spans.

Among individual studies, Conti, Heckman, and Urzua (2010a, 2010b) estimate a multifactor model of schooling, earnings, and health outcomes using data from the British Cohort Study. They find that cognitive ability is not a very important determinant of smoking decisions or obesity but that noncognitive competencies are generally more important for smoking, obesity, and self-reported health. More recently, Hauser and Palloni (2011) studied the relationship between high school class ranking, cognitive ability, and mortality in a large sample of American high school graduates. They found that the relationship between cognitive ability (IQ) and survival was entirely explained by a measure of cumulative academic performance (rank in high school class) that was only moderately associated with IQ. Moreover, the effect of class ranking on survival was three times greater than that of IQ. The authors' interpretation of these findings is that higher cognitive ability improves the chances of survival by encouraging responsible, well-organized, timely behaviors appropriate to the situation—both in terms of high school academics and in later-life health behaviors.

COMPETENCIES AND HEALTHY
RELATIONSHIPS IN ADULTHOOD

Insights into the importance of transferable competencies for healthy marriages and other relationships in adulthood can be gleaned from the literature in a number of areas. Our review concentrates on three: (1) studies of couple satisfaction and marriage duration, (2) programs designed to promote healthy marriages, and (3) programs targeting teen relationship building.

A literature review by Halford et al. (2003; see also Gonzaga, Campos, and Bradbury, 2007) suggests four broad classes of variables that impact the trajectory of relationship satisfaction over time: couple interaction, life events impinging upon the couple, enduring individual characteristics of the partners, and contextual variables. Most relevant to the committee charge are the enduring individual characteristics and interactions.

Behavioral genetic studies show substantial heritabilities for divorce in adulthood (McGue and Lykken, 1992; Jockin, McGue, and Lykken, 1996). A handful of studies have examined early childhood correlates of adult relationship stability. Two of the most relevant drew data from the Dunedon birth cohort study. Newman et al. (1997) found that undercontrolled temperament observed at age 3 predicted greater levels of conflict in romantic relationships at age 21. Relatedly, Moffitt et al. (2011) found that childhood self-control predicts the likelihood of being a single parent.

Most personality traits are not very predictive of relationship satisfaction (e.g., Gottman, 1994; Karney and Bradbury, 1995). However, low neuroticism (i.e., high ability to regulate negative affect) as an adult has been found to predict high relationship satisfaction (Karney and Bradbury, 1997). In addition, Davila and Bradbury (2001) find that low anxiety over abandonment and comfort with emotional closeness are also predictive.

Among the elements of couple interaction, effective communication competencies has predicted relationship satisfaction in numerous studies although, interestingly enough, prospectively and not concurrently (Karney and Bradbury, 1995).

Insights into needed skills can also be gleaned from the curricula of effective adult couple relationship education programs. Many such programs attempt to boost couples' positive communication, conflict management, and positive expressions of affection (Halford et al., 2003). In contrast, curricula for teen relationship programs promote positive attitudes and beliefs rather than skills, although, as with adult programs, some also target relationship behavior (Karney et al., 2007).

IMPORTANCE TO CIVIC PARTICIPATION

Civic engagement is variously understood to include involvement in activities focused on improving one's community, involvement in electoral activities (voting, working on campaigns, etc.), and efforts to exercise voice and opinion (e.g., protests, writing to elected officials, etc.) (Zukin et al., 2006). Academics, foundations, and policy makers have expressed concern about decreasing levels of political engagement in the United States, particularly among youth. For example, political scientist Robert Putnam (2000) drew attention to Americans' lack of connection through clubs, civic associations, and other groups in his influential book *Bowling Alone*.

In response to these concerns, there has been a resurgence of interest in the development of the knowledge, skills, and dispositions that facilitate civic engagement—this cluster of knowledge, skills, and dispositions is sometimes referred to as "civic literacy." Studies are looking at the roles played by peers, schools, the media, and other factors in civic literacy and engagement (Delli Carpini and Keeter, 1997; Niemi and Junn, 1998). A recent review of this literature (Garcia Bedolla, 2010) finds that schools have a greater impact on civic literacy than was previously thought, and it has also pointed to the importance of parents and neighborhoods. However, these studies have focused on young people's attitudes, dispositions, or intentions about future political behavior, and have not linked school-based civics programs with later voting behavior and other civic activities in adulthood.

Prevalence of Civic Participation

Recent survey data suggest that some forms of engagement are fairly widespread (e.g., voting in general elections, volunteerism, consumer boycotts). A majority of young people report that they regularly follow public affairs (Lopez et al., 2006). But upward of 60 percent of young people are unable to describe activities that they can attribute to civic or political engagement, and a significant percentage is "highly disengaged." These young people do not generally believe their civic or political actions are likely to make much difference. Another type of civic participation is direct political action—protest, work on political campaigns, and the like. Overall, just 13 percent of young people are reported as being intensely involved in politics at this level—survey data indicate they are motivated by a desire to address a social or political problem.

Factors Associated with Civic Participation

Studies have shed light on the factors that correlate with political engagement, focusing on the role of family, schools, and peers in the development of children's political attitudes and behaviors. Early studies found that families tend to be more important than schools, as political orientations and other attitudes and perspectives appeared to be socially inherited from parents to children (Abramowitz, 1983; Achen, 2002). Indeed, research over four decades has demonstrated that socioeconomic status (SES) is a strong predictor of engagement and participation (Garcia Bedolla, 2010). More recent studies underscore the importance of parents and neighborhoods in the socialization process; they also indicate that schools can play a more important role than was previously believed (Niemi and Junn, 1998; Kahne and Sporte, 2008).

The literature linking years of schooling with civic outcomes is extensive. However, as with labor market and health outcomes, studies providing convincing causal estimates are relatively rare. Lochner (2011) provides a review of these rigorous studies and concludes that this literature suggests important effects of completed schooling on a wide range of political behaviors in the United States, but not in the United Kingdom or Germany. The U.S. impacts are found for voting registration and behavior, political interest, and the acquisition of political information.

Smith (1999) examined the effects of early investments in young people's social capital on political involvement and "civic virtue" in young adulthood. Using longitudinal data, she examined parental involvement, youth religious involvement, and participation in voluntary associations. She found that early extensive connections to others, close family relationships, and participation in religious activities and extracurricular activities during adolescence were significant predictors of greater political and civic involvement in young adulthood.

EDUCATIONAL ATTAINMENT AND
TRANSFER IN THE LABOR MARKET

A general theme of the evidence presented in this chapter is that measurable cognitive competencies, personality traits, and other intrapersonal and interpersonal competencies developed in childhood and adolescence are, at best, modestly predictive of adult successes, particularly labor market productivity. Cognitive ability does appear to matter and, among personality traits, so, apparently, does conscientiousness. But, in the research to date, their predictive power is modest. In terms of "transfer," we are unable to point to a particular set of competencies or behaviors that have been shown to transfer well to the labor market. (Boosting these skills may increase educational attainment, however, as discussed in the following chapters.)

Education attainment, in contrast, is strongly predictive of labor market success, even in research approaches designed to approximate random assignment experiments. Measurable cognitive, intrapersonal, and interpersonal competencies account for surprisingly little of the impact of education on future productivity. But even if we do not know exactly what it is about spending an additional year in school that makes people more productive, a policy approach designed to promote attainment might be promising, particularly if it can be shown that attainment promotes competencies that are transferable across jobs or across an individual's entire career.

Prior to the human capital revolution of the 1960s, the manpower planning approach assumed that each job and occupation required a specific level and type of education. Education policy planners produced projections of economic output by sector multiplied by a fixed formula of occupational requirements per unit of output that was further translated into a rigid formula of educational needs of a future labor force. Needless to say, the manpower forecasts failed, largely because of the rigid assumptions relating educational requirements to occupation and occupational requirements to economic output. Changes in technology, organization, and the market prices of labor and capital, and error-prone projections of sectoral output all undermined the accuracy of the projections of educational need.[9]

Becker's (1964) early work on human capital took a more general approach by distinguishing between general and specific human capital. He proposed that education developed "general" human capital that was valuable across different firms, while training and experience within a firm work developed "specific" human capital, valuable only in a particular firm. Becker's (1964) human capital model depended upon market dynamics in which adjustments would take place through responses to the costs and productivity of different kinds of labor. Labor supply and demand were expected to adapt, as any changes in demand for human capital resulting from changes in the firm's organization, technology, and mix of outputs would be met by individual and company investments in education, job training, and on-the-job learning.

There is considerable evidence that labor supply, allocation, and productivity are widely adaptable to changes in the economy, especially over the long run. This is because education increases the capacity of workers to learn on the job, benefit from further training, and respond to productive needs as they arise. Workers with more education are generally able to learn their jobs more quickly and do them more proficiently. They can work more intelligently and with greater precision and can accomplish more within the same time period. Greater levels of education increase their ability to benefit from training for more complex job situations, and this is evidenced in the literature on training.[10] The research demonstrating the overall impact of education on productivity and economic outcomes did not address precisely what competencies were developed by educational investments. However, an important insight was established by Nelson and Phelps (1966), who suggested that a major contribution of education was to enable workers to adapt to technological change.

Welch (1970) and Schultz (1975) generalized this insight to suggest that investments in more educated workers had an even greater impact on a firm's ability to adapt to technological change. They argued that hiring more educated workers can improve a firm's productivity not only because, relative to less educated workers, these workers are more productive in

---

[9]See Blaug (1975) for a trenchant critique of this type of approach.
[10]See Lynch (1992); Leuven and Oosterbeek (1997); Blundell et al. (1999).

their current jobs and can be more quickly and easily trained for complex jobs, but also because they can allocate their time and other resources more efficiently in their own jobs and in related jobs in ways that increase the overall productivity of the firm. In this way, the contributions of more educated workers go beyond their own job performance to impact the overall performance of the organization. For both Welch and Schultz, these benefits represent the greatest opportunity for investments in more educated workers to pay off for the firm.

More education, and higher education in particular, appears to develop workers' abilities to master an understanding of the production process and to tacitly make adjustments to changes in prices, technology, the productivity of inputs, or mix of outputs. These continuous adjustments allow the firm to "return to equilibrium" (in economic terms), maximizing productivities and profits. Neither Welch nor Schultz addressed which specific aspects of schooling contributed to the ability of workers to make the tacit adjustments to production that will increase productivity and profitability. It is possible that schooling develops not only cognitive competencies but also intrapersonal and interpersonal competencies that enable workers to make decisions that benefit the firm.

Welch (1970) and Schultz (1975) provide many examples of how investments in more educated workers may help firms adjust to optimize their productivity and profits, but there are also many examples of adjustments to disequilibria in the overall labor market. During the Second World War, women replaced males in the labor force in what had been male occupations, continuing the high rates of productivity needed to support both the war effort and the economy (Goldin, 1991). Chung (1990) studied vocationally trained workers for particular occupations who had been employed in those occupations or in occupations that were not matched specifically to their training. He found that workers who had received vocational training for a declining manufacturing industry, textiles, were substantially switching to a growing and thriving manufacturing industry, electronics, and were receiving considerably higher earnings in the latter than in the former. That is, the supply of workers was adapting in the short run to the changes in demand, and in the longer run the occupational training choice of workers was adapting too.

The historical evidence suggests that education is transferable across occupations because many occupations require common skills. For example, Gathmann and Schonberg (2010) found that competencies developed at work (which Becker viewed as "specific" and not valuable outside the firm) were more portable than previously thought. Analyzing data on the complete job histories and wages of over 100,000 German workers, along with detailed information on the tasks used in different occupations, they found that workers developed task-specific knowledge and skills and were rewarded accordingly, with higher wages as they gained experience in an occupation. On average, workers who changed occupations—whether voluntarily or because they were laid off—were more likely to move to an occupation requiring similar tasks (and attendant competencies) to their previous occupation than to a "distant" occupation requiring very different competencies. Laid-off workers who were unable to find work in similar occupations and were forced to move to a distant occupation experienced higher wage losses than those who were able to find work in similar occupations.

The authors found that university graduates appeared to gain more task-specific knowledge and skills than less educated workers and to be rewarded accordingly with higher wages. However, when more highly educated workers were required to move to distant occupations, their wages declined more than did the wages of less highly educated workers who had to move to a distant occupation. This suggests that the deep task-specific competencies developed by the highly educated workers were less transferable than the shallower competencies developed by the less educated workers. Overall, the study suggests that workers are more easily able to transfer competencies developed on the job to a similar occupation, involving similar tasks, than to a dissimilar occupation. This is analogous to research findings from the learning sciences, which have found that transfer of learning to a new task or problem is facilitated when the new task or problem has similar elements to the learned task (see Chapter 4).

Other evidence suggests that even workers with relatively lower levels of education may be able to adapt to the demands of complex jobs. One measure of adaptability is the substitutability among workers with different levels of education. Economists measure employers' ability to substitute workers at one level of education for jobs that normally are associated with a higher level of education by examining how the mix of more and less educated workers changes as relative wages for different educational levels change. Historical studies in the United States suggest that each 10 percent increase in the labor costs of a higher level of education is associated with a 15 percent decrease in employment at that educational level and increase in workers with less education to replace them (Ciccone and Peri, 2005). This implies that employers view workers as highly adaptable to perform jobs that traditionally require more education, when relative wages encourage such substitution.

CONCLUSIONS AND RECOMMENDATIONS

The research evidence related to the relationship between various cognitive, intrapersonal, and interpersonal competencies is limited and uneven in quality. Some of the evidence reviewed in this chapter is correlational in nature and should be considered, at best, suggestive of possible causal linkages. Other evidence, from longitudinal studies, is more suggestive of causal connections than the correlational evidence, but it is still prone to biases from a variety of sources. The strongest causal evidence, particularly the evidence of the impacts of years of completed schooling on adult outcomes, comes from statistical methods that are designed to approximate experiments.

- Conclusion: The available research evidence is limited and primarily correlational in nature; to date, only a few studies have demonstrated a causal relationship between one or more 21st century competencies and adult outcomes. The research has examined a wide range of different competencies that are not always clearly defined or distinguished from related competencies.

Many more studies of the relationships between various competencies and outcomes (in education, the labor market, health, and other domains) have focused on the role of general cognitive ability (IQ) than on specific intrapersonal and interpersonal skills (see Table 3-1). Economists who conduct such studies tend to lump all competencies other than IQ into the category of "noncognitive skills," while personality and developmental psychologists have developed a much more refined taxonomy of them. All three groups have investigated the relationships between cognitive, intrapersonal, and interpersonal competencies and outcomes in adolescence and adulthood.

- Conclusion: Cognitive competencies have been more extensively studied than intrapersonal and interpersonal competencies, showing consistent, positive correlations (of modest size) with desirable educational, career, and health outcomes. Early academic competencies are also positively correlated with these outcomes.

- Conclusion: Among intrapersonal and interpersonal competencies, conscientiousness (staying organized, responsible, and hardworking) is most highly correlated with desirable outcomes in education and the workplace. Antisocial behavior, which has both intrapersonal and interpersonal dimensions, is negatively correlated with these outcomes.

Across the available studies, the relative size of the correlations with the three different domains of skills is mixed. There is some evidence that better measurement of noncognitive competencies might result in a higher estimate of their importance in education and in the workplace.

A general theme of the evidence presented in this chapter is that measurable cognitive skills, personality traits, and other intrapersonal and interpersonal competencies developed in childhood and adolescence are, at best, modestly predictive of adult successes, particularly in the labor market. Educational attainment, in contrast, is strongly predictive of labor market success, even in research approaches designed to approximate random assignment experiments. Measurable cognitive, intrapersonal, and interpersonal competencies account for surprisingly little of the impact of education on future wages (wages, in economic theory, reflect productivity).

Studies by economists have found that more highly educated workers are more productive than those with less years of schooling are because more highly educated workers are better able to accomplish a given set of work tasks and are also more able to benefit from training for more complex tasks. In addition, more highly educated workers have the capacity to allocate resources more efficiently in their own work activities and in behalf of the enterprise in which they work than do workers with fewer years of schooling.

- **Conclusion: Educational attainment—the number of years a person spends in school—strongly predicts adult earnings, and also predicts health and civic engagement. Moreover, individuals with higher levels of education appear to gain more knowledge and skills on the job than do those with lower levels of education and they are able, to some extent, to transfer what they learn across occupations. Since it is not known what mixture of cognitive, intrapersonal, and interpersonal competencies accounts for the labor market benefits of additional schooling, promoting educational attainment itself may constitute a useful complementary strategy for developing 21st century competencies.**

The limited and uneven quality of the research reviewed in this chapter limits our understanding of the relationships between various cognitive, intrapersonal, and interpersonal competencies and adult outcomes.

- **Recommendation 1: Foundations and federal agencies should support further research designed to increase our understanding of the relationships between 21st century competencies and successful adult outcomes. To provide stronger causal evidence about such relationships, the programs of research should move beyond simple correlational studies to include more longitudinal studies with controls for differences in individuals' family backgrounds and more studies using statistical methods that are designed to approximate** experiments. Such research would benefit from efforts to achieve common definitions of 21st century competencies and an associated set of activities designed to produce valid and reliable assessments of the various individual competencies.

4

Perspectives on Deeper Learning

This chapter returns to the discussion begun in Chapter 2 about the nature of deeper learning and 21st century skills. It opens with an introduction that includes a brief discussion of the goals of deeper learning and a brief discussion of the history of theory and research on transfer. The second and longest section of the chapter discusses cognitive perspectives on deeper learning, reviewing work in cognitive and educational psychology in support of our argument that deeper learning is the process of developing durable, transferable knowledge that can be applied to new situations. In the third section, we offer an example of a learning environment that promotes the processes of deeper learning and develops cognitive, intrapersonal, and interpersonal competencies. In the fourth and fifth sections, we discuss the intrapersonal and interpersonal domains, considering how 21st century competencies in these two domains support the process of deeper learning. The sixth section briefly discusses the implications of the research reviewed throughout the chapter for teaching of deeper learning and 21st century competencies, and the chapter ends with conclusions.

A CLASSIC CONCERN: LEARNING FOR TRANSFER

The committee views the broad call for deeper learning and 21st century skills as reflecting a long-standing issue in education and training—the desire that individuals develop transferable knowledge and skills. Associated with this is the challenge of creating learning environments that support development of the cognitive, intrapersonal, and interpersonal competencies that enable learners to transfer what they have learned to new situations and new problems. These competencies include both knowledge in a domain and knowledge of how, why, and when to apply this knowledge to answer questions and solve problems—integrated forms of knowledge that we refer to as 21st century competencies and discuss further below.

If the goal of instruction is to prepare students to accomplish tasks or solve problems exactly like the ones addressed during instruction, then deeper learning is not needed. For example, if someone's job calls for adding lists of numbers accurately, that individual needs to learn to become proficient in using the addition procedure but does not need deeper learning about the nature of number and number theory that will allow transfer to new situations that involve the application of mathematical principles. As discussed in the previous chapter, today's technology has reduced demand for such routine skills (e.g., Autor, Levy, and Murnane, 2003). Success in work and life in the 21st century is associated with cognitive, intrapersonal, and interpersonal competencies that allow individuals to adapt effectively to changing situations rather than to rely solely on well-worn procedures.

When the goal is to prepare students to be able to be successful in solving new problems and adapting to new situations, then deeper learning is called for. Calls for such 21st century skills as innovation, creativity, and creative problem solving can also be seen as calls for deeper learning—helping students develop transferable knowledge that can be applied to solve new problems or respond effectively to new situations. Before turning to a discussion of the relationship between deeper learning and 21st century competencies in terms of theories and research on learning and knowing and the implications for transfer, we briefly discuss some of the rich history of work on the nature and extent of transfer.

Brief Historical Overview of Theory and Research on Transfer

Transfer was one of the first topics on the research agendas of both psychology and education, and it has remained as perhaps the central topic in the research on learning and instruction for more than 100 years. Research to date suggests that despite our desire for broad forms of transfer, knowledge does not transfer very readily, but it also illuminates instructional conditions that support forms of transfer that are desirable and attainable.

Specific transfer is the idea that learning A affects one's learning of B only to the extent that A and B have elements in common. For example, learning Latin may help someone learn Spanish solely because some of the vocabulary words are very similar and the verb conjugations are very similar. In contrast, general transfer is the idea that learning A affects one's learning of B because learning A strengthens general characteristics or knowledge in the learner that are broadly relevant (such as mental discipline or general principles). On the general transfer side of the controversy was the *doctrine of formal discipline,* which held that learning certain school subjects such as Latin and geometry would improve the mind in general (i.e., teach *proper habits of mind*) and thereby improve learning and performance in other unrelated subjects. On the specific transfer side of the controversy was E.L. Thorndike, largely recognized as the founder of educational psychology, who sought to put the issue to an empirical test. In a famous set of early studies, Thorndike and Woodworth (1901) found that students who were taught a cognitive skill showed a large improvement on the taught tasks but not on other tasks. Thorndike was able to claim strong support for specific rather than general transfer: "Improvement in any single mental function rarely brings about equal improvement in any other function, no matter how similar" (Thorndike, 1903, p. 91).

This was not a good outcome for those dedicated to helping students develop the ability to exhibit general transfer—that is, to apply what they have learned in one situation to a novel situation. Subsequent work by Judd (1908) offered some hope by showing that transfer to new situations depended on the instructional method used during initial learning, with some instructional methods supporting transfer to new situations and others not. An important aspect of Judd's finding is that transfer was restricted to new situations that required the same general principles as required in the original task, although it could be applied to situations requiring different behaviors.

Judd's finding has been replicated in many contexts. For example, Singley and Anderson (1989) report on an experiment designed to study the acquisition and transfer of skills in text editing. A group of 24 young women (aged 18-30) from a secretarial school were first taught to use either one or two line editors (text editing software used to change individual lines of text) and then a screen editor (text editing software used to scroll throughout a page of text), while control groups spent similar amounts of time either learning and using one of the screen editors or simply typing a manuscript. The authors observed positive transfer, both from one line editor to the next and from the line editors to the screen editor, as indicated by reductions in total learning time, keystrokes, residual errors, and other measures in comparison to the control groups. They proposed that the very high level of transfer from one line editor to the next line editor was due to the fact that, although the surface features of the commands used in the two editors were different, the underlying principles were nearly identical. In addition, they proposed that the moderate level of transfer from the line editors to the screen editor reflected the fact that the procedures used in the two line editors are largely different from those used by the screen editor. Nevertheless, the two line editors and the screen editor do share several decision rules, enabling the moderate level of transfer. It is important to note that this research examined transfer within a single subject or topic area—text editing. Research to date has not found evidence of transfer across subjects or disciplines.

Although there is little support in the research literature for general transfer in the broadest sense, there is encouraging evidence for what could be called "specific transfer of general principles" within a subject area or topic when effective instructional methods are used. Understanding how to promote this type of specific transfer is a continuing goal of research. Much of contemporary work continues to follow a line of thinking originally developed by the gestalt psychologists (e.g., Katona, 1942; Wertheimer, 1959) working in the first half of the 20th century. They were the first to propose a distinction between reproductive thinking (i.e., applying a previously learned procedure to solve a new problem) and productive thinking (i.e., inventing a new solution method to solve a new problem). Insight— moving from a state of not knowing how to solve a problem to a state of knowing how to solve it—is at the heart of productive thinking and was a major research theme of gestalt psychology (Duncker, 1945; Mayer, 1995). The gestaltists also emphasized the distinction between rote learning (which involved learning to blindly follow a procedure) and meaningful learning (which involved deeper understanding of the structure of the problem and the solution method), and they provided evidence that meaningful learning leads to transfer, whereas rote learning does not (Katona, 1940). For example, Wertheimer showed that in learning to solve for the area of a parallelogram, students could be taught how to apply the formula *area* = *height* × *base* (learning by rote), or they could be shown that they could cut off a triangle from one end and place it on the other end to form a rectangle (learning by understanding). According to Wertheimer, both kinds of instruction enabled students to perform well on problems like those given during instruction (i.e., retention tests), but only learning by understanding could promote problem solving on unusually shaped parallelograms and related nonparallelogram shapes (i.e., transfer tests).

Overall, one of the continuing goals of research and theory is to elucidate what is meant by learning with understanding—the processes that produce such learning as well as the outcomes in terms of knowledge representations—as well as how the products of such "deeper learning" processes lead to productive thinking in the context of transfer situations (see, e.g., Schwartz, Bransford, and Sears, 2005). In the next section, we consider the relationship between deeper learning and 21st century skills from the perspective of contemporary research and theory on the nature of the mental structures and cognitive processes associated with learning as well as the sociocultural nature of learning and knowing.

THE RELATIONSHIP BETWEEN DEEPER LEARNING AND COGNITIVE COMPETENCIES

To clarify the meaning of "deeper learning" and illuminate its relationship to 21st century competencies in the cognitive domain, the committee turned to two important strands of research and theory on the nature of human thinking and learning, the *cognitive* perspective and the *sociocultural* perspective, also referred to as the "situated" perspective (Greeno, Pearson, and Schoenfeld, 1996). In contrast to the differential perspective discussed in Chapter 2, which focuses on differences among individuals in knowledge or skill, the cognitive perspective focuses on types of knowledge and how they are structured in an individual's mind, including the processes that govern perception, learning, memory, and human performance. Research from the cognitive perspective investigates the mechanisms of learning and the nature of the products—the types of knowledge and skill—that result from those mechanisms, as well as how that knowledge and skill is drawn upon to perform a range of simple to complex tasks. The goal is theory and models that apply to all individuals, accepting the fact that there will be variation across individuals in execution of the processes and in the resultant products.

The sociocultural perspective emerged in response to the perception that research and theory within the cognitive perspective was too narrowly focused on individual thinking and learning. In the sociocultural perspective, learning takes place as individuals participate in the practices of a community, using the tools, language, and other cultural artifacts of the community. From this perspective, learning is "situated" within, and emerges from, the practices in different settings and communities. A community may be large or small and may be located inside or outside of a traditional school context. It might range, for example, from colleagues in a company's Information Technology department to a single elementary school classroom or a global society of plant biologists.

Such research has important implications for how academic disciplines are taught in school. From the sociocultural perspective, the disciplines are distinct communities that engage in shared practices of ongoing knowledge creation, understanding, and revision. It is now widely recognized that science is both a body of established knowledge and a social process through which individual scientists and communities of scientists continually create, revise, and elaborate scientific theories and ideas (Polanyi, 1958; National Research Council, 2007). In one illustration of the social dimensions of science, Dunbar (2000) found that scientists' interactions with their peers, particularly how they responded to questions from other scientists, influenced their success in making discoveries.

The idea that each discipline is a community with its own culture, language, tools, and modes of discourse has influenced teaching and learning. For example, Moje (2008) has called for reconceptualizing high school literacy instruction to develop disciplinary literacy programs, based on research into what it means to write and read in mathematics, history and science and what constitutes knowledge in these subjects. Moje (2008) argues that students' understanding of how knowledge is produced in the subject areas is more important than the knowledge itself.

Sociocultural perspectives are reflected in new disciplinary frameworks and standards for K-12 education. In science, for example, *A Framework for K-12 Science Education: Practices, Crosscutting Concepts, and Core Ideas* (hereafter referred to as the NRC science framework; National Research Council, 2012) calls for integrated development of science practices, crosscutting concepts, and core ideas. The Common Core State Standards in English language arts (Common Core State Standards Initiative, 2010a) reflect an integrated view of reading, writing, speaking/listening, and language and also respond to Moje's (2008) call for disciplinary literacy by providing separate English language arts standards for history and science. Based on the view of each discipline as a community engaged in ongoing discourse and knowledge creation, the NRC science framework and the standards in English language arts and mathematics include expectations for learning of intrapersonal and interpersonal competencies along with cognitive competencies (see Chapter 5 for further discussion).

In the committee's view, and informed by both perspectives, the link between deeper learning and 21st century competencies lies in the classic concept of transfer—the ability to use prior learning to support new learning or problem solving in culturally relevant contexts. We define deeper learning not as a product but as processing—both within individual minds and through social interactions in a community—and 21st century competencies as the learning outcomes of this processing in the form of transferable knowledge and skills that result. The transferable knowledge and skills encompass all three domains of competency: cognitive, intrapersonal, and interpersonal, in part reflecting the sociocultural perspective of learning as a process grounded in social relationships.

To support our proposed definitions of deeper learning and 21st century competencies, we first draw on concepts and principles derived from work in cognitive psychology. Based on this review of the research, we describe the nature of deeper learning and briefly discuss instruction that supports deeper learning and transfer (we elaborate on teaching for transfer in Chapters 5 and 6).

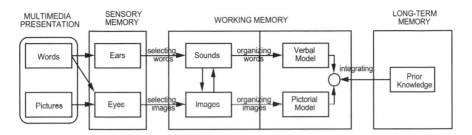

FIGURE 4-1 An information processing model memory.
SOURCE: Mayer, Heiser, and Lonn (2001). Copyright 2001 by the American Psychological Association. Reproduced with permission. The use of APA information does not imply endorsement by APA.

Components of Cognitive Architecture[1]

One of the chief theoretical advances to emerge from research and theory is the notion of *cognitive* architecture—the information processing system that determines the flow of information and how it is acquired, stored, represented, revised, and accessed in the mind. Figure 4-1 shows the main components of this architecture. Research has identified the distinguishing characteristics of the various types of memory shown in Figure 4-1 and the mechanisms by which they interact with each other.

Working Memory

Working memory is what people use to process and act on information immediately before them (Baddeley, 1986). Working memory is a conscious system that receives input from memory buffers associated with the various sensory systems. There is also considerable evidence that working memory can receive input from the long-term memory system.

The key variable for working memory is capacity—how much information it can hold at any given time. Controlled (also defined as conscious) human thought involves ordering and rearranging ideas in working memory and is consequently restricted by the finite capacity of working memory. Simply stated, working memory refers to the currently active portion of long-term memory. But there are limits to such activity, and these limits are governed primarily by how information is organized. Although few people can remember a randomly generated string of 16 digits, anyone with a slight knowledge of American history is likely to be able to recall the string 1492-1776-1865-1945. This is just one example of an important concept:

---

[1]This section of the chapter draws heavily on National Research Council (2001, pp. 65-68).

namely, that knowledge stored in long-term memory can have a profound effect on what appears, at first glance, to be the capacity constraint in working memory.

Long-Term Memory

Long-term memory contains two distinct types of information—semantic information about "the way the world is" and procedural information about "how things are done." Unlike working memory, long-term memory is, for all practical purposes, an effectively limitless store of information. It therefore makes sense to try to move the burden of problem solving from working memory to long-term memory. What matters most in learning situations is not the capacity of working memory—although that is a factor in speed of processing—but how well one can evoke the knowledge stored in long-term memory and apply it to address information and problems in the present.

Contents of Memory

Contemporary theories also characterize the types of cognitive content that are processed by the architecture of the mind. The nature and organization of this content is extremely critical for understanding how people answer questions and solve problems, and how they differ in this regard as a function of the conditions of instruction and learning. An important distinction in cognitive content is between domain-general knowledge, which is applicable to a range of situations, and domain-specific knowledge, which is relevant to a particular problem area.

Domain-General Knowledge and Problem-Solving Processes

Cognitive research has shown that general problem-solving procedures, not specific to a particular domain of knowledge, are generally slow and inefficient. Newell and Simon (1972) developed a computer program to test such general procedures, known as "weak methods," identifying their limitations as follows:

- Hill climbing: One solves a problem by taking one step at a time toward the overarching goal or task. This approach is inflexible and may be inefficient, as selecting whatever step takes one uphill (or in a particular direction) may cause the problem solver to climb a foothill, ignoring the much more efficient procedure of going around it. More sophisticated problem-solving strategies, such as those used by expert chess players, require one to *look ahead* many steps to see potential problems well in advance and avoid them.

- Means-ends analysis: One solves a problem by considering the obstacles that stand between the initial problem state and the goal state. The problem solver then identifies subgoals related to the elimination of each these obstacles. When all of the subgoals have been achieved (all of the obstacles have been eliminated), then the main goal of interest has been achieved. Because the subgoals have been identified through a focus on the main goal, means-ends analysis can be viewed as a strategy in which the long-range goal is always kept in mind to guide problem solving. It is not as near-sighted as other search techniques, like hill climbing.

- Analogy: One solves a problem by using the solution of a similar problem. However, evidence shows that, generally, people who have learned to solve a first problem are not better at solving a second problem analogous to the first. Even when given explicit instructions about the relationship between the two problems, individuals do not always find it easier to solve the second problem.

- Trial and error: One solves a problem by randomly trying out solutions until one has reached the goal. Trial-and-error approaches can be very inefficient, as many of the random solutions may be incorrect, and there is no boundary to narrow the search for possible solutions.

Problem solvers confronted by a problem outside their area of expertise use these weak methods to try to constrain what would otherwise be very large search spaces when they are solving novel problems. In most situations, however, learners are expected to use *strong methods*—relatively specific algorithms particular to the domain that will make it possible to solve problems efficiently. Strong methods, when available, find solutions with little or no search. For example, someone who knows calculus can find the maximum of a function by applying a known algorithm (taking the derivative and setting it equal to zero). As discussed further below, experts are able to quickly solve novel problems within their domain of expertise because they can readily retrieve relevant knowledge, including the appropriate, strong methods to apply. Paradoxically, although one of the hallmarks of expertise is access to a vast store of strong methods in a particular domain, both children and scientists fall back on their repertoire of weak methods when faced with truly novel problems (Klahr and Simon, 1999).

Knowledge Organization: Schemas and Expert-Novice Differences[2]

Although weak methods remain the last resort when one is faced with novel situations, people generally strive to interpret situations so that they can apply *schemas*—previously learned and somewhat specialized techniques (i.e., strong methods) for organizing knowledge in memory in ways that are useful for solving problems. Schemas help people interpret complex data by weaving them into sensible patterns. A schema may be as simple as "Thirty days hath September" or more complex, such as the structure of a chemical formula. Schemas help move the burden of thinking from working memory to long-term memory. They enable competent performers to recognize situations as instances of problems they already know how to solve; to represent such problems accurately, according to their meaning and underlying principles; and to know which strategies to use to solve them.

The existence of problem-solving schemas has been demonstrated in a wide variety of contexts. Extensive research shows that the ways students mentally "represent" (form a mental model of) the information given in a math or science problem or in a text that they read depends on the organization of their existing knowledge. As learning occurs, increasingly well-structured and qualitatively different organizations of knowledge develop. These structures enable individuals to build a representation or mental model that guides problem solution and further learning, avoid trial-and-error solution strategies, and formulate analogies and draw inferences that readily result in new learning and effective problem solving (Glaser and Baxter, 1999). The impact of schematic knowledge is powerfully demonstrated by research on the nature of expertise.

Research conducted over the past five decades has generated a vast body of knowledge about how people learn the content and procedures of specific subject domains. Researchers have probed deeply the nature of expertise and how people acquire large bodies of knowledge over long periods of time. Studies have revealed much about the kinds of mental structures that support problem solving and learning in various domains ranging from chess to physics; what it means to develop expertise in a domain; and how the thinking of experts differs from that of novices.

The notion of expertise is inextricably linked with subject-matter domains: experts must have expertise in *something*. Research on how people develop expertise has provided considerable insight into the nature of thinking and problem solving. Although every person cannot be expected to become an expert in a given domain, findings from cognitive science about the nature of expertise can shed light on what successful learning looks like and guide the development of effective instruction and assessment.

---

[2]This section of the chapter draws heavily on National Research Council (2001, pp. 70-73).

What distinguishes expert from novice performers is not simply general mental abilities, such as memory or fluid intelligence, or general problem-solving strategies. Experts have acquired extensive stores of knowledge and skill in a particular domain, and perhaps more significantly, they have organized this knowledge in ways that make it readily retrievable and useful.

In fields ranging from medicine to music, studies of expertise have shown repeatedly that experts commit to long-term memory large banks of well-organized facts and procedures, particularly deep, specialized knowledge of their subject matter (Chi, Glaser, and Rees, 1982; Chi and Koeske, 1983). Most important, they have efficiently coded and organized this information into well-connected schemas. These methods of encoding and organizing help experts interpret new information and notice features and meaningful patterns of information that might be overlooked by less competent learners. These schemas also enable experts, when confronted with a problem, to retrieve the relevant aspects of their knowledge.

Of particular interest to researchers is the way experts encode, or chunk, information into meaningful units based on common underlying features or functions. Doing so effectively moves the burden of thought from the limited capacity of working memory to long-term memory. Experts can represent problems accurately according to their underlying principles, and they quickly know when to apply various procedures and strategies to solve them. They then go on to derive solutions by manipulating those meaningful units. For example, chess experts encode mid-game situations in terms of meaningful clusters of pieces (Chase and Simon, 1973).

The knowledge that experts have cannot be reduced to sets of isolated facts or propositions. Rather, their knowledge has been encoded in a way that closely links it with the contexts and conditions for its use. Because the knowledge of experts is "conditionalized," they do not have to search through the vast repertoire of everything they know when confronted with a problem. Instead, they can readily activate and retrieve the subset of their knowledge that is relevant to the task at hand (Simon, 1979; Glaser, 1992). These and other related findings suggest that teachers should place more emphasis on the conditions for applying the facts or procedures being taught, and that assessment should address whether students know when, where, and how to use their knowledge.

Practice and Feedback[3]

Every domain of knowledge and skill has its own body of concepts, factual content, procedures, and other items that together constitute the knowledge of that field. In many domains, including areas of literature,

---

[3]This section of the chapter draws heavily on National Research Council (2001, pp. 84-87).

history, mathematics, and science, this knowledge is complex and multifaceted, requiring sustained effort and focused instruction to master. Developing deep knowledge of a domain such as that exhibited by experts, along with conditions for its use, takes time and focus and requires opportunities for practice with feedback.

Whether considering the acquisition of some highly specific piece of knowledge or skill such as the process of adding two numbers, or some larger schema for solving a mathematics or physics problem, certain laws of skill acquisition always apply. The first of these is the *power law of practice*: acquiring skill takes time, often requiring hundreds or thousands of instances of practice in retrieving a piece of information or executing a procedure. This law operates across a broad range of tasks, from typing on a keyboard to solving geometry problems (Rosenbloom and Newell, 1987). According to the power law of practice, the speed and accuracy of performing a simple or complex cognitive operation increases in a systematic nonlinear fashion over successive attempts (see Figure 4-2). This pattern is characterized by an initial rapid improvement in performance, followed by subsequent and continuous improvements that accrue at a slower and slower rate.

The power law of practice is fully consistent with theories of cognitive skill acquisition, according to which individuals go through different stages in acquiring the specific knowledge associated with a given cognitive skill (e.g., Anderson, 1982). Early on in this process, performance requires effort because it is heavily dependent on the limitations of working memory. Individuals must create a representation of the task they are supposed to perform, and they often verbally mediate or "talk their way through the task" while it is being executed. Once the components of the skill are well represented in long-term memory, the heavy reliance on working memory, and the problems associated with its limited capacity, can be bypassed. As a consequence, exercise of the skill can become fluent and then automatic. In the latter case, the skill requires very little conscious monitoring, and thus mental capacity is available to focus on other matters. Evidence indicates that with each repetition of a cognitive skill, as in accessing a concept in long-term memory from a printed word, retrieving an addition fact, or applying a schema for solving differential equations, some additional knowledge strengthening occurs that produces continual small improvements.

Practice, however, is not enough to ensure that a skill will be acquired. The conditions of practice are also important. The second major law of skill acquisition involves *knowledge of results*. Individuals acquire a skill much more rapidly if they receive feedback about the correctness of what they have done. If incorrect, they need to know the nature of their mistake. It was demonstrated long ago that practice without feedback produces little learning (Thorndike, 1927). One of the persistent dilemmas in education

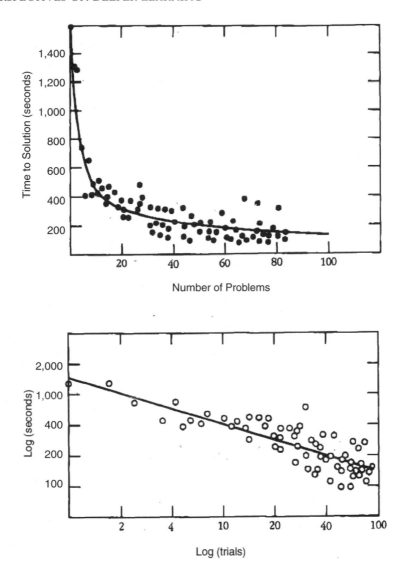

FIGURE 4-2 Skill acquisition curves.
SOURCE: Anderson (1990, p. 262). Reprinted with permission from W.H. Freeman and Company, from J.R. Anderson. *Cognitive psychology and its implications.* Permission conveyed through Copyright Clearance Center, Inc.

is that students often spend time practicing incorrect skills with little or no feedback. Furthermore, the feedback they ultimately receive is often neither timely nor informative. For the less able student, unguided practice (e.g., homework in math) can be practice in doing tasks incorrectly.

The timing and quality of feedback influences its effectiveness in speeding acquisition of skills or knowledge (Pashler et al., 2005; Shute, 2008). The optimal timing of feedback appears to differ depending on the type and complexity of the learning task and the characteristics of the learner. For example, immediate feedback can quickly prevent further incorrect practice, but it also has potential limitations, including posing a threat to motivation and reducing opportunities for learners to correct their own errors and develop self-regulated learning skills. There is growing evidence that feedback that explains why the practice is incorrect is more valuable for learning than feedback that simply flags errors (Roscoe and Chi, 2007; Shute, 2008; National Research Council, 2011a). The value of explanatory feedback has been demonstrated through research conducted in both digital and nondigital learning environments. For example, Moreno and Mayer (2005) compared two different versions of an interactive science learning game in which students traveled to different planets with different environmental conditions and were asked to design a plant that could survive in these conditions. The authors found that students who received explanatory feedback performed significantly better than did students who received only corrective feedback on a test designed to measure both retention of the targeted botany concepts and transfer of these concepts to new problems of plant design based on the same general principles.

The Nature of Deeper Learning

The review of research thus far in this chapter allows us to more clearly describe the nature of deeper learning. First, the history of research on transfer suggests that there are limits to how far the knowledge and skills developed through deeper learning can transfer. Transfer is possible within subject area or domain of knowledge, when effective instructional methods are used. Second, the research on expertise suggests that deeper learning involves the development of well-organized knowledge in a domain that can be readily retrieved to apply (transfer) to new problems in that domain. Third, the research suggests that deeper learning requires extensive practice, aided by explanatory feedback that helps learners correct errors and practice correct procedures, and that multimedia learning environments can provide such feedback. Fourth, the work of the gestalt psychologists discussed above allows us to distinguish between rote learning and meaningful learning (or deeper learning). Meaningful learning (which develops deeper understanding of the structure of the problem and the solution method) leads to transfer, while rote learning does not (Katona, 1940).

Building on the research of the Gestalt psychologists, we can distinguish between different types of tests and the learning they measure. Retention tests are designed to assess learners' memory for the presented material using recall tasks (e.g., "What is the definition of deeper learning?") or recognition tasks (e.g., "Which of the following is not part of the definition of deeper learning? A. learning that facilitates future learning, B. learning that facilitates future problem solving, C. learning that promotes transfer, D. learning that is fun."). While retention and recognition tests are often used in educational settings, experimental psychologists use transfer tests to assess learners' ability to use what they learned in new situations to solve problems or to learn something new (e.g., "Write a transfer test item to evaluate someone's knowledge of deeper learning.").

Although using the senses to attend to relevant information may be all that is required for success on retention tasks, success on transfer tasks requires deeper processing that includes organizing new information and integrating it with prior knowledge in one's mind (see Figure 4-1). This deeper cognitive process develops 21st century skills—knowledge in a learner's long-term memory that can be used in new situations.

Results from the two different types of assessments can be used to distinguish between three different types of learning outcomes—no learning, rote learning, and meaningful learning (see Table 4-1; also Mayer, 2010). No learning is indicated by poor performance on retention and transfer tests. Rote learning is indicated by good retention performance and poor transfer performance. Meaningful learning (which also could be called deeper learning) is indicated by good retention performance and good transfer performance. Thus the distinguishing feature of meaningful learning (or deeper learning) is the learner's ability to transfer what was learned to new situations.

TABLE 4-1 Three Types of Learning Outcomes

Type of Outcome	Retention Performance	Transfer Performance
No learning	Poor	Poor
Rote learning	Good	Poor
Meaningful (deeper) learning	Good	Good

SOURCE: R.E. Mayer, *Applying the science of learning, 1st edition*, © 2010. Reprinted (2010) by permission of Pearson Education, Inc., Upper Saddle River, NJ.

Components of Deeper Learning

Researchers have characterized the suite of knowledge and abilities that are used in the process of deeper learning in various ways. For example, when Anderson et al. (2001) updated Bloom's 1956 taxonomy of learning objectives, they included three types of knowledge and skills: (1) knowledge (e.g., facts and concepts); (2) skills (e.g., procedures and strategies); and (3) attitudes (e.g., beliefs). In Chapter 2, we proposed that knowledge and skills can be divided into three broad domains of competence: cognitive, intrapersonal, and interpersonal.

Mayer (2011a) suggested that deeper learning involves developing an interconnected network of five types of knowledge:

- Facts, statements about the characteristics or relationships of elements in the universe;
- Concepts, which are categories, schemas, models, or principals;
- Procedures, or step-by-step processes;
- Strategies, general methods; and
- Beliefs about one's own learning.

Earlier in this chapter, we noted that mentally organizing knowledge helps an individual to quickly identify and retrieve the relevant knowledge when trying to solve a novel problem (i.e., when trying to transfer the knowledge). In light of these research findings, Mayer (2010) proposed that the way in which a learner organizes these five types of knowledge influences whether the knowledge leads to deeper learning and transfer. For example, factual knowledge is more likely to transfer if it is integrated, rather than existing as isolated bits of information, and conceptual knowledge is more likely to transfer if it is mentally organized around schemas, models, or general principles. As the research on expertise and the power law of practice would indicate, procedures that have been practiced until they become automatic and embedded within long-term memory are more readily transferred to new problems than those that require much thought and effort. In addition, specific cognitive and metacognitive strategies (discussed later in this chapter) promote transfer. Finally, development of transferable 21st century skills is more likely if the learner has productive beliefs about his or her ability to learn and about the value of learning—a topic we return to later, in the section on the intrapersonal domain.

Table 4-2 outlines the cognitive processing of the five types of integrated knowledge and dispositions that, working closely together, support deeper learning and transfer.

Deeper learning involves coordinating all five types of knowledge. The learner acquires an interconnected network of specific facts, automates

TABLE 4-2 What Is Transferable Knowledge?

Type of Knowledge	Format or Cognitive Processing
Factual	Integrated, rather than separate facts
Conceptual	Schemas, models, principles
Procedures	Automated, rather than effortful
Strategies	Specific cognitive and metacognitive strategies
Beliefs	Productive beliefs about learning

SOURCE: Adapted from Mayer (2010).

procedures, refines schemas and mental models, and refines cognitive and metacognitive strategies, while at the same time developing productive beliefs about learning. Through this process, the learner develops transferable knowledge, which encompasses not only the facts and procedures that support retention but also the concepts, strategies, and beliefs needed for success in transfer tasks. We view these concepts, thinking strategies, and beliefs as 21st century skills.

This proposed model of transferable knowledge reflects the research on development of expertise, which, as noted above, has distinguished differences in the knowledge of experts and novices in domains such as physics, chess, and medicine (see Table 4-3). Novices tend to store facts as isolated units, whereas experts store them in an interconnected network. Novices tend to create categories based on surface features, whereas experts create categories based in structural features. Novices need to expend conscious effort in applying procedures, whereas experts have automated basic procedures, thereby freeing them of the need to expend conscious effort in applying them. Novices tend to use general problem-solving strategies such as means-ends analysis, which require a backward strategy starting from the goal, whereas experts tend to use specific problem-solving strategies tailored to specific kinds of problems in a domain, which involve a forward strategy starting from what is given. Finally, novices may hold unproductive beliefs, such as the idea that their performance depends on ability, whereas

TABLE 4-3 Expert-Novice Differences on Five Kinds of Knowledge

Knowledge	Novices	Experts
Facts	fragmented	integrated
Concepts	surface	structural
Procedures	effortful	automated
Strategies	general	specific
Beliefs	unproductive	productive

SOURCE: Adapted from Mayer (2010).

experts may hold productive beliefs, such as the idea that if they try hard enough they can solve the problem. In short, analysis of learning outcomes in terms of five types of knowledge has proven helpful in addressing the question of what expert problem solvers know that novice problem solvers do not know.

AN ILLUSTRATION OF DEEPER LEARNING AND THE DEVELOPMENT OF 21ST CENTURY COMPETENCIES

Before turning to discussions of deeper learning and 21st century competencies in the intrapersonal and interpersonal domains, we offer a description of a learning environment designed to develop mathematics competencies. Although the instruction focused on knowledge of high school mathematics, the teaching practices used to advance this goal led to development of intrapersonal and interpersonal competencies as well. We offer this case as illustrative (not definitive) of how learning and instruction in traditional school subjects might be organized in ways that produce multiple forms of transferable knowledge and skill (additional examples are provided in Chapter 5).

Our example is derived from Boaler and Staples' (2008) 5-year longitudinal study of approximately 700 students at three high schools. Railside was an urban, ethnically diverse school, where 30 percent of students were English language learners and 30 percent of students qualified for free or reduced meals. Hilltop was a more rural school where approximately half of the students were Latino and half white, 20 percent of students were English language learners, and 20 percent qualified for free or reduced meals. Greendale was a predominantly white school in a small coastal community, with no English language learners, and only 10 percent of students qualifying for free or reduced meals. The sample of schools was chosen intentionally to allow the researchers to observe different mathematics teaching approaches, and the research team gathered a wide range of data over 4 years, including videotapes of classroom activities, assessments of mathematics content, and interviews with students and teachers.

The mathematics teachers at Railside worked collaboratively to develop and implement a mixed-ability curriculum in algebra and geometry classes and made more modest changes to advanced algebra classes. They had high expectations for all students and engaged them in a common, cognitively challenging curriculum. Students spent most of their time working together small, mixed-ability groups to address complex problems. Students at the other two high schools experienced more traditional mathematics instruction, including teacher lectures, whole-class, question-and-answer sessions, and individual practice solving relatively short, closed-ended problems.

At the beginning of the study, when incoming freshmen at all three schools took an assessment of middle school mathematics knowledge, Railside students scored significantly lower than students from the other two schools. Nevertheless, all Railside students were placed in algebra classes, with a curriculum organized around themes, such as "What is a linear function?" The teachers restructured the traditionally rigid sequence of mathematics classes so that students could take two courses within a single year (e.g., algebra and geometry). They also implemented many teaching practices designed to create a new culture of learning within the algebra classrooms. For example, teachers explicitly and publicly valued many different dimensions of mathematical work, recognized the intellectual contributions of students within a group who might otherwise be thought of as low status, and modeled for students the importance of asking good questions. The teachers conveyed to the students that there were many different methods and paths to solve the complex problems and required students to justify their answers.

One important teaching practice focused on encouraging students to be responsible for each other's mathematics learning. Teachers did this in several ways. First, when placing students into groups, they assigned them to particular roles—such as facilitator, team captain, recorder, or resource manager—to convey the idea that all students have important contributions to make. As they circulated around the classroom, teachers frequently emphasized the different roles, for example, by reminding facilitators to help group members check their answers or show their work. In addition, the teachers encouraged students to be responsible for each other's learning through their assessment practices, which included, at times, assigning grades based on the quality of a group's conversations. At other times, teachers asked one member of the group a question and, if that group member could not answer, gave the group some time to help that member find the solution (without providing hints or the answer, so that the group members were required to struggle through to the answer).

At the end of each of school year, all students took content-focused assessments designed by researchers to include topics that had been addressed across the three different schools and teaching approaches (algebra at the end of year 1, geometry at the end of year 2, and advanced algebra and geometry at the end of year 3). In addition, the researcher administered open-ended project assessments in each year of the study, with longer, more applied problems that students worked on in groups. By the end of year 1, the Railside students were approaching comparable levels in algebra to students at the other two schools. By the end of year 2, the Railside students' scores were significantly higher than those of the students in the traditional mathematics classes. At the end of year 3, the Railside students' scores were higher, but not significantly so (perhaps because the year 3 curriculum had not been developed as much by the teachers). In year 4, 41 percent of seniors at Railside were enrolled in calculus, compared with approximately 27 percent in the two other schools.

Railside students also scored higher than students at the other two schools on the California Standards test, a curriculum-aligned test, although they did not do as well on the CAT 6, a standardized state test, perhaps because that test requires strong English language skills and cultural knowledge. In addition, the Railside approach was successful at improving equity. Significant disparities in the mathematics achievement of incoming white, black, and Latino students at Railside disappeared over the course of the study period, although achievement differences between different ethnic groups continued at the other two schools.

These findings begin to illuminate both the process of deeper learning and its role in developing transferable skills and knowledge. Clearly, the innovative approach led to gains in cognitive competencies in mathematics. At the same time, interview data showed that students developed positive dispositions towards mathematics and conscientiousness in addressing mathematics problems—important intrapersonal competencies. For example, 84 percent of Railside students agreed with the statement, "Anyone can be really good at math if they try," compared to 52 percent of students in the traditional classes at the other two schools. Data from the videotaped project assessments showed that Railside students persisted in working through difficult problems for longer time periods than students from the other two schools. Railside students also gained important interpersonal skills, learning to value group work not only for how it aided their own learning but also for helping others. In interviews, they expressed enjoyment in helping others and did not describe others as smart or dumb, slow or quick. Although the focus of their conversations was on mathematics, they learned to appreciate the different perspectives, insights, methods, and approaches offered by students from different cultures and circumstances.

THE INTRAPERSONAL DOMAIN[4]

The model of the suite of knowledge and skills developed through deeper learning shown in Table 4-2 above (Mayer, 2010) includes intrapersonal facets—specifically, productive beliefs about learning—as well as cognitive dimensions. Here, we further explore the intrapersonal dimensions of learning.

The intrapersonal domain encompasses a broad range of competencies that reside within an individual and operate across a variety of different life contexts and situations, including learning situations. We have

---

[4]This section of the chapter draws heavily on National Research Council (2001, pp. 88-89).

proposed in Chapter 2 that this domain includes three clusters of 21st century competencies:

- Intellectual openness (aligned with the personality factor of openness to experience), including such skills as flexibility, adaptability, artistic and cultural appreciation, and personal and social responsibility
- Work ethic (aligned with the personality factor of conscientiousness), including such skills as initiative and self-direction, responsibility, Type 1 self-regulation (metacognition, including forethought, performance, and self-reflection), and perseverance
- Core self-evaluation (aligned with the personality factor of neuroticism and its opposite, emotional stability), including such skills as Type 2 self-regulation (self-monitoring, self-evaluation, self-reinforcement), and physical and psychological health

Below, we discuss research and theory by investigating how these competencies support learning, including evidence suggesting that they support deeper learning and transfer. We also briefly describe the broader construct of self-regulation and research in child and adolescent development and economics that suggest that competence in self-regulation transfers across a variety of life situations.

The Role of Beliefs and Motivation in Learning

In our discussion of the cognitive domain above, we noted that motivation helps learners to mentally organize and integrate information in the cognitive processing that is central to deeper learning (this is sometimes referred to as "generative processing"). We also argued that productive beliefs about learning are an essential component of transferable knowledge. Here, we explore further how beliefs and motivation support deeper learning.

The beliefs students hold about learning can significantly affect learning and performance (e.g., Dweck and Leggett, 1988). For example, many students believe, on the basis of their typical classroom and homework assignments, that any math problem can be solved in 5 minutes or less, and if they cannot find a solution in that time, they will give up. Many young people and adults also believe that talent in mathematics and science is innate, which gives them little incentive to persist if they do not understand something in these subjects immediately. Conversely, people who believe they are capable of making sense of unfamiliar things often succeed because they invest more sustained effort in doing so.

A recent review of research on social-psychological interventions designed to change students' beliefs and feelings of self-efficacy as learners provides evidence that motivation and related intrapersonal skills enhance deeper learning (Yaeger and Walton, 2011). The authors found that relatively brief interventions can lead to large and sustained gains in student achievement, as students develop durable, transferable intrapersonal skills and apply them to new learning challenges in a positive, self-reinforcing cycle of academic improvement.

Some of the experiments target students' "attributions"—how they explain the causes of events and experiences. Research in social psychology shows that if students attribute poor school performance to traits they view as fixed (such as general low intelligence or a more specific lack of aptitude in mathematics), they will not invest time and effort to improve their performance. This leads to an "exacerbation cycle" of negative attributions and poor performance (Storms and Nisbett, 1970).

Wilson and Linville (1982, 1985) studied a brief intervention designed to change attributions among college freshmen. They brought two groups of struggling freshmen into the laboratory to view videos of upperclassmen discussing their transition to the college. In the videos viewed by the experimental group, upperclassmen said that their grades were low at first, due to transient factors such as a lack of familiarity with the demands of college, but that their grades improved with time. In the videos viewed by the control group, upperclassmen talked about their academic and social interests but did not mention first-year grades. One year later, students in the treatment group had earned significantly higher grade point averages (0.27 percent higher) than students in the control group, and the effect increased over the following semesters. Ultimately, students in the treatment group were 80 percent less likely to drop out of college than the control group.

In another example, Blackwell, Trzesniewski, and Dweck (2007) studied an intervention designed to change attributions among low-income minority seventh-grade students in an urban school. In an 8-week period at the beginning of the school year, the students took part in eight workshops on brain function and study skills. Students in the experimental group were taught that the brain can get stronger when a person works on challenging tasks, while those in the control group learned only study skills. At the end of the academic year, the students in the experimental group earned significantly higher mathematics grades than those in the control group (a mean increase of 0.30 grade points), reversing the normal pattern of declining mathematics grades over the course of seventh grade. Noting that the effectiveness of interventions targeting attributions has been replicated with different student populations, Yaeger and Walton (2011) observe that these studies support the hypothesis that changes in attributions can lead to a positive, self-reinforcing cycle of improvement. Students who attribute a low grade to transitory factors, such as a temporary lack of effort, rather than to a lack of general intelligence or mathematics ability, are more motivated to work harder in their classes. This leads to improved grades, which, in turn, reinforce students' view that they can succeed academically and make them less likely to attribute any low grades to factors beyond their control.

Other experiments are designed to reduce "stereotype threat," the worry that one is perceived as having low intelligence as a member of a stereotyped group, which has been shown to negatively affect academic performance. Yaeger and Walton (2011) describe an intervention based on self-affirmation theory, which posits that people who reflect on their positive attributes will view negative events as less threatening, experience less stress, and function more effectively than they otherwise would. Cohen et al. (2006, 2009) asked white and black seventh-grade students to complete a brief, 15-20-minute writing exercise at the beginning of the school year. The experimental group wrote about why two or three values were personally important to them, while the control group wrote about values that were not personally important. By the end of the first semester, black students in the experimental group had significantly higher grade point averages than their peers in the control group, reducing the black-white achievement gap by about 40 percent. With a few more of these exercises, the black students' gain relative to the control group persisted for 2 years.

These brief interventions appear to work by engaging students as active participants. For example, when students write about values that are important, they are actually generating the self-affirmation intervention. Although they are intentionally brief, to avoid conveying to students that they need intensive help or remediation, the interventions "can induce deep processing and prepare students to transfer the content to new settings" (Yaeger and Walton, 2011, p. 284). The study findings showing that the interventions have led to changes in students' academic trajectories demonstrate transfer of students' learning to new school or college assignments.

The Importance of Metacognition

In his book on unified theories of cognition, Newell (1990) points out that there are two layers of problem solving—applying a strategy to the problem at hand, and selecting and monitoring that strategy. Good problem solving, Newell observed, often depends as much on the selection and monitoring of a strategy as on its execution. The term *metacognition* (literally "thinking about thinking") is commonly used to refer to the selection and monitoring processes, as well as to more general activities of reflecting on and directing one's own thinking.

Experts have strong metacognitive skills (Hatano, 1990). They monitor their problem solving, question limitations in their knowledge, and avoid simple interpretations of a problem. In the course of learning and problem solving, experts display certain kinds of regulatory performance such as knowing when to apply a procedure or rule, predicting the correctness or outcomes of an action, planning ahead, and efficiently apportioning cognitive resources and time. This capability for self-regulation and self-instruction enables advanced learners to profit a great deal from work and practice by themselves and in group efforts.

Studies of metacognition have shown that people who monitor their own understanding during the learning phase of an experiment show better recall performance when their memories are tested (Nelson, 1996). Similar metacognitive strategies distinguish stronger from less competent learners. Strong learners can explain which strategies they used to solve a problem and why, while less competent students monitor their own thinking sporadically and ineffectively and offer incomplete explanations (Chi et al., 1989; Chi and VanLehn, 1991).

There is ample evidence that metacognition develops over the school years; for example, older children are better than younger ones at planning for tasks they are asked to do (Karmiloff-Smith, 1979). Metacognitive skills can also be taught. For example, people can learn mental devices that help them stay on task, monitor their own progress, reflect on their strengths and weaknesses, and self-correct errors. It is important to note, however, that the teaching of metacognitive skills is often best accomplished in specific content areas since the ability to monitor one's understanding is closely tied to domain-specific knowledge and expertise (National Research Council, 1999).

Self-Regulated Learning and Self-Regulation

Student beliefs about learning, motivation, and metacognition are all dimensions of the broader construct of self-regulated learning, which focuses on understanding how learners take an active, purposeful role in learning, by setting goals and working to achieve them.

In a recent review of the research on self-regulated learning, Wolters (2010) observes that, although there are several different models of such learning, the most prominent is that developed by Pintrich and colleagues (Pintrich, 2000, 2004). In this model, learners engage in four phases of self-regulation, not necessarily in sequential order: forethought or planning (setting learning goals); monitoring (keeping track of progress in a learning activity); regulation (using, managing, or changing learning strategies to achieve the learning goals; and reflection (generating new knowledge about the learning tasks or oneself as a learner). These phases overlap substantially with the elements of Type 1 self-regulation included in our proposed cluster of Work Ethic/Conscientiousness skills (see Table 2-2). As the learner engages in the different phases of self-regulation, he or she may regulate one or more of several interrelated dimensions of learning, including cognition (for example, by using cognitive and metacognitive learning strategies); motivation and affect (for example, by planning to reward himself or herself after studying); learning behavior; and the learning context or environment (such as deciding where to study, and who to study with).

Comparing these dimensions of self-regulated learning with a list of 21st century skills proposed by Ananiadou and Claro (2009), Wolters found a high degree of conceptual overlap. The 21st century skills of initiation and self-direction were congruent with self-regulated learning, as the ability to set learning goals and manage the pursuit of those goals is a hallmark of a self-regulated learner. The 21st century skill of adaptability, including the ability to respond effectively to feedback, is very similar (or identical) to what the learner does in the monitoring and reflection phases of self-regulated learning. Learners who are strong in self-regulated learning are seen as particularly adept at using different forms of feedback to continue and complete learning activities. Earlier in this chapter, we noted that development of expertise requires not only extensive practice but also feedback. Accordingly, development of self-regulated learning skills should aid development of expertise in a domain.

Wolters (2010) identified a moderate degree of overlap between self-regulated learning and the interpersonal skills of collaboration and communication. He notes that research on self-regulated learning has begun to explore the interpersonal dimensions of this "intrapersonal" skill, finding that the abilities and beliefs underlying self-regulated learning are developed through social processes. In addition, self-regulated learners are effective at seeking help from peers or teachers, working in groups, and other aspects of collaboration (Newman, 2008). Wolters (2010) concluded that the conceptual similarities between 21st century skills and dimensions of self-regulated learning lend support to the critical importance of competencies such as self-direction, adaptability, flexibility, and collaboration, and suggested drawing on the self-regulated learning research to improve understanding of the 21st century skills.

The construct of self-regulated learning has been used to design instructional interventions that have improved academic outcomes among diverse populations of students, from early elementary school through college. These interventions have led to improvements in class grades and other measures of achievement in writing, reading, mathematics, and science (Wolters, 2010).

Further research is needed to more clearly define the dimensions of self-regulated learning, the relationship between this construct and 21st century skills, and how development of self-regulated learning influences academic engagement and attainment for diverse groups of students (Wolters, 2010). Longitudinal research or other research to improve our understanding of the developmental trajectory of different dimensions of self-regulated learning, such as time management and goal-setting, would help to determine the age level at which students should begin to develop these dimensions. In addition, research is needed to develop more unified assessments of self-regulated learning. The currently available measures (using self-reports, observational, and other methods) suffer from shortcomings and are not fully aligned with current views of self-regulated learning.

Self-Regulation

Self-regulated learning is one facet of the broader skill of self-regulation, which is related to conscientiousness. Self-regulation encompasses setting and pursuing short- and long-term goals and staying on course despite internal and external challenges; it includes managing one's emotions (Hoyle and Davisson, 2011). What an individual uses to overcome internal challenges, such as counterproductive impulses, or external challenges that may arise in different situations requires a set of strategies that, taken together, comprise self-regulation.

Research on self-regulation is growing rapidly, with hundreds of articles and five major edited volumes published since 2000 (Hoyle and Davisson, 2011). Reflecting the breadth of the construct, researchers have studied self-regulation in various life contexts, such as emotion, chronic illness, smoking, exercise, eating, and shopping (Wolters, 2010). To date, there is no consensus in the research on how to define self-regulation. In a review of 114 chapters in edited volumes, Hoyle and Davisson (2011) found that some provided no definition at all, there was no evidence of a common definition, and the same authors sometimes proposed different definitions in different chapters. Because the different definitions include a large number of behavioral variables, further research is needed to more clearly delimit the construct and to exclude variables that are not a critical element of self-regulation.

In the previous chapter, we summarized research indicating that attention, a dimension of self-regulation, is related to reading and math achievement. Attention is the ability to control impulses and focus on tasks (e.g., Raver, 2004), and plays an important role in avoiding antisocial behavior. Specifically, we noted that attention, measured at school entry, predicts later reading and mathematics achievement in elementary school (Duncan et al., 2007). In addition, children who are weak in self-regulation, as indicated by persistently high levels of antisocial behavior across the elementary school years, are significantly less likely to graduate from high school and to attend college than children who never had these problems (Duncan and Magnuson, 2011). Developmental psychologists have developed measures of self-regulation in young children that focus on the ability to delay gratification. Longitudinal studies have found that measures of this dimension of self-regulation in early childhood predict academic and social competence in adolescence (Mischel, Shoda, and Peake, 1988; Shoda, Mischel, and Peake, 1990). Conversely, children who lacked self-regulation in early childhood are more likely at age 18 to be impulsive, to seek danger, to be aggressive, and to be alienated from others (Arsenault et al., 2000).

Given the importance of self-regulation, greater consensus on how to conceptualize this broad construct is needed. The current disagreement in the literature about how to define the foundations, process, and consequences of self-regulation poses a major barrier to the development of accurate assessments of it (Hoyle and Davisson, 2011). As we discuss in the following chapter, teaching for deeper learning and transfer begins with a model of student learning, representing the desired outcomes, and includes assessments to measure student progress toward these outcomes. Agreement on definitions is an essential first step toward teaching and learning of self-regulation.

THE INTERPERSONAL DOMAIN

The sociocultural perspective that learning is "situated" within unique social contexts and communities illuminates the importance of the interpersonal domain for deeper learning. This domain encompasses a broad range of skills and abilities that an individual draws on when interacting with others. We have proposed in Chapter 2 that it includes two skill clusters:

- Teamwork and collaboration (aligned with the personality factor of agreeableness), including such skills as communication, collaboration, teamwork, cooperation, interpersonal skills, and empathy
- Leadership (aligned with the personality factor of extroversion), including such skills as leadership and responsibility, assertive communication, self-presentation, and social influence

This preliminary taxonomy of the interpersonal domain represents an initial step toward addressing the problem of a lack of clear, agreed-upon definitions of interpersonal skills and processes. Below, we discuss the role of interpersonal skills in deeper learning, and then return to the definitional problem.

Much of what humans learn, beginning informally at birth and continuing in more structured educational and work environments, is acquired through discourse and interactions with others. For example, development of new knowledge in science, mathematics, and other disciplines is often shaped by collaborative work among peers (e.g., Dunbar, 2000). Through such interactions, individuals build communities of practice, test their own theories, and build on the learning of others. Individuals who are using a naive strategy can learn by observing others who have figured out a more productive one. The social nature of learning contrasts with many school situations in which students are often required to work independently. Yet the display and modeling of cognitive competence through group participation and social interaction is an important mechanism for the internalizing of knowledge and skill (National Research Council, 1999).

An example of the importance of social context can be found in the 1994 work of Ochs, Jacoby, and Gonzales. They studied the activities of a physics laboratory research group whose members included a senior physicist, a postdoctoral researcher, technical staff, and predoctoral students. They found that workers' contributions to the laboratory depended significantly on their participatory skills in a collaborative setting—that is, on their ability to formulate and understand questions and problems, to construct arguments, and to contribute to the construction of shared meanings and conclusions.

Lave and Wenger (1991) proposed that much of knowledge is embedded within shared systems of representation, discourse, and physical activity in "communities of practice" and that such communities support the development of identity—one is what one practices, to some extent. In this view, school is just one of the many contexts that can support learning. Several studies have supported the idea that knowledge and skills are developed and applied in communities of practice. For example, some researchers have analyzed the use of mathematical reasoning skills in workplace and other everyday contexts (Lave, 1988; Ochs, Jacoby, and Gonzales, 1994). One such study found that workers who packed crates in a warehouse applied sophisticated mathematical reasoning in their heads to make the most efficient use of storage space, even though they may not have been able to solve the same problem expressed as a standard numerical equation (Scribner, 1984). The rewards and meaning that people derive from becoming deeply involved in a community can provide a strong motive to learn.

Studies of the social context of learning show that, in a responsive social setting, learners observe the criteria that others use to judge competence and can adopt these criteria. Learners then apply these criteria to judge and perfect the adequacy of their own performance. Shared performance promotes a sense of goal orientation as learning becomes attuned to the constraints and resources of the environment. In school, students develop facility in giving and accepting help (and stimulation) from others. Social contexts for learning make the thinking of the learner apparent to teachers and other students so that it can be examined, questioned, and built on as part of constructive learning.

Social Dimensions of Motivation and Self-Regulated Learning

Earlier in this chapter, we discussed interventions designed to change students' beliefs about themselves as learners and also their motivation for learning (Yaeger and Walton, 2011). Although these interventions target intrapersonal skills and attitudes as a way to enhance cognitive learning, they are based on research and theory from social psychology. The interventions are carefully designed to tap into social communities and relationships that are important and meaningful to the targeted audiences. For example, the intervention by Wilson and Linville (1982, 1985) used videos of upperclassmen to convey an important message to struggling freshmen because upperclassmen are viewed as trusted sources of information by freshmen. Similarly, we noted that the abilities and beliefs underlying self-regulated learning are developed through social processes and that self-regulated learners are effective at seeking help from peers or teachers, working in groups, and other aspects of collaboration (Newman, 2008). In Chapter 3, we observed that children lacking interpersonal skills, as reflected in persistent patterns of antisocial behavior over the elementary school years, are significantly less likely to graduate from high school and to attend college than children who never had these problems (Duncan and Magnuson, 2011). Clearly, social and interpersonal skills support deeper learning that transfers to new classes and problems, enhancing academic achievement.

IMPLICATIONS FOR INSTRUCTION

Findings from the research reviewed in this chapter have important implications for how to organize teaching and learning to facilitate deeper learning and development of transferable 21st century competencies. Here, we briefly summarize some of the implications, and in Chapter 6, we discuss in greater detail how to design instruction to support deeper learning.

As summarized by a previous NRC committee, research conducted over the past century has (National Research Council, 2001, p. 87):

> clarified the principles for structuring learning so that people will be better able to use what they have learned in new settings. If knowledge is to be transferred successfully, practice and feedback need to take a certain form. Learners must develop an understanding of when (under what conditions) it is appropriate to apply what they have learned. Recognition plays an important role here. Indeed, one of the major differences between novices and experts is that experts can recognize novel situations as minor variants of situations to which they already know how to apply strong methods.

Experts' ability to recognize familiar elements in novel problems allows them to apply (or transfer) their knowledge to solve such problems. The research has also clarified that transfer is also more likely to occur when the person understands the underlying principles of what was learned. The models children develop to represent a problem mentally, and the fluency with which they can move back and forth among representations, are other important dimensions of transfer that can be enhanced through instruction.

The main challenge in designing instruction for transfer is to create learning experiences for learners that will prime appropriate cognitive processing during learning without overloading the learner's information-processing system. Research on learning with multimedia tools has led to the development of the cognitive theory of multimedia learning (Mayer, 2009, 2011a), derived from the cognitive load theory (Sweller, 1999; Plass, Moreno, and Brünken, 2010). This theory posits that learners experience cognitive demands during learning, but their limited processing capacity restricts the amount of cognitive processing they can engage in at any one time. According to both theories, learning experiences may place three different types of demands on learners' limited working memory: (1) extraneous processing, (2) essential processing, and (3) generative processing (Sweller, 1999; Mayer, 2009, 2011a; Plass, Moreno, and Brünken, 2010). Extraneous processing does not serve the learning goals and is caused by poor instructional design. Essential processing is necessary if a learner is to mentally represent the essential material in the lesson, and it is required to address the material's complexity. Generative processing involves making sense of the material (e.g., mentally organizing it and relating it to relevant prior knowledge) and depends on the learner's motivation to exert effort during learning.

Depending on how it is designed, instruction may lead to one of three types of cognitive processing: extraneous overload, essential overload, and generative underuse (Mayer, 2011a). If instruction creates an extraneous overload situation, the amount of extraneous, essential, and generative processing required by the instructional task exceeds the learner's cognitive capacity for processing in working memory. An appropriate instructional goal for extraneous overload situations is to reduce extraneous processing (thereby freeing up cognitive capacity for essential and generative processing). If instruction creates an essential overload situation, the amount of essential and generative processing required by the instructional task exceeds the learner's cognitive capacity, even though extraneous processing demands have been reduced or eliminated. An appropriate instructional goal for essential overload situations is to manage essential processing (as it cannot be cut because it is essential for the instructional objective). Finally, if instruction creates a situation of generative underuse, the learner does not engage in sufficient generative processing even though cognitive capacity is available. An appropriate instructional goal for generative underuse situations is to foster generative processing.

In Chapter 6, we discuss evidence-based instructional methods for reducing extraneous processing, managing essential processing, and promoting generative processing. That chapter describes examples of techniques that have been successful in teaching for transfer, including findings from specific educational interventions.

CONCLUSIONS

Deeper learning occurs when the learner is able to transfer what was learned to new situations. Research on teaching for transfer, which primarily reflects the cognitive perspective on learning, has a long history in psychology and education. This research indicates that learning for transfer requires knowledge that is mentally organized, understanding of the broad principles of the knowledge, and skills for using this knowledge to solve problems. Other, more recent research indicates that intrapersonal skills and dispositions, such as motivation and self-regulation, support deeper learning and that these valuable skills and dispositions can be taught and learned. Sociocultural perspectives on learning illuminate the potential for developing intrapersonal and interpersonal skills within instruction focused on cognitive mastery of school subjects; such perspectives provide further evidence that skills in all three domains play important roles in deeper learning and development of transferable knowledge.

- Conclusion: The process of deeper learning is essential for the development of 21st century competencies (including both skills and knowledge), and the application of transferable 21st century competencies, in turn, supports the process of deeper learning in a recursive, mutually reinforcing cycle.

In Chapter 3, the committee concluded that educational attainment is strongly predictive of positive adult outcomes in the labor market, health, and civic engagement. The research reviewed in this chapter indicates that individuals both apply and develop intertwined cognitive, intrapersonal, and interpersonal competencies in the process of deeper learning, including the learning of school subjects. Through deeper learning, individuals develop transferable 21st century competencies that facilitate improvements in academic achievement and that increase years of educational attainment. Thus the research reviewed in this chapter supports the argument that deeper learning and 21st century skills prepare young people for adult success.

At the same time, this chapter finds a lack of clear, agreed-upon definitions of specific cognitive, intrapersonal, and interpersonal competencies. This lack of shared definitions is greatest for competencies in the intrapersonal and interpersonal domains.

5

Deeper Learning of English Language Arts, Mathematics, and Science

This chapter addresses the second question in the study charge by analyzing how deeper learning and 21st century skills relate to academic skills and content in the disciplines of reading, mathematics, and science,[1] especially as the content and skill goals are described in the Common Core State Standards for English language arts and mathematics and NRC's *A Framework for K-12 Science Education* (hereafter referred to as the NRC science framework; National Research Council, 2012).

The existing Common Core State Standards, as well as the Next Generation Science Standards that are under development in 2012 based on the NRC science framework (National Research Council, 2012), are expected to strongly influence teaching and learning in the three disciplines, including efforts to support deeper learning and development of 21st century skills. The English language arts and mathematics standards were developed by state education leaders, through their membership in the National Governors Association and the Council of Chief State School Officers, and have been adopted by nearly all (45) states, along with 2 territories and the District of Columbia. The Next Generation Science Standards are being developed through a similar process and are also likely to be widely adopted by the states.

---

[1]In keeping with its charge, the committee explored deeper learning in the individual disciplines of reading, mathematics, and science. It only briefly addressed integrated approaches to teaching across disciplines (see Box 5-2), as this topic lay outside its charge. A separate NRC committee has been charged to review the relevant research and develop a research agenda for integrated teaching of science, technology, engineering, and mathematics (STEM).

The first, second, and third sections of the chapter focus, respectively, on English language arts, mathematics, and science and engineering. For each discipline we

- discuss how "deeper learning" has been characterized in the discipline, including issues and controversies that have played out over time;
- describe the relevant parts of the Common Core State Standards or the NRC science framework (along with selected other reports outlining expectations for student learning) in light of the historical context; and
- analyze how the new standards and framework map to our characterization of deeper learning and to the clusters of 21st century skills defined in Chapter 2.

In the final section of the chapter, we present conclusions and recommendations based on a broad look across all three disciplines. In this broad look, we compare the expectations included in the Common Core State Standards and the NRC science framework with deeper learning (as characterized within each discipline) and 21st century skills.

ENGLISH LANGUAGE ARTS

The Context: A History of Controversy

Discussions of how to teach reading and writing in the United States have a reputation for contentiousness, reflected in the military metaphors used to describe them, such as "the reading wars" or "a curricular battleground." The public debates surrounding the fairly regular pendulum swings of the curriculum reveal fundamental differences in philosophy and widely variant interpretations of a very large but sometimes inconsistent research base.

Divergent Positions on Reading for Understanding

Beliefs about how to develop reading for understanding diverge greatly, with the spectrum of opinions defined by two extreme positions. One position, which we will refer to as the simple view of reading, holds that reading comprehension is the product of listening comprehension and decoding. Proponents of this position argue that students in the early grades should learn all of the letters of the alphabet and their corresponding sounds to a high degree of accuracy and automaticity. Agile decoding combined with a strong oral language (i.e., listening vocabulary) base will lead to fluent reading for understanding, limited only by the reader's store of knowledge and language comprehension. After the code is mastered, further development of reading for understanding is expected through either or both of (a) a wide reading of literature and nonfiction to gather new ideas and insights about the natural and social world and (b) solid instruction in the disciplines—the sciences, the social sciences, mathematics, and the humanities.

The polar opposite position, which might best be labeled a utilitarian view of reading, writing, and language, contends that from the outset of kindergarten, educators should engage children in a systematic quest to make sense of their world through deep engagement with the big ideas that have puzzled humankind for centuries. These are, of course, the very ideas that prompted humans to develop the disciplinary tools we use to understand and improve the natural and social world in which we live. Proponents of the utilitarian view argue that students will need to use, and hence refine, their reading and writing skills as they seek information to better understand and shape their worlds. Once students feel the need to learn to read, it will be much easier to teach students the lower-level skills needed to transform print into meaning. A side benefit is that students will have learned an important lesson about the purpose of reading—that it is always about making meaning and critiquing information on the way to acquiring knowledge.

Disagreements Over Curricular Focus, Integration, and Complexity

Disagreements on curriculum and epistemology both confound and intensify the polarized views on teaching reading for understanding. One area of disagreement is curricular focus. Instructional approaches based on the simple view tend to be curriculum centered. All students are expected to march through the same lessons and assessments, and whole-class instruction is commonplace. By contrast, instructional approaches based on the utilitarian view tend to be student centered, and each student may consume a slightly different pedagogical diet. Teachers differentiate activities and assignments for individual students based on feedback about how they are progressing, and instruction is more likely to be delivered in small groups or individualized settings.

A second area of disagreement focuses on whether the English language arts curriculum should be integrated with or separate from instruction in other disciplines. In the simple view, reading, writing, and language skills should be taught separately from the disciplinary curriculum, at least in the early stages of reading, until these fundamental skills become highly automatic. Then and only then, the argument goes, will students be ready to meet the challenges of disciplinary learning from text. The utilitarian view, by contrast, calls for integration between English language arts and disciplinary learning from the earliest stages. Acquiring disciplinary knowledge plus discourse and inquiry skills is the goal to which reading, writing, and language skills are bound, even as they are still being acquired.

A third area of disagreement centers on strategies for coping with complexity. Advocates for the simple view argue for decomposing complex processes into component parts. For example, to help students learn to read words in connected text, they propose that teachers should first focus on teaching the parts of reading—the correspondences between individual letters (or groups of letters) and sounds. Only when students have learned these correspondences to a high degree of accuracy and automaticity should they be asked to synthesize the letters and corresponding sounds into words by reading aloud. Similarly, in writing, advocates of the simple view argue that teachers should first help students learn the parts—the correspondences between the sounds within spoken words and letters that represent these sounds. Only after students have mastered these correspondences should teachers ask them to synthesize the sounds and corresponding letters into the spelling of words.

In contrast, advocates for the utilitarian view would cope with complexity through scaffolding. They argue that students should be encouraged to perform the ultimate target task, such as reading words in connected text. Teachers should scaffold students' performance of the task with various tools, such as reading aloud to convey the "whole of the story"; repeated readings (I'll read a sentence, then you read it); choral readings; and encouraging students to use context and picture cues to figure out pronunciations and word meanings. In writing, students would be encouraged to get their ideas on paper and to spell things the way they sound, with the expectation that later they would, with teacher guidance, transform their sound-based spellings into conventional spellings so that others will be able to read their stories. Students would also be expected to share their written pieces with peers even before they can write and spell fluently, in an effort to represent their attempts to communicate complex ideas.

A fourth area of disagreement centers on where the locus of meaning lies—in the text, the reader, the context in which the reading is completed, or a hybrid space involving all three. A committee chaired by Snow (2002) specified a hybrid space by defining reading comprehension as "the process of simultaneously extracting and constructing meaning through interaction and involvement with written language." The committee viewed the text as an important but insufficient determinant of reading comprehension. Kintsch (1998), in his widely accepted "construction–integration" model of reading comprehension, also discussed the importance of both extracting and constructing meaning, viewing the text as an important but insufficient resource for constructing a model of meaning. He proposed that readers construct a mental representation of what they thought the text said (a text base) and then integrate it with key concepts from memory to create a representation (what he called the situation model) of what they thought the text meant.

Pedagogical approaches reflect these different views of where meaning lies. Approaches based on the simple view tend to stay very close to the text. Teachers pose questions to lay out the "facts" of the text prior to any interpretation, critique, or application of what was learned through reading to accomplish a new task. Approaches based on the utilitarian view may engage students in using the text as a reservoir of evidence to evaluate the validity of different claims, interpretations, critiques, or uses of the text.

The research base for reading, as reflected in key summary documents in the field—such as the report of the National Institute of Child Health and Human Development (2000), the National Academy of Sciences' *Preventing Reading Difficulties in Young Children* (National Research Council, 1998), and the four volumes of the *Handbook of Reading Research* (Pearson et al., 1984; Barr et al., 1991; Kamil et al., 2000, 2011)—tend to provide consistent support for a balanced position that emphasizes both basic and more advanced processes. Such a balanced approach strongly emphasizes the basic skills of phonemic awareness, alphabet knowledge, and decoding for accurate word learning in the early stages of reading acquisition, but places an equal emphasis on reading for meaning at all stages of learning to read. As students mature and the demands of school curriculum focus more on the acquisition of disciplinary knowledge, the emphasis on reading for meaning increases. Thus the polar views that define the extremes of the continuum of views on reading acquisition and pedagogy ultimately converge in a more comprehensive view of written language acquisition. For the all-important early stages of reading, while there is strong support for early emphasis on the basics, there is no evidence that such an emphasis should preclude an equally strong emphasis on learning to use the range of skills and knowledge acquired early on to engage in transfer to new situations and in monitoring one's reading and writing to see if it makes sense.

Summary

Although all the parties in the debate share the goal of deeper learning in English language arts, they propose different routes. Some want to start with shallower or more basic tasks as a foundation for deeper or higher-order tasks. Others want to start with the deeper learning tasks and engage the more basic tasks and information as resources to help students complete the more challenging tasks. In the final analysis, the research supports a more balanced view that incorporates both the "basics" and the need to monitor reading and writing for sense-making and to apply whatever is learned about reading and writing to the acquisition of knowledge within disciplinary settings.

The Four Resources Model as an Approach to Defining Deeper Learning

In the early 1990s, Australian scholars Freebody and Luke took an important step forward in reconciling the various controversies described above (Freebody and Luke, 1990; Luke and Freebody, 1997). They created what is now known as the "four resources model." The model consists of a set of different stances that readers can take toward a text, each of which approaches reading from a different point of view: that of the text, the reader, the task, or the context. Taken together, the stances constitute a complete "theory" of a reader who is capable of managing all of the resources at his or her disposal. The authors propose that any reader can assume any one of these four stances in the quest to make meaning in response to a text. The confluence of reader factors (how much a reader knows or is interested in a topic), text (an assessment of the complexity and topical challenge of the text), task (what a reader is supposed to do with the topic), and context (what is the purpose or challenge in dealing with this text) will determine the particular stance a reader assumes when reading a particular text. That stance can change from text to text, situation to situation, or even moment to moment when reading a given text. The various stances (resources) and the key questions associated with each are

- The reader as decoder, who asks: What does the text say? In the process, the reader builds a coherent text base where each idea is tested for coherence with all of the previous ideas gleaned from a close reading of the text.
- The reader as meaning maker, who asks: What does the text mean? In answering that question, the reader seeks to develop meaning based on: (a) the ideas currently in the text base and (b) the reader's prior knowledge.
- The reader as text analyst, who asks: What tools does the author use to achieve his or her goals and purposes? The text analyst considers how the author's choice of words, form, and structure shape our regard for different characters or our stance toward an issue, a person, or a group. The text analyst reads through the texts to get to the author and tries to evaluate the validity of the arguments, ideas, and images presented.
- The reader as text critic, who asks questions about intentions, subtexts, and political motives. The text critic assumes that no texts are ideologically neutral, asking such questions as: Whose interests are served or not served by this text? Who is privileged,

marginalized, or simply absent? What are the political, economic, epistcmological, or cthical goals of the author?

When the stances of the text critic and the text analyst are combined, the goals of truly critical reading can be achieved. The reader can examine both the assumptions (what knowledge base is required to make sense of the text) and consequences (whose views are privileged and whose are ignored) of a text.

All four stances are in play as well when a writer creates texts for others to read. Writers have various conceptual intentions toward their readers—to inform, for example, or to entertain, persuade, or inspire. They sometimes focus on the code in getting the words on paper. They always employ the two standards of the meaning maker—that what they write in any given segment is consistent with the ideas in the text up to this point, and that it is consistent with the assumed knowledge of the ideal reader. Writers are most expert at handling the form-function (or purpose-structure) relationship of the text analyst; in fact, the crux of the author's craft is to seek and find just the right formal realization of each particular conceptual intention toward the reader. Finally, writers have ulterior motives along with transparent ones. They privilege, marginalize, omit, or focus—sometimes intentionally and other times unwittingly as agents of the cultural forces that shape their work.

The four resources model allows us to define deeper learning in English language arts in a way that recognizes the controversies in the discipline yet meets the need for a balanced approach that equips the reader or writer to take different stances toward the reading or writing of a text depending on the purposes, the context, and the actual task confronting the reader or writer. Reading and writing are simultaneously code-breaking, meaning making, analytic, and critical activities; which stance dominates at a particular moment in processing depends upon the alignment of reader, text, task, and contextual factors. This perspective on deeper learning, recognizing that the reader or writer may adopt various stances from moment to moment, contrasts sharply with the "simple view" of reading and writing. The simple view would limit beginning readers to the code-breaking stance and limit beginning writers to codifying language, by putting down letters and words.

Drawing on the four resources model, we can now define deeper learning in English language arts from two perspectives: (1) as privileging activities that are successively higher on the list—in which the reader acts as meaning maker, text analyst, or text critic; or (2) as privileging the management of all four stances in relation to the reader's assessment of the difficulty of the text or task and the reader's purpose and knowledge resources. In the first perspective on deeper learning, analysis and critique take precedence over making meaning, which takes precedence over decoding. Such a hierarchy is consistent with the research base we will discuss in Chapter 6, in which we will describe the pedagogy of deeper learning as encouraging generative processing, elaboration, and questioning—all of which would lead us down the pathway toward meaning making, analysis, and critique. Indeed, the research on discussion protocols in reading text suggests that the effects of discussion questions are highly specific—that unless one focuses directly on analysis and critique, it is not likely to emerge on its own (Murphy et al., 2009). In the second perspective on deeper learning, reflecting on and managing one's own knowledge matters most in shaping the particular stance that one takes toward the understanding or construction of a text. This perspective builds on other principles of deeper learning elaborated in Chapter 4, namely, the notions of developing metacognitive strategies, self-monitoring, and self-explanation—all dispositions that encourage the learner to intentionally engage in his or her own comprehension and learning processes. This view also suggests that deeper learning involves knowing when and why to privilege lower-order over higher-order skills in pursuit of understanding or problem solving.

These two perspectives on deeper learning in English language arts are not mutually exclusive. Deeper learning could involve the deliberate selection of a stance that elicits the skills and processes that best fit the situation and problem that a learner faces at any given moment *and* also suggest a procedural preference for always selecting the highest level among alternative stances when the situation or problem allows more than one approach. For example, if assuming either the meaning making stance or the analysis stance will allow the learner to solve a reading or writing problem, the learner should opt for an analytic stance to complete the task. From either perspective, beginning readers and writers as well as those who are more advanced, can engage in deeper learning.

Common Core State Standards

The widely adopted Common Core State Standards in English language arts (CCSS-ELA; Common Core State Standards Initiative, 2010a) are likely to shape any attempt to infuse deeper learning initiatives into school curricula. In other words, it is likely that whatever purchase deeper learning initiatives accrue in the next decade will be filtered through this set of standards. From this perspective, the prospects for reading and writing instruction aligned with the four resources model seem promising.

The full title of the CCSS-ELA, *Standards for English Language Arts and Literacy in History/Social Studies, Science, and Technical Subjects* (Common Core State Standards Initiative, 2010a), provides the first indication that these standards will be different from state English language arts

(ELA) standards created before 2010. The title signals the adoption of an integrated view of the topics of reading, writing, speaking/listening, and language. This integrated view is applied to two domains—literature and informational text—for reading and writing in grades K-5. The standards for grades 6-12 are first organized by ELA topic and then by subject matter (history and science) to distinguish which standards are the responsibility of the ELA teacher and which might better be addressed by science and history teachers. Within ELA, the four topics are again applied to the domains of literature and informational text. By contrast, the subject area sections address only the topics of reading and writing, broken down according to history/social studies and science/technical subjects.

This integrated view of ELA contrasts sharply with the heavy emphasis that in recent years has been placed on reading as a separate subject, almost to the exclusion of other language arts topics and other school subjects. The integration of reading with other topics and subjects represents a dramatic shift away from the "big five" approach—phonemic awareness, phonics, fluency, vocabulary, and comprehension—which has dominated reading instruction for over a decade (National Institute of Child Health and Human Development, 2000). The new standards present reading, writing, and oral language as tools for knowledge acquisition, effective argumentation, and clear communication across the disciplines of literature, science (and technical subjects), and history (and social studies). The standards address phonemic awareness, phonics, and fluency primarily in the foundational skills addendum to the K-5 standards. Vocabulary is highlighted in the language strand, and comprehension, alongside composition, is emphasized throughout. This combined with the standards' focus on reading and writing in the disciplines of history and science indicates that the CCSS-ELA can be interpreted as calling for a major shift from the current emphasis on decoding to comprehension of and learning with text.

The CCSS-ELA include 10 college and career readiness anchor standards, representing the "end state"—what high school graduates should know and be able to do if all of the specific grade-level and disciplinary variations of these 10 standards were to be successfully implemented. As shown in Box 5-1, the 10 anchor standards for reading are arranged in four clusters.

The mapping of these standards onto the four resources model (Luke and Freebody, 1997) is reasonably transparent. The three standards in Cluster 1, Key Ideas and Details, reflect the stance of the reader as decoder, with a hint of reader as meaning maker (because of the requirement of invoking prior knowledge to complete each task). The three standards in Cluster 2, Craft and Structure, reflect the stance of the reader as text analyst, focusing on form-function (or purpose-structure) relationships. The three standards in Cluster 3, Integration of Knowledge and Ideas, entail

BOX 5-1
College and Career Readiness Anchor Standards for Reading

Key Ideas and Details

1. Read closely to determine what the text says explicitly and to make logical inferences from it; cite specific textual evidence when writing or speaking to support conclusions drawn from the text.
2. Determine central ideas or themes of a text and analyze their development; summarize the key supporting details and ideas.
3. Analyze in detail where, when, why, and how events, ideas, and characters develop and interact over the course of a text.

Craft and Structure

4. Interpret words and phrases as they are used in a text, including determining technical, connotative, and figurative meanings, and explain how specific word choices shape meaning or tone.
5. Analyze the structure of texts, including how specific sentences, paragraphs, and larger portions of the text (e.g., a section or chapter) relate to each other and the whole.
6. Assess how point of view or purpose shapes the content and style of a text.

Integration of Knowledge and Ideas

7. Synthesize and apply information presented in diverse ways (e.g., through words, images, graphs, and video) in print and digital sources in order to answer questions, solve problems, or compare modes of presentation.
8. Delineate and evaluate the reasoning and rhetoric within a text, including assessing whether the evidence provided is relevant and sufficient to support the text's claims.
9. Analyze how two or more texts address similar themes or topics in order to build knowledge or to compare the approaches the authors take.

Range and Level of Text Complexity

10. Read complex texts independently, proficiently, and fluently, sustaining concentration, monitoring comprehension, and, when useful, rereading.

SOURCE: Common Core State Standards Initiative (2010a). © Copyright 2010. National Governors Association Center for Best Practices and Council of Chief State School Officers. All rights reserved. Reprinted with permission.

all four stances—decoder, meaning maker, analyst, and critic, but favor the text critic (especially 8) and meaning maker (especially 7 and 9). And, of course, the standard in Cluster 4, Range and Level of Text Complexity, involves all four stances in constant interaction.[2]

Relating the Standards to Deeper Learning and 21st Century Skills

The CCSS-ELA offer a policy framework that is highly supportive of deeper learning (as reflected in the four resources model) in English language arts. On the other hand, it remains to be seen whether the assessments that emerge from the two state assessment consortia, which have been funded by the Department of Education to develop next-generation assessments aligned to the Common Core State Standards, will be equally supportive of the goal of deeper learning, a question we will return to in Chapter 7.

In the previous chapters, we identified three broad domains of 21st century skills—cognitive, intrapersonal, and interpersonal. To examine the relationship between these clusters of 21st century skills and the various disciplinary standards documents, the committee created a list of some of the most frequently cited 21st century and deeper learning skills and then examined the standards for the degree of support provided for these skills.[3] The domain of cognitive 21st century skills, developed through deeper learning, is well represented in the CCSS-ELA. What is missing, both from the new CCSS and from the larger discussion of goals for reading and writing instruction presented above, is any serious consideration of the intrapersonal and interpersonal domains (see Figure 5-1).

Although the word "motivation" appears three times in the CCSS-ELA, the new standards do not seriously address the motivational factors (engagement, interest, identity, and self-efficacy) and dispositional factors (conscientiousness, stamina, persistence, collaboration) that we know

---

[2]It is fortunate that we can continue this mapping of cognitive constructs of CCSS onto the NAEP infrastructure for cognitive targets for reading assessment. NAEP's *locate and recall* target corresponds quite closely to the *key ideas and details* CCSS category. NAEP's *integrate and interpret* corresponds to CCSS's *integration of knowledge and ideas*, and NAEP's *critique and evaluate* incorporates much of what falls into CCSS's *craft and structure* (though it entails much more than craft and structure). This set of correspondences should facilitate longitudinal analyses of the course of reform engendered by the CCSS.

[3]The classifications in the figures in this chapter represent common sense judgments by an expert in each discipline who is familiar with the standards, with curriculum and practice, and with the cognitive and educational research literatures in the discipline. Undoubtedly other judges would classify some components differently. The study committee was not charged with conducting a more elaborate analytic study with multiple independent raters and assessments of reliability. Thus these diagrams and observations are meant to represent a plausible illustrative view rather than a definitive analysis.

English Language Arts

Deeper Learning/21st Century Skills Only	Areas of Strongest Overlap	Discipline-Based Standards Documents Only

• Systems thinking
• Complex communication II (social/interpersonal aspects)
• Cultural sensitivity, valuing diversity
• Motivation, persistence
• Identity
• Attitudes
• Self-development
• Collaboration/team-work
• Adaptability
	• Constructing and evaluating evidence-based arguments
	• Nonroutine problem solving
	• Complex communication I
	  ○ Disciplinary discourse
	  ○ Critical reading
	• Critical thinking
		• Disciplinary content of literature (saga of human experience)
		• Conventions of written and oral language
		• Literal text comprehension
		• Rhetorical effectiveness

FIGURE 5-1 Overlap between ELA-CCSS standards and 21st century skills. SOURCE: Created by the committee.

support deeper learning. However, recent research in English language arts illustrates the potential for developing these intrapersonal factors, as well as interpersonal factors. One example is described in Box 5-2 below, and another is found in the work of Guthrie, Wigfield, and You (2012). As noted in Chapter 4, the development of self-regulated strategies in writing—including motivation and feelings of self-efficacy—has been shown to improve writing performance among diverse groups of learners (Graham, 2006). The most probable explanation for the conspicuous absence of these factors from the standards is that, as noted in Chapter 6, they represent skills that are difficult to measure, at least without a very heavy reliance on human judgment. Therefore, these factors are unlikely candidates for systematic monitoring in accountability systems, which have traditionally relied on standardized measures that minimize reliance on human judgment. Presumably the authors of the standards were aware of research showing that reading and writing instruction focused on domain-specific learning goals can develop motivation and positive dispositions toward disciplinary learning, such as the example presented below, but felt that this was beyond the purview of the ELA standards.

MATHEMATICS

The Context: Typical Mathematics Instruction

Research studies provide a clear, consistent picture of typical school mathematics instruction in the United States. What we know is largely derived from two kinds of data and associated research analyses. One type of study that has been carried out over several decades has involved direct observation of classroom teaching (e.g., Stake and Easley, 1978; Stodolsky, 1988; Stigler et al., 1999; Hiebert et al., 2005), and another has used teacher self-report data from surveys (e.g., Weiss et al., 2001; Grouws, Smith, and Sztajn, 2004).

These studies present a remarkably consistent characterization of mathematics teaching in upper elementary school and middle-grade classrooms in the United States: Students generally work alone and in silence, with little opportunity for discussion and collaboration and little or no access to suitable computational or visualization tools. They focus on low-level tasks that require memorizing and recalling facts and procedures rather than tasks requiring high-level cognitive processes, such as reasoning about and connecting ideas or solving complex problems. The curriculum includes a narrow band of mathematics content (e.g., arithmetic in the elementary and middle grades) that is disconnected from real-world situations, and a primary goal for students is to produce answers quickly and efficiently without much attention to explanation, justification, or the development of meaning (e.g., Stodolsky, 1988; Stigler and Hiebert, 1999). As earlier chapters in this volume have indicated, reflecting research evidence regarding how people learn best when the goal is developing understanding (National Research Council, 1999), such pedagogy is at odds with goals aimed at deeper learning and transfer.

Although this pervasive approach to mathematics teaching has not been directly established as the cause of the generally low levels of student achievement, it is difficult to deny the plausibility of such a connection. In response, an array of reform initiatives has been aimed at changing what and how mathematics is taught and learned in American schools. Although reformers have disagreed on some issues, they share the goal of enhancing students' opportunities to learn mathematics with understanding and hence the attendant goal of promoting teaching mathematics for understanding. These goals reflect a focus on deeper learning in school mathematics.

Evolution of National Standards in Mathematics

School mathematics reform has a long history that cannot be adequately described in the limited space here, so we focus on the most recent

BOX 5-2
An Example of Deeper Learning in English Language Arts

The Common Core State Standards for English language arts (Common Core State Standards Initiative, 2010a) provide many opportunities to enact the principles of deeper learning embodied in this report. First, they promote a double vision of integration—(a) that reading, writing, and discourse ought to support one another's development, and (b) that reading, writing, and language practices are best taught and learned when they are employed as tools to acquire knowledge and inquiry skills and strategies within disciplinary contexts, such as science, history, or literature. Hence the standards for reading, writing, and language are unpacked in grades 6 through 12 within the three domains of literature, science and technology, and history. Further, a common criterion for rigorous thinking embedded in the standards centers on developing argumentation skill—the ability to understand, critique, and construct arguments that are valid within the norms of each discipline. Students are asked to deal with what counts as evidence, how arguments are constructed, what constitutes a counter claim and counter evidence—in short, both the structure and substance of reasoning is privileged. While not as ubiquitous as cognitive skills, interpersonal skills are strongly implicated in the speaking and listening standards, with an emphasis on collaboration and listening with care to understand and evaluate others' utterances as a part of rigorous discourse.

At the elementary level, project-based learning has a long history dating back to days of John Dewey and the progressive education movement in schools, a tradition in which the goal was to minimize the distance between school learning and the learning that occurs in the enactment of everyday life outside of school. In one (of many) modern instantiation of this tradition, literacy and science educational researchers at the University of California-Berkeley's Lawrence Hall of Science and in the Graduate School of Education have worked with elementary classroom teachers on an NSF-sponsored curriculum in which reading, writing, and academic language are used as tools to support the acquisition of science knowledge, inquiry strategies, and argumentation skills (Cervetti et al., 2012). Aptly named *Seeds of Science/Roots of Reading*, the program combines hands-on science activities (e.g., designing mixtures such as glue or hair gel from everyday household ingredients or using models to understand the formation of sand on a beach) with a host of reading, writing, and oral discourse activities to support and extend students' investigations and projects. Over the course of an 8-week unit, students read nine different types of books about various aspects of the topic (e.g., the science of sand, light, soil habitats) in a range of genres. These genres may include reference books, brief biographies of scientists, information pieces, books that model an aspect of either a scientific or a literacy process, and books that connect science to everyday life. All of the books are coordinated with specific subtopics within the unit. For example, a hands-on investigation of snails' preferred habitats is paired with a parallel trade book about a science class that collects and analyzes data about the same investigation. Similarly, the students' investigation of "mystery" sand is paired with a biography of a sand scientist that describes how he investigates the size, shape, color, texture, and origin of sand.

Students write in their science journals almost daily and engage in spirited discussions and debates (they call them discourse circles) about unsettled issues that arise from hands-on investigations and/or readings (e.g., they might hold a debate about the origin of a mystery sand). In a typical week in this approach, students will spend about 50 percent of their time in science activities and about 50 percent in reading, writing about their investigations, and talking about their reading, and their personal writing. Several times a week, students are asked to reflect on the quality and focus of their personal learning and participation as well as the learning and participation of their work groups—and even the class as a whole.

The curriculum is designed to foster deeper learning in the cognitive domain, through all of the reading, writing, and inquiry activities. At the same time, deeper learning of intrapersonal competencies is supported by the individual and group reflection activities, which encourage metacognition, taking personal responsibility for one's learning, stamina, and persistence. In the interpersonal domain, deeper learning is fostered by ongoing collaboration, including the discussions about the readings, the small group collaborative investigations, the discourse circles, and even in the division of labor students work out for extended investigations or projects. Reflection activities encourage students to reflect not only on their learning but also on how well their group cooperated and how they could improve their discussions.

The approach was tested in 94 fourth-grade classrooms in one Southern state. Half of the teachers taught the integrated science-literacy curriculum, while the other half of the teachers taught the two topics separately, covering the same science content with materials provided by their school districts along with their regular literacy instruction. Students in the integrated lessons made significantly greater gains on measures of science understanding, science vocabulary, and science writing, and both groups made comparable gains in science reading comprehension. Examples like these demonstrate that cognitive outcomes, which are clearly emphasized in most educational testing and accountability schemes in our country, need not suffer—indeed can prosper—when they are taught and learned in a context in which inter- and intrapersonal skills and practices are equally emphasized. Such examples also demonstrate that at least some disciplines—in this case, English language arts—can benefit from being taught in another disciplinary context, like science. Research has demonstrated the effectiveness of similar curricula integrating English language arts in the disciplines of literature (Guthrie et al., 2004) and social studies (De La Paz, 2005).

SOURCE: Adapted from Cervetti et al. (2012).

reform efforts. In 1989, the National Council of Teachers of Mathematics (NCTM) published the *Curriculum and Evaluation Standards for School Mathematics* (*CESSM*), which was the first attempt to lay out comprehensive national goals for mathematics learning. The curriculum goals portion of the document was divided into three sections representing grade-level clusters: 1-4, 5-8, and 9-12. Each section contained goals for all students and additional goals for college-intending students. *CESSM* promoted a view of mathematics as accessible to all students if instruction were changed to place greater emphasis on understanding and applicable knowledge and less emphasis on the memorization of facts and procedures.

CESSM, serving as the first national model of content expectations in school mathematics, had substantial influence on the mathematics instructional goals and frameworks later developed by a number of individual states. Nevertheless, over time it became clear that *CESSM* lacked the specificity needed by state policy makers to set objectives at and across grade levels and by teachers to implement the report's pedagogical and curricular ideas in their classrooms. In response to these perceived limitations, in 2000 the NCTM developed and published a successor document, *Principles and Standards for School Mathematics* (*PSSM*) (National Council of Teachers of Mathematics, 2000).

While *PSSM* preserved the essential tenets of the earlier *CESSM*, especially its emphasis on the importance of learning mathematics with understanding, it also added several enhancements. To provide more grade-level-specific clarity and guidance, *PSSM* was divided into narrower grade-level bands: K-2, 3-5, 6-8, and 9-12. For each band, *PSSM* presented only one set of goals for all students. *PSSM* also had a common set of overarching curricular expectations across the K-12 spectrum, which was intended to help state officials develop logical progressions of instruction from grade to grade for inclusion in state curriculum guidelines. *PSSM* was much more specific than the *CESSM* about the research basis for its recommendations, and the NCTM published a companion document that reviewed research in a number of areas directly related to the content of *PSSM*.

PSSM was subjected to extensive field review prior to publication, and it was generally well received when published in 2000, but it arrived at the dawn of the No Child Left Behind (NCLB) era in American education. Because extant standardized tests of school mathematics were not well aligned with *PSSM*, and because NCLB regulations required that these tests be a regular feature of every school year in grades 3-8 in order to determine whether adequate yearly progress was being made, *PSSM* had far less impact on states, schools, teachers, and students than had been envisioned by the NCTM.

One decade later, the move toward national guidance regarding expectations for school mathematics learning took a giant leap forward with the publication of the *Common Core State Standards for Mathematics* (CCSSM; Common Core State Standards Initiative, 2010b). CCSSM presents grade-level-specific expectations that are intended to be the core expectations for mathematics learning in the United States. *CCSSM* diverges from *CESSM* and *PSSM* in certain ways, including how it names the strands of content to be taught and learned and how it distributes certain content across the grades, but it retains the same focus on the importance of teaching in ways that enable students to learn mathematics with understanding. The *CCSSM* states, "These Standards define what students should understand and be able to do in their study of mathematics" (Common Core State Standards Initiative, 2010b, p. 4). Not only is this a consistent theme across the reform documents, it is also a topic that has received considerable attention from the research community.

Research Perspectives on Teaching Mathematics for Understanding

Studies conducted over the past 60 years provide a solid body of evidence concerning the benefits of teaching mathematics for understanding. As summarized in Silver and Mesa (2011, p. 69), teaching mathematics for understanding is sometimes referred to as:

> authentic instruction, ambitious instruction, higher order instruction, problem-solving instruction, and sense-making instruction (e.g., Brownell and Moser, 1949; Brownell and Sims, 1946; Carpenter, Fennema, and Franke, 1996; Carpenter et al., 1989; Cohen, 1990; Cohen, McLaughlin, and Talbert, 1993; Fuson and Briars, 1990; Hiebert and Wearne, 1993; Hiebert et al., 1996; Newmann and Associates, 1996). Although there are many unanswered questions about precisely how teaching practices are linked to students' learning with understanding (see Hiebert and Grouws, 2007), the mathematics education community has begun to emphasize teaching that aims for this goal.

Among the hallmarks of this conceptually oriented version of instruction are (a) mathematical features, or tasks that are drawn from a broad array of content domains and are cognitively demanding, and (b) pedagogical features, or teaching practices that are suitable to support multiperson collaboration and mathematical discourse among students, as well as their engagement with mathematical reasoning and explanation, consideration of real-world applications, and use of technology or physical models (e.g., Hiebert and Carpenter, 1992; Fennema and Romberg, 1999).

Mathematical Features

The mathematics curriculum in the United States, especially in elementary and middle grades, has long been characterized as incoherent, cursory, and repetitive (e.g., Balfanz, Mac Ivar, and Byrnes, 2006). Many have argued that the excessive attention paid to numbers and operations has restricted students' opportunities to learn other interesting and important mathematics content. Reflecting this concern, the National Council of Teachers of Mathematics standards (1989, 2000) noted the importance of including topics in algebra, geometry, measurement, and data analysis in the middle grades. Broader coverage is expected not only to enrich mathematics learning by exposing students to more topics but also to make salient the connections that exist among different content domains and topics—connections that are viewed by psychologists as hallmarks of student understanding (National Research Council, 1999).

Reformers have also called for a new approach to the mathematics tasks that provide daily opportunities for student learning. For example, the *Professional Standards for Teaching Mathematics* (National Council of Teachers of Mathematics, 1991) claimed that student learning of mathematics with understanding depended to a great extent on the teacher using "mathematical tasks that engage students' interests and intellect" (p. 1). Although such tasks can help students develop understanding, establish and maintain curiosity, and communicate with others about mathematical ideas, mathematics teachers in grades K-8 usually present cognitively undemanding tasks, such as recalling facts and applying well-rehearsed procedures to answer simple questions (Stake and Easley, 1978; Stodolsky, 1988; Porter, 1989; Stigler and Hiebert, 1999). Research has shown that it is not easy for teachers to use cognitively demanding tasks well in mathematics classrooms (Stein, Grover, and Henningsen, 1996; Henningsen and Stein, 1997). However, the regular use of such tasks to maintain high levels of cognitive demand can lead to increased student understanding and the development of problem solving and reasoning (Stein and Lane, 1996) and greater overall student achievement (Hiebert et al., 2005).

Pedagogical Features

Reformers have also advocated a broader array of pedagogical strategies to increase students' understanding of mathematics, moving beyond the limited current practices described above. As noted earlier in this chapter, current practice is at odds with research findings about how people learn with understanding (National Research Council, 1999). Silver and Mesa (2011) describe the goals of the reformers as follows:

Advocates for conceptually oriented teaching in school mathematics (e.g., National Council of Teachers of Mathematics, 1989, 2000) have suggested the potential value of fostering communication and interaction among students in mathematics classrooms through the use of complex tasks that are suitable for cooperative group work and that provide settings in which students need to explain and justify their solutions. Moreover, to increase students' engagement with mathematical tasks and their understanding of concepts, instructional reform efforts have also encouraged the use of hands-on learning activities and technological tools, as well as connecting work done in the mathematics classroom to other subjects and to the world outside school. Beyond exhortations, there is also some research evidence to support these hypotheses about pedagogy that might support students' development of mathematical understanding (e.g., Boaler, 1998; Fawcett, 1938; Fuson and Briars, 1990; Good, Grouws, and Ebmeier, 1983; Hiebert and Wearne, 1993; Stein and Lane, 1996). (Silver and Mesa, 2011, p. 69)

Two examples of instruction incorporating these types of pedagogical features are found in Box 5-3.

Deeper Learning Expectations in Mathematics

As noted earlier, the three major reform documents in school mathematics—*CESSM*, *PSSM*, and *CCSSM*—all emphasize deeper learning of mathematics, learning with understanding, and the development of usable, applicable, transferable knowledge and skills. These themes are in line with the broader statements we discussed earlier regarding the importance of 21st century learning skills. Generally speaking, the mathematics curriculum reform documents are much more explicit about expectations in the cognitive domain than they are about expectations in the intrapersonal and interpersonal domains. Yet, even in the domains less explicitly dealt with in the curriculum reform documents, one finds attention to some key 21st century goals, such as collaborative work, self-regulation, and the formation of positive attitudes and a mathematical identity. Moreover, there is a robust research literature on the matters of collaboration, metacognition, attitudes, motivation, and identity as they pertain to the teaching and learning of school mathematics. Chapter 3 of *Engaging Schools: Fostering High School Students' Motivation to Learn* (National Research Council and Institute of Medicine, 2004) provides an analysis of how many of these factors might interact with issues of race and culture to affect the learning of mathematics.

To implement the first principle, children explore five different lands at each grade level. In each land, they learn about a particular form of number

---

BOX 5-3
Examples of Deeper Learning in Mathematics

In Chapter 4, we provided an illustration of deeper learning of mathematics at the high school level (Boaler and Staples, 2008). Here, we focus on early mathematics learning. The weak performance of U.S. 15-year-olds on the mathematics component of the Programme for International Student Assessment (PISA) test (OECD, 2010) reflects the weakness of early math education in the United States. Deeper learning of mathematics in early childhood could potentially reverse the problem of persistent gaps in mathematics knowledge between children from low-income and middle-income backgrounds.

Example 1: Using Board Games for Early Mathematics Learning

One approach to helping preschoolers learn basic number concepts and strategies involves the use of board games. Playing board games with linearly arranged, consecutively numbered, equal-size spaces provides young children with multiple cues about the magnitude of the numbers. Ramani and Siegler (2011) compared the number knowledge of middle-income preschoolers who played a linear board game to the number knowledge of preschoolers from low-income backgrounds who also played this game. Among both groups of preschoolers, those with less initial knowledge of numbers gained more in understanding than those with greater initial knowledge. Significantly, the children from low-income backgrounds learned at least as much, and on several measures more, than preschoolers from middle-income backgrounds.

The study built on an earlier study of low-income preschoolers (Ramani and Siegler, 2008; Siegler and Ramani, 2009), which found that a brief game-playing intervention led to greater improvements in numeracy than alternative numerical activities lasting the same amount of time. The low-income preschoolers showed gains in their ability to estimate number lines, compare magnitudes, identify numerals, and in basic arithmetic, and these gains were stable over a 9-week period. Those who had earlier played the linear board game learned more from subsequent practice and feedback on addition problems than their peers who engaged in other numerical activities, suggesting that they were able to transfer the knowledge they had gained through game play.

---

representation while simultaneously addressing specific knowledge goals (developmental milestones) for that grade level. They begin in Object Land, where they initially work with real objects and then move on to work with pictures of objects. Next, they visit Picture Land, where numbers are represented as semiabstract patterns of dots that are equivalent to mathematical sets. By playing various card and dice games, the students gradually come to think of these patterns in the same way that they think of the words they use to talk about numbers. Third, they explore Line Land, where numbers are represented as segments along a line, and they play linear games. Later,

A higher percentage of preschoolers from middle-income families than from low-income families report playing board games at home (Ramani and Siegler, 2011), and this difference may contribute to the gap in mathematics knowledge between young children from low-income and middle-income backgrounds. The authors suggest that parents and teachers more frequently engage young children in playing linear board games, which require minimal time to play and are extremely inexpensive.

Example 2: Restructuring the Elementary School Mathematics Classroom

Deeper learning as called for in the Common Core State Standards and other documents reviewed above remains rare in U.S. classrooms. In the 2005 NRC report *How Students Learn: History, Mathematics, and Science in the Classroom*, Griffin (2005) describes very different mathematics classroom activities that are part of the research-based program, *Number Worlds*, for prekindergarten through grade 2. The program is based on six guiding principles (National Research Council, 2005, p. 283), and we describe illustrative activities related to a few of these principles below:

1. Expose children to the major ways that numbers are represented and talked about.
2. Provide opportunities to link the "world of quantity" with the "world of counting numbers" and the "world of formal symbols."
3. Provide visual and spatial analogs of number representations that children can actively explore in hands-on fashion.
4. Engage children and capture their imagination so knowledge constructed is embedded not only in their minds but also in their hopes, fears, and passions.
5. Provide opportunities to acquire computational fluency as well as conceptual understanding.
6. Encourage the use of metacognitive processes (e.g., problem solving, communication, reasoning) that will facilitate knowledge construction.

they visit Sky Land, where numbers are represented with vertical bar graphs and scales, and Circle Land, where numbers are represented by sundials and clocks, and they learn that numbers are used to measure time and the seasons of the year.

All of the activities are designed to help early elementary students mentally link physical quantities with counting numbers and formal symbols (design principle 2) as illustrated by the game "Plus Pup." To start, the teacher and children put a certain number of cookies into a lunch bag, and then the teacher or a child takes a walk with the bag. Along the way, the teacher or child picks up the Plus Pup card, and receives one more cookie. The teacher then invites the children to figure out how many cookies are in the bag. At first, the children open up the bag and count the cookies, but as they continue to replay the game, they gradually realize that they can use numbers to find the answer.

To support metacognitive processes (design principle 6), the program includes question cards that draw children's attention to the changes in quantities they enact during game play and prompt children to perform any calculations necessary to answer the questions. Additional follow-up questions encourage children to reflect on their own reasoning. The teacher usually uses the question cards at first, but over time, the children gradually begin to pose the questions themselves, assuming greater responsibility for their own learning. In a wrap-up period at the end of each lesson, a reporter from each small group first describes what the group did and learned and then takes questions from the rest of the class. This time for communication and reflection supports significant learning.

Evaluation studies indicate that the program is effective in helping diverse young children develop number knowledge that is deep, lasting, and transferable to further mathematics learning. A longitudinal 3-year study compared the performance of three groups of kindergarten through ninth grade students: (1) an urban, low-income group who participated in Number Worlds; (2) a low-income group who had been tested and identified as high achievers in mathematics; and (3) a largely middle-class group, also tested and designated as high achievers, who were enrolled in a magnet school with an enriched mathematics program. Over the course of the study period, from kindergarten entry to the end of second grade, the mathematics achievement of the Number Worlds group first caught up with, and then gradually exceeded, the achievement of the other two groups.

In addition to clearly enhancing mathematics achievement in the cognitive domain, the program generates positive dispositions toward mathematics among both students and teachers in the intrapersonal domain (Griffin, 2005) as well as enhances the interpersonal skills of communication, collaboration, and teamwork.

Again, the committee mapped the reform documents and the lists of 21st century learning skills to ascertain areas of overlap and emphasis. A summary is provided in Figure 5-2, and outcomes of the mapping process are elaborated briefly below.

Cognitive Skills

In mathematics, as is the case with the other content areas treated in this chapter, the cognitive domain affords the strongest correspondence between 21st century skills and school learning goals for the subject. In

Mathematics

Deeper Learning/21st Century Skills Only	Areas of Strongest Overlap	Discipline-Based Standards Documents Only

• Complex communication II (social/inter-personal aspects)
• Cultural sensitivity, valuing diversity
• Adaptability
• Complex communication I
  ○ Critical reading
	• Constructing and evaluating evidence-based arguments
	• Nonroutine problem solving
	• Complex communication I
	  ○ Disciplinary discourse
	• Systems thinking
	• Critical thinking
	• Motivation, persistence
	• Identity
	• Attitudes
	• Self-development
	• Collaboration/teamwork
	• Self-regulation, executive functioning
		• Disciplinary content, including specific forms of representation
		• Discipline-specific entailments of reasoning/ argument (e.g., mathematical proof; mathematical induction)

FIGURE 5-2 Overlap between CCSS mathematics standards and 21st century skills. SOURCE: Created by the committee.

particular, the *CCSSM*, *PSSM*, and *CESSM* documents all consider critical thinking, problem solving, constructing and evaluating evidence-based arguments, systems thinking, and complex communication to be important learning goals for mathematics, though there is some variation in how these skills are treated and the relative emphasis placed on each.

The two most prominent areas of overlap between 21st century skills and learning goals for school mathematics are found for the themes of argumentation/reasoning and problem solving. Problem solving and reasoning are central to mathematics and have long been viewed as key leverage points in efforts to teach mathematics for understanding (Fawcett, 1938; Schoenfeld, 1985; Silver, 1985, 1994; Charles and Silver, 1988).

As the *PSSM* reasoning and proof standard states

Being able to reason is essential to understanding mathematics. . . . [I]nstructional programs across PK-12 should enable students to . . . recognize reasoning and proof as fundamental aspects of mathematics; make and investigate mathematical conjectures; develop and evaluate mathematical arguments and claims; and select and use various types of reasoning and methods of proof. (National Council of Teachers of Mathematics, 2000, p. 56)

Students are expected to have opportunities to explore mathematical patterns in order to detect regularities, to formulate conjectures and hypotheses based on observed patterns and regularities, and to investigate and test the validity of these conjectures and hypotheses using mathematical reasoning. Students should learn to use varieties of mathematical reasoning and argumentation (e.g., probabilistic, geometric, algebraic, and proportional reasoning) and to generate mathematically valid proof arguments and counterarguments (e.g., develop validity justifications and produce a counterexample) (National Council of Teachers of Mathematics, 2000, pp. 56-59).

This theme of argumentation and reasoning is touched on explicitly in two of the *CCSSM* standards for mathematical practice: "Reason abstractly and quantitatively," and "Construct viable arguments and critique the reasoning of others." In discussing the latter standard, *CCSSM* states

> Mathematically proficient students understand and use stated assumptions, definitions, and previously established results in constructing arguments. They make conjectures and build a logical progression of statements to explore the truth of their conjectures. They are able to analyze situations by breaking them into cases, and can recognize and use counterexamples. They justify their conclusions, communicate them to others, and respond to the arguments of others. . . . Students at all grades can listen to or read the arguments of others, decide whether they make sense, and ask useful questions to clarify or improve the arguments. (Common Core State Standards Initiative, 2010b, p. 6)

The *CCSSM* also deals explicitly with problem solving. Its first standard in the category of mathematic practice is "Make sense of problems and persevere in solving them." In discussing this standard, *CCSSM* states

> Mathematically proficient students start by explaining to themselves the meaning of a problem and looking for entry points to its solution. They analyze givens, constraints, relationships, and goals. They make conjectures about the form and meaning of the solution and plan a solution pathway rather than simply jumping into a solution attempt. They consider analogous problems, and try special cases and simpler forms of the original problem in order to gain insight into its solution. They monitor and evaluate their progress and change course if necessary. . . . They can understand the approaches of others to solving complex problems and identify correspondences between different approaches. (Common Core State Standards Initiative, 2010b, p. 6)

This view that problem-solving processes play a central role in mathematical activity is resonant with the earlier characterization provided in *PSSM*'s problem-solving standard:

> Problem solving means engaging in a task for which the solution method is not known in advance. In order to find a solution, students must draw on their knowledge, and through this process, they will often develop new mathematical understandings. Solving problems is not only a goal of learning mathematics but also a major means of doing so . . . instructional programs across PK-12 should enable students to . . . build new mathematical knowledge through problem solving, solve problems that arise in mathematics and in other contexts, apply and adapt a variety of appropriate strategies to solve problems, and monitor and reflect on the process of mathematical problem solving. (National Council of Teachers of Mathematics, 2000, p. 52)

Students should learn to recognize classes of problems that can be solved using routine procedures and should also learn to use a wide range of problem-solving strategies (e.g., heuristic processes such as drawing a diagram, considering special cases, working backward, solving a simpler problem, and looking for patterns and regularities) that can be useful in solving nonroutine problems.

Intrapersonal and Interpersonal Skills

Unlike skills in the cognitive domain, those in the intrapersonal and interpersonal domains are not particularly prominent in the mathematics curriculum reform documents. Historically the interpersonal and intrapersonal domains have been represented in research conducted on mathematics teaching and learning (McLeod and Adams, 1989; McLeod, 1992; Schoenfeld, 1992), but they have tended to receive less attention as curricular or instructional outcomes. The two prominent areas of overlap between 21st century skills and learning goals for school mathematics in these domains are self-regulation and motivation/persistence.

The theme of self-regulation is evident in the *CCSSM* standard of mathematical practice, "Make sense of problems and persevere in solving them." The expectation is clear that students must learn to monitor and evaluate their progress when solving problems, and to change course if necessary. Within this *CCSSM* standard one also finds explicit attention to persistence, as the earlier quote illustrates. Students are expected to spend time examining a problem, considering pathways, reflecting on progress, and adjusting solution approaches rather than leaping immediately onto a solution path and then abandoning it at the first obstacle.

SCIENCE AND ENGINEERING

The Context: Evolution of National Standards in Science

National initiatives to outline disciplinary content standards for K-12 science education have undergone significant evolution over the past two decades. The American Association for the Advancement of Science's (AAAS's) reports *Science for All Americans* (American Association for the Advancement of Science, 1989) and *Benchmarks for Science Literacy* (American Association for the Advancement of Science, 1993) and the National Research Council's *National Science Education Standards* (National Research Council, 1996) were ambitious efforts to lay out systematic guidelines and standards for science literacy for K-12 education based on reviews of research by national panels of experts. More recently, in July 2011, the National Research Council released the NRC science framework (National Research Council, 2012), and Achieve, Inc., has been commissioned by the Carnegie Corporation to develop a full set of standards based on this framework. These standards are intended to be the science education counterpart of the Common Core State Standards in English language arts and mathematics, and it is expected that they too will be adopted in many states.

The following analysis of the correspondence between disciplinary standards for science education and 21st century skills is based primarily on the NRC science framework as well as on several recent volumes published by the NRC that review and synthesize current research on students' learning and on curricular and pedagogical models in science. These reports include *How Students Learn: History, Mathematics, and Science in the Classroom* (National Research Council, 2005); *America's Lab Report: Investigations in High School Science* (National Research Council, 2006); *Taking Science to School: Learning and Teaching Science in Grades K-8* (National Research Council, 2007); and *Exploring the Intersection of Science Education and 21st Century Skills* (National Research Council, 2010).

Science Content and Process

One of the long-standing issues in science education has been the relative emphasis that should be placed on—and the nature of the relationship between—"content" (facts, formulas, concepts, and theories) and "process" (scientific method, inquiry, discourse). AAAS's Project 2061 aimed to transform science education in the United States by placing a heavy emphasis on inquiry, often interpreted primarily as hands-on investigation, as a corrective to the overemphasis on isolated factual content common in so many science classrooms (American Association for the Advancement of Science, 1989, 1993). The *National Science Education Standards*, too, called for engaging students in inquiry, both to motivate their interest in science and to help them learn about science content and the nature of science (National Research Council, 1996).

As these calls for more inquiry in science classrooms have been acted upon in recent decades, certain trends have emerged that indicate a need to further articulate what is meant by scientific inquiry. One trend was that inquiry in some circles came to be associated primarily with "hands-on" science, often reflecting a commitment by education practitioners to a change in the pedagogy from passive, teacher-led instruction to active, student-driven discovery. "Hands-on" laboratory activities can effectively support science learning if they are designed with clear learning goals in mind; are thoughtfully sequenced into the flow of science instruction; integrate learning of science content with learning about the processes of science; and incorporate time for student reflection and discussion (National Research Council, 2006). However, such approaches are not typical in American high schools. Instead, the calls for more inquiry sometimes resulted in a particular neglect of critical reasoning, analysis of evidence, development of models, and written and oral discourse associated with constructing and evaluating arguments and explanations—all aspects of inquiry that may be downplayed when "hands-on" activities are not carefully designed and scaffolded.

A second trend was the tendency to treat scientific methodology as divorced from content (National Research Council, 2007). Many students, for instance, are introduced to a generic "scientific method," which is presented as a fixed linear sequence of steps, emphasizing experimental investigations, which the students are often asked to apply in a superficial or scripted way. This approach to the scientific method often obscures or distorts the processes of inquiry as they are practiced by scientists. Practices, such as reasoning carefully about the implications of models and theories; framing questions and hypotheses so that they can be productively investigated; systematically analyzing and integrating data to serve as evidence to evaluate claims; and communicating and critiquing ideas in a scientific community are vital parts of inquiry. However, they tend to be missed when students are taught a scripted procedure designed to obtain a particular result in a decontextualized investigation. Furthermore, these higher-level reasoning and problem-solving practices require a reasonable depth of familiarity with the content of a given scientific topic if students are to engage in them in a meaningful way.

Debates over content versus process are not in step with the current views of the nature of science. Philosophers of science and scientists themselves now view science as both a body of established knowledge and an ongoing process of scientific discovery that can lead to revisions in that body of knowledge (National Research Council, 2005). Science is seen as a fundamentally social enterprise that is aimed at advancing knowledge through the development of theories and models that have explanatory and predictive power and that are grounded in evidence. In practice this means that the content and the process are deeply intertwined. Similarly, as highlighted in Chapters 4 and 6, strategies involving higher-order thinking and problem solving tend to be domain specific and are best developed and practiced in a suitably rich content domain (National Research Council, 2005).

Understanding the Structure of Scientific Knowledge

In recent decades, our understanding of what constitutes an appropriate foundation of factual and conceptual knowledge in science has been further developed. Research in cognitive science has emphasized that sophisticated scientific knowledge is characterized by a rich, conceptually organized, well-connected, and fluently integrated set of representations (National Research Council, 2005, 2007). An important hallmark of these integrated webs or networks of knowledge is that the facts, concepts, theories, and procedures that are organized in this way can be meaningfully understood, usefully applied, and productively added to or further developed on an ongoing basis. In this respect there is significant congruence among how scientific knowledge is construed within the discipline, how it is construed within the NRC science framework, and in the committee's definition of deeper learning as learning that can be successfully transferred and applied in new situations (see Chapter 4).

The development of sophisticated scientific knowledge involves simultaneous and mutually reinforcing learning of both content knowledge and process skills. For example, a review of science learning in grades K-8 proposed that students who are proficient in science (National Research Council, 2007, p. 2) have the following capabilities:

1. Know, use, and interpret scientific explanations of the natural world.
2. Generate and evaluate scientific evidence and explanations.
3. Understand the nature and development of scientific knowledge.
4. Participate productively in scientific practices and discourse.

Both of these reviews reflect a view of science as a body of knowledge as well as an ongoing process.

Current Science Instruction

Today's K-12 science classrooms generally reflect neither the calls for more fully developed inquiry experiences in national science standards nor the research evidence on how students learn science. As in mathematics, the curriculum has been criticized as being "a mile wide and an inch deep." The authors of *Taking Science to School* (National Research Council, 2007) offered this summary of K-8 science instruction: "Typical classroom activities convey either a passive and narrow view of science learning or an activity-oriented approach devoid of question-probing and only loosely related to conceptual learning goals" (p. 253). Large science textbooks cover many topics with little depth, providing little guidance on how to place science in the context of meaningful problems. As teachers try to cover the broad curriculum, they give insufficient attention to students' understanding and instead focus on superficial recall-level questions (Weiss et al., 2003; Weiss and Pasley, 2004). The patterns are similar to those observed in mathematics classrooms (Stigler and Hiebert, 1999).

Similarly, at the high school level, laboratory activities that typically take up about one science class period each are disconnected from the flow of science instruction. Instead of focusing on clear learning objectives, laboratory manuals and teachers often emphasize procedures, leaving students uncertain about what they are supposed to learn. Furthermore, these activities are rarely designed to integrate learning of science content and processes. During the rest of the week, students spend time listening to lectures, reading textbooks, and preparing for tests that emphasize many different topics (National Research Council, 2006).

Making matters worse, in the past decade time and resources for science education have often been cut back since science test scores have not counted in the formulations for whether schools are making adequate yearly progress under the NCLB legislation. This lack of emphasis has further limited the development of new capacity for high-level science instruction in K-12 schools and has thus also limited the potential impact of deeper learning goals within the state and national standards currently in use.

A limited number of small-scale studies (e.g., Herrenkohl et al., 1999; Kolodner et al., 2003; Klahr and Nigam, 2004; Krajcik et al., 2008; Cobern et al., 2010), reviews and syntheses (e.g., Linn, Davis, and Bell, 2004; Mayer, 2004; Kirschner, Sweller, and Clark, 2006), and meta-analyses (Minner, Levy, and Century, 2010) of thoughtfully implemented science instruction have shed some light on the current debates about the most appropriate pedagogical practices for science teaching and learning. The current synthesis based on available evidence does not dictate a particular pedagogical approach as uniformly superior. Scaffolding, modeling, guided inquiry, explicit instruction, individual study and practice, computer-mediated learning, and group problem solving and discussion have all been shown to be effective in various circumstances. The choice of instructional strategy often depends on the particular goals of a specific lesson or unit (National Research Council, 2000, 2007). As in other domains of learning, the research base indicates that one rarely gets something for nothing: If we want students to be skillful at reading and interpreting scientific materials, engaging in both written and oral scientific discourse, working fluently with quantitative data, constructing models, and problem solving effectively with peers, then we must give them the particular opportunities, models, and guidance needed to develop each of those sets of skills.

The Framework: Relating Scientific Practices and Concepts

The NRC science framework uses the term "practices" (in the plural) instead of process or skills to capture (1) the essential integration of knowledge and skills in action, and (2) the variety of activities, competencies, and dispositions involved in doing science productively, including habits of reasoning, discourse norms of communities and institutions, attitudes, values, epistemological understanding, and recognition of multiple methodologies (e.g., observation, field work, and modeling, in addition to laboratory experiments). The authors contrast this diversity with the thin procedural treatment of a single uniform "scientific method" that is commonly presented in science classrooms. They also note that modeling, communication, critique, and evaluation require particular attention and experiences to cultivate and that these experiences are often lacking in approaches that emphasize the hands-on aspects of inquiry as well as those that focus too narrowly on manipulating and controlling variables.

An overarching goal expressed in the NRC science framework is to ensure that all students—whether they pursue advanced education and careers in STEM fields or not—"possess sufficient knowledge of science and engineering to engage in public discussions on related issues; are careful consumers of scientific and technological information related to their everyday lives; [and] are able to continue to learn about science outside school" (National Research Council, 2012, p. 1). To these ends, they should have sufficiently deep understanding of core concepts in science, such as matter, energy, forces, earth and solar systems, organisms, and ecosystems, to think productively and to avoid common myths and misconceptions. They should also have sufficient experience with and understanding of a spectrum of scientific methods, including experimental, observational, and modeling approaches, to be able to evaluate and critique the quality and completeness of the available evidence and the relative degrees of certainty or uncertainty associated with it.

The NRC science framework is unequivocal in stating that the practices of science are inextricably tied to both *learning* and *doing* science. Science practices cannot and should not be taught in isolation, and, as new science standards based on the framework are developed, the practices should be infused throughout the standards for content knowledge. Participating in these practices is intended to simultaneously advance students' understanding of scientific methods, of the nature of science, of applications of science, and of particular foundational scientific concepts. In comparing the abilities described in the NRC science framework with 21st century skills, a key point to note is that the area of greatest overlap is found in the science and engineering practices. By considering how the framework connects disciplinary content to practices in this area of overlap, we can gain insight both into the meaning of "deep" in deeper learning and into certain clusters of 21st century skills.

The NRC science framework makes several important assertions about science and engineering education: (1) that disciplinary knowledge and skills (as exemplified in the "practices") are essentially intertwined and must be simultaneously coordinated in science and engineering education; (2) that engaging in the practices of science and engineering advances students' understanding of the nature of scientific knowledge, the variety of methodologies used in science and engineering, and areas of meaningful application; and (3) that participating in science or engineering practices also affects disciplinary learning by engaging students' interest and increasing their motivation.

This argument that engaging in science and engineering practices is necessary and beneficial for learning disciplinary content is noteworthy because such a connection is not made in a strong way within current frameworks of deeper learning and 21st century skills, such as the Hewlett Foundation's description of deeper learning[4] or the Partnership for 21st Century Skills framework.[5] These formulations generally note the importance of learning in core academic disciplines but give no guidance as to how or whether the learning of disciplinary content connects to the development of the other 21st century skills. The framework thus provides a rationale for connecting the "deep" learning of disciplinary content in science and engineering with at least some 21st century skills.

---

[4]See http://www.hewlett.org/programs/education-program/deeper-learning for description [April 2012].

[5]See http://www.p21.org/overview/skills-framework/57 for description [April 2012].

Organization of the NRC Science Framework

The NRC science framework includes engineering as well as science and notes that while the two disciplines have distinctly different goals, they share important features, such as reasoning and problem-solving processes, the testing and evaluation of outcomes and products, and the use of cognitive tools, such as analogical reasoning, systems thinking, and mental and physical models. In what follows the comments about science teaching and learning are generally intended to apply to engineering education as well. Where a distinction between science and engineering education seems important, it is noted.

The science framework is laid out in three dimensions, which are conceptually distinct but integrated in practice in the teaching, learning, and doing of science and engineering. The three dimensions are

- core disciplinary ideas,
- crosscutting concepts, and
- scientific and engineering practices

Core Disciplinary Ideas

One goal of the revision to the *National Science Education Standards* was to reduce the long catalog of factual knowledge students are expected to master in order to place a deeper and more sustained focus on a much smaller set of core ideas that have broad importance across scientific disciplines and that are key for developing more complex ideas. Drawing on recent research on cognition, development, and learning in science,[6] the new framework adopts a "learning progressions" approach to the core disciplinary ideas. In this approach, the learning standards are organized as integrated, continuous progressions of ideas that increase in sophistication over multiple years, from the early elementary grades through high school. The core ideas are grouped according to life sciences, earth and space sciences, physical sciences, and engineering and technology.

Crosscutting Concepts

The NRC science framework identifies seven crosscutting concepts, which are important scientific concepts that bridge across multiple disciplines. They include patterns; cause and effect; scale, proportion, and

---

[6]A comprehensive list of research references is included in an appendix that accompanies the NRC science framework.

quantity; systems and system models; energy and matter; structure and function; and stability and change.

Scientific and Engineering Practices

The NRC science framework conceptualizes practices as occurring in and connecting across three "spaces":

1. **Investigation and empirical inquiry,** in which the dominant practices are observing phenomena, planning experiments and data collection, deciding what and how to measure, and identifying sources of uncertainty. This space involves interaction with the natural or physical world.
2. **Construction of explanations or designs,** a conceptual theory-building space, focused on developing hypotheses, models, and solutions.
3. **Evaluation space,** focused on analysis, argument, and evaluation, in which the dominant practices are the analysis and construction of arguments and the critique of fit of evidence in relation to predictions (science) or of design outcomes to constraints and goals (engineering).

Eight key practices, which collectively span these spaces, are highlighted in the framework. Each is fairly richly described, so they are perhaps best thought of as complex activities rather than discrete skills. The key practices are as follows (National Research Council, 2012, p. 42):

1. Asking questions (for science) and defining problems (for engineering)
2. Developing and using models
3. Planning and carrying out investigations
4. Analyzing and interpreting data
5. Using mathematics, information and computer technology, and computational thinking
6. Constructing explanations (for science) and designing solutions (for engineering)
7. Engaging in argument from evidence
8. Obtaining, evaluating, and communicating information

While the three dimensions of the NRC science framework (i.e., core disciplinary ideas, crosscutting concepts, and science and engineering practices) and the way in which they are conceptually organized do not map in a tidy way to 21st century skills, there is significant overlap. Furthermore, the framework allows (indeed, forces) distinct discipline-based interpretations of what some of these skills mean in the context of science education.

In the *Taking Science to School* report (National Research Council, 2007), an expert committee identified four strands of science proficiency: knowing, using, and interpreting scientific explanations of the natural world; generating and evaluating scientific evidence and explanations; understanding the nature and development of scientific knowledge; and participating productively in scientific practices and discourse. There are significant similarities between these strands for scientific proficiency and the framework's three-dimensional organization, and the framework authors explicitly cite many of the findings summarized in *Taking Science to School* as the basis for similar recommendations. The framework is more detailed and specific than the *Taking Science to School* report in addressing the knowledge and practices students need to develop over the K-12 span.

The framework also makes important connections to other disciplines—most notably English language arts and mathematics. The crosscutting concepts include a special focus on the mathematical concepts of scale, quantity, and proportion, with the observation that scientific systems and processes span remarkable ranges of magnitudes on dimensions of time (e.g., nanoscale to geologic time) and space (e.g., atoms to galaxies). Students need to be fluent with systems of measurement for different types of quantities, with ratio relationships among different quantities, and with the relative magnitudes associated with various scientific concepts and phenomena. They also need to be able to create, interpret, and manipulate a variety of representations for quantitative data.

Similarly, the framework emphasizes the importance of reading, writing, and speaking skills in science and engineering. It notes that scientists and engineers typically spend half of their working time reading, interpreting, and producing text. As noted above, the integration of literacy activities in disciplinary contexts provides students with opportunities to master the particular challenges posed by disciplinary materials. In science, for example, texts often include unfamiliar vocabulary and complex sentence structures and are also often multimodal, incorporating diagrams, tables, graphs, images, and mathematical expressions. Students must also learn discourse norms for discussion and critique in science—discerning, for instance, that a scientific "argument" is not the same thing as an interpersonal disagreement (see Box 5-4). Varying interpretations are adjudicated through reasoning with evidence, and changing one's mind because of convincing evidence presented by a peer does not mean that one "lost the fight."

Relating the NRC Science Framework to Deeper Learning and 21st Century Skills

We asked how, from the point of view of the framework, a proposed 21st century skill might be characterized within science and engineering and what degree of support the framework would provide for incorporating such a skill as part of teaching and learning in the discipline. Our findings are shown in Figure 5-3 and discussed below.

Cognitive Competencies

Drawing on the framework (as well as other sources mentioned above), we found the strongest correspondence—and hence the strongest support—in the cluster of 21st century skills categorized as "cognitive." In particular, critical thinking, nonroutine problem solving, constructing and evaluating evidence-based arguments, systems thinking, and complex communication were all strongly supported in the framework and were construed as being central and indispensible to the disciplines of science and engineering.

However, each of these abilities tends to be embodied in particular ways in the science and engineering standards. For example, "complex communication" entails mastering the discourse norms for framing and communicating scientific questions and hypotheses or engineering problems and design proposals. The framework emphasizes communicating findings and interpretations clearly and participating constructively in peer critiques and reviews as well as the capacity to engage in critical reading (including quantitative comprehension) of discipline-based texts, data archives, and other scientific information sources.

Similarly, "constructing and evaluating evidence-based arguments" is framed in terms of generating, evaluating, and testing scientific hypotheses or engineering designs. In particular, the framework highlights the importance of distinguishing scientific from nonscientific questions; distinguishing evidence from claims; and evaluating the reliability, completeness, and degree of uncertainty associated with evidence and interpretations.

Intrapersonal Competencies

In some respects, the intrapersonal category is the most difficult domain of skills to evaluate. Metacognitive reasoning about one's own thinking and working processes and the capacity to engage in self-directed learning throughout one's lifetime receive explicit support in the framework. However, the degree of support for such factors as motivation and persistence, attitudes, identity and value issues, and self-regulation (if construed as a person being punctual, organized, taking on responsibility, and so forth) is weaker or more indirect. At the same time, though, there is no obvious

---

BOX 5-4
An Example of Deeper Learning in Science

Many of the elements of the vision for science education outlined in *A Framework for K-12 Science Education* are currently uncommon in science instruction
in U.S. classrooms. These include the sustained development of a smaller set of
core disciplinary ideas over longer periods of time, the cultivation of reasoning and
problem-solving skills even in earlier grades, attention to scientific communication
(both written and oral) that explicitly involves developing explanatory theories
and models and using data as evidence to construct and evaluate explanations
and arguments, and development of an understanding of the nature of scientific
knowledge. What might this look like as realized in the classroom?

One particularly rich illustration comes from the work of Herrenkohl et al.
(1999) who conducted a study of an extended unit of science instruction with third
through fifth graders investigating sinking and floating. Over a period of 10 weeks,
students worked in small groups to carry out a series of investigations based
on cognitive research on the conceptual pathway that students follow in coming
to understand when and why various objects will sink or float (Smith, Snir, and
Grosslight, 1992; Smith et al., 1994). Conceptual development in this domain involves understanding and relating concepts of mass, volume, density, and relative
density and is known to be conceptually challenging for many students. Students'
investigations were carefully scaffolded to support reasoning practices in science
and were also interspersed with teacher-guided whole-class discussions in which
students gained experience communicating, monitoring, and critiquing their own
thinking and the thinking of their peers as they developed, tested, and evaluated
theoretical explanations for the phenomena they were observing.

The team of researchers, along with the classroom teachers, incorporated a
number of instructional tools and practices. As students conducted their investigations, they were introduced to explicit strategies in science, including predicting

---

conflict or lack of compatibility between the vision of science education
presented by the framework and these 21st century skills. The NRC science framework is not mute on such topics as valuing diversity, being a
conscientious and self-motivated learner, or appreciating the intellectual
values of science and engineering. Rather, it seems to situate the issues as
something other than disciplinary learning goals for individual students.
Issues of diversity and equity, for instance, are treated as goals that are important for the communal enterprise of science and its relation to societal
needs and values. Personal qualities, such as engagement and persistence,
seem to be viewed as means that can help support successful science learning for more students, rather than as stand-alone end goals or outcomes of
science education.

and theorizing, summarizing results, and relating predictions and theories to the results obtained. Through classroom discussions and repeated opportunities to practice these science strategies, students came to be able to distinguish between predictions and theories, to develop theory-based explanations of their observations, and to use evidence to evaluate their theories, rejecting some and refining others. During whole-class discussion, as small groups reported on their work, students also became experienced at taking on several "audience roles," taking responsibility for checking their peers' predictions and theories; summarizing results; and assessing the relation between the reporters' predictions, theories, and results. Public documents in the classroom, such as a theory chart used to help students track the development of their thinking over time, and a questions chart, which they used to catalog good questions for the audience to ask reporters, were used to scaffold students' awareness of how scientific thinking and knowledge develop and change over time and of the kinds of strategies that lead to progress.

The researchers described their approach as "sociocognitive," and we note that it requires students to develop and practice strategies from the cognitive, interpersonal, and intrapersonal domains. Students learned to apply explicit reasoning and planning strategies for designing, conducting, and interpreting their investigations. They also became better able to monitor their thinking and to recognize when their ideas were or were not well developed or justified. They also became more comfortable with scientific discourse, learning not to become defensive when questioned by peers and learning the norms and expectations for scientific reasoning and discussion. Results from coded videotapes of classroom activities and discussions and from pretests and posttests indicated that students' notions of scientific theorizing and their ability to engage in it evolved significantly, as did their conceptual understanding of the phenomena of floating and sinking.

SOURCE: Created by the committee, based on Herrenkohl et al. (1999).

To some degree, the difficulties encountered in aligning intrapersonal and interpersonal skills with disciplinary standards may be ontological in nature: The science and engineering standards are intended to characterize a set of knowledge and skills that students are expected to master during the K-12 years, while at least some of the deeper learning and 21st century skills are intended to characterize desired qualities of a person as a lifelong learner, as a citizen, and as a member of the workforce (Conley, 2011). In this respect, some of these skills would be expected to be complementary to, rather than overlapping with, disciplinary standards—a view that is compatible with the vision presented in the NRC science framework.

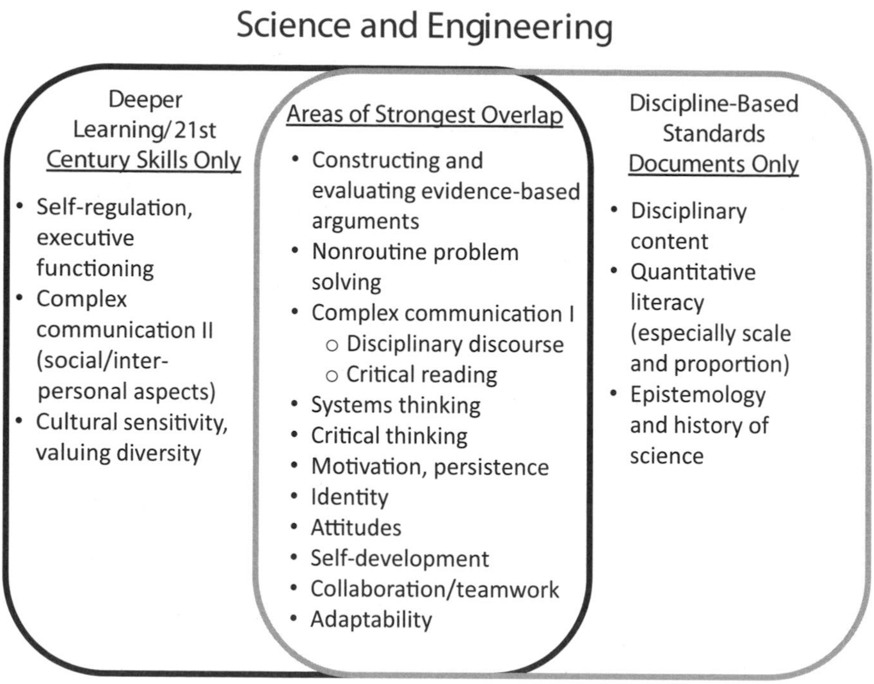

Science and Engineering

FIGURE 5-3 Overlap between science standards framework and 21st century skills.
SOURCE: Created by the committee.

Interpersonal Competencies

Within the domain of interpersonal skills, the framework provides strong support for collaboration and teamwork. A pervasive theme in the framework is the importance of understanding science and engineering as norm-governed enterprises conducted within a community, requiring well-developed skills for collaborating and communicating. In addition, the framework supports adaptability, construed as the ability and inclination to revise one's thinking or strategy in response to evidence or peer review.

There is less attention paid to interpersonal social skills and values, such as cultural sensitivity or valuing diversity. While these are not seen as being in conflict with learning about and practicing science and engineering, they are not strongly supported as explicit learning goals for students in the disciplines. Indeed, these almost seem to be emphasized more as important skills for teachers to use in engaging diverse students in science learning than as disciplinary learning goals for the students themselves.

Findings

Several important observations emerge from our mapping of science and engineering standards with 21st century skills. First, some of these skills correspond with the disciplinary standards, and standards documents value these skills highly as important for learning and practicing science and engineering. However, the standards documents value specific interpretations of these skills from a disciplinary perspective, and there may be other interpretations of these skills that differ substantially from these disciplinary interpretations. For example, there is very strong support in the framework for "complex communication" when viewed as sophisticated discourse within the discipline or as critical reading and quantitative literacy skills; however, there is considerably less support for complex communication skills if they are construed as involving interpersonal sensitivity, cultural awareness, or negotiation and persuasion skills.

Another key observation is that, aside from the possible divergence of interpretations just mentioned, there is little in statements of 21st century skills that would be viewed as directly in competition with or incompatible with standards for teaching and learning science and engineering. Of course, there is always room for conflict over relative emphasis and the competition for ever-scarce classroom time, and there would also likely be some potential for conflict depending on certain choices of pedagogical strategies, which are not strictly dictated by the framework. We note, however, that one theme of a recent National Research Council workshop (National Research Council, 2010) was that those science education initiatives that aligned particularly well with 21st century skills tended to emphasize project-based and problem-solving approaches to curriculum and learning. The emphasis on the eight key practices in the Framework would converge in this direction as well.

CONCLUSIONS AND RECOMMENDATIONS

While we found substantial support for deeper learning and 21st century skills in the various standards documents and supporting research literature, we also found a certain degree of unevenness in their prominence and coverage. A cluster of skills, primarily from the cognitive domain, appeared as central in each of the three disciplines, although the particular interpretations of them varied from discipline to discipline. This set included critical reasoning, the ability to construct and evaluate arguments in relation to evidence, nonroutine problem solving, and complex communication (both written and oral) involving the discourse standards of the various disciplinary communities. However, the definitions of argumentation and standards of evidence differed across the three disciplines.

- Conclusion: Some 21st century competencies are found in standards documents, indicating that disciplinary goals have expanded beyond their traditional focus on basic academic content. A cluster of cognitive competencies—including critical thinking, nonroutine problem solving, and constructing and evaluating evidence-based arguments—is strongly supported in standards documents across all three disciplines.

Intrapersonal skills and characteristics, such as persistence, self-efficacy, self-regulation, and one's identity as a capable learner, were treated more variably across the standards documents, although the research literature on teaching and learning in the disciplines provides some support for their importance. We note that the smaller degree of attention paid to noncognitive dimensions in the standards documents stands in contrast to the evidence discussed in Chapter 3, which indicates that they are important for larger educational and workforce goals, such as staying in school, completing degrees, and attaining higher levels of education. However, we also observe that they may be less likely to be emphasized in disciplinary standards because they may be crosscutting competencies and thus not unique to or distinctively expressed within a given discipline.

- Conclusion: Coverage of other 21st century competencies—particularly those in the intrapersonal and interpersonal domains—is uneven. For example, standards documents across all three disciplines include cognitive and interpersonal competencies related to discourse structures and argumentation, but the disciplines differ in their view of what counts as evidence and what the rules of argumentation are. This uneven coverage could potentially lead to learning environments for different subjects that do not equally support the development of 21st century competencies.

Our review of the research on how the disciplines have characterized "deeper learning" and sought to foster it indicates that instruction for deeper learning is rare in current English language arts, mathematics, and science classrooms.

- Conclusion: Development of higher-order 21st century competencies within the disciplines will require systematic instruction and sustained practice. It will be necessary to devote additional instructional time and resources to advance these sophisticated disciplinary learning goals over what is common in current practice.

The committee's review of research on learning goals in the three disciplines indicates that people in each of the disciplines desire to develop skills and knowledge that will transfer beyond the classroom. However, the goals for transfer are specific to each discipline. For example, the NRC science framework envisions that, by the end of twelfth grade, students will be prepared "to engage in public discussions on science-related issues, to be critical consumers of scientific information related to their everyday lives, and to continue to learn about science throughout their lives" (National Research Council, 2012, pp. 1-2). As we discuss further in Chapter 6, attempts to cultivate general problem-solving skills in the absence of substantive disciplinary or topical knowledge have not typically been effective. We speculate that there may be a mismatch between the expectations of employers in this regard and what is known about learning and transfer. It is an open question as to whether a student who becomes an adept problem solver across a variety of academic disciplines would be better able to transfer problem-solving abilities to new areas than a student who was strong in just one discipline, or whether particular kinds of instructional practices and experiences in the K-12 setting would increase the likelihood of transfer of advanced skills across domains. More research is needed to address these questions.

- **Conclusion: Teaching for transfer within each discipline aims to increase transfer within that discipline. Research to date provides little guidance about how to help learners aggregate transferable knowledge and skills across disciplines. This may be a shortcoming in the research or a reflection of the domain-specific nature of transfer.**

- **Recommendation 2: Foundations and federal agencies should support programs of research designed to illuminate whether, and to what extent, teaching for transfer within an academic discipline can facilitate transfer across disciplines.**

6

Teaching and Assessing for Transfer

The prior chapters have established transfer as the defining characteristic of deeper learning; discussed the importance of cognitive, intrapersonal, and interpersonal skills for adult success; and expanded our description of deeper learning, including both the process of deeper learning and its manifestation in the disciplines of English language arts, mathematics, and science. This chapter takes the argument one step further by reviewing research on teaching for transfer. The first section discusses the importance of specifying clear definitions of the intended learning goals and the need for accompanying valid outcome measures if we are to teach and assess for transfer. Accepting that there are limitations in the research, the next section describes emerging evidence indicating that it is possible to support deeper learning and development of transferable knowledge and skills in all three domains. The third section then summarizes what is known about how to support deeper learning and the development of transferable cognitive competencies, identifying features that may serve as indicators that an intervention is likely to develop these competencies in a substantial and meaningful way. The fourth section then discusses what is known about how to support deeper learning in the intrapersonal and interpersonal domains. The fifth section returns to issues of assessment and discusses the role of assessment in support of deeper learning. The final section offers conclusions and recommendations.

THE NEED FOR CLEAR LEARNING
GOALS AND VALID MEASURES

Educational interventions may reflect different theoretical perspectives on learning and may target different skills or domains of competence. In all cases, however, the design of instruction for transfer should start with a clear delineation of the learning goals and a well-defined model of how learning is expected to develop (National Research Council, 2001). The model—which may be hypothesized or established by research—provides a solid foundation for the coordinated design of instruction and assessment aimed at supporting students' acquisition and transfer of targeted competencies.

Designing measures to evaluate student accomplishment of the particular learning goals can be an important starting point for the development process because outcome measures can provide a concrete representation of the ultimate student learning performances that are expected and of the key junctures along the way, which in turn can enable the close coordination of intended goals, learning environment characteristics, programmatic strategies, and performance outcomes. Such assessments also communicate to educators and learners—as well as designers—what knowledge, skills, and capabilities are valued (Resnick and Resnick, 1992; Herman, 2008).

An evidence-based approach to assessment rests on three pillars that need to be closely synchronized (National Research Council, 2001, p. 44):

- A *model* of how students represent knowledge and develop competence in a domain
- Tasks or situations that allow one to *observe* student performance relative to the model
- An *interpretation* framework for drawing inferences from student performance

Developing that first pillar—a model of the learning outcomes to be assessed—offers a first challenge in the assessment of cognitive, intrapersonal, and interpersonal competencies. Within each of these three broad domains, theorists have defined and conducted research on a wealth of individual constructs. In the previous chapters, we noted that the research literature on cognitive and noncognitive competencies has used a wide variety of definitions, particularly in the intrapersonal and interpersonal domains. In Chapter 2, we suggested certain clusters of competencies within each domain as the targets of assessment and instruction and offered preliminary definitions. Questions remain, however, about the implications of these definitions. For example, the range of contexts and situations across which the learning of these competencies should transfer remains unclear.

A second challenge arises from the existing assessment models and methodologies used to observe and interpret students' responses relative to these constructs. It is widely acknowledged that most current large-scale measures of educational achievement do not do a good job of reflecting deeper learning goals in part because of constraints on testing formats and testing time (Webb, 1999; also see Chapter 7). While a variety of well-developed exemplars exist for constructs in the cognitive domain, those for intrapersonal and interpersonal competencies are less well developed. Below, we briefly discuss examples of measures for each domain of competence. (For a fuller discussion of this topic, see National Research Council, 2011a.)

Measures of Cognitive Competence

Promising examples of measures focused on important cognitive competencies can be found in national and international assessments, in training and licensing tests, and in initiatives currently under way in K-12. One example is the computerized problem-solving component of the Programme for International Student Assessment (PISA), which is scheduled for operational administration in 2012 (National Research Council, 2011b). In this 40-minute test, items are grouped in units around a common problem, which keeps reading and numeracy demands to a minimum. The problems are presented within realistic, everyday contexts, such as refueling a moped, playing on a handball team, mixing elements in a chemistry lab, and taking care of a pet. The difficulty of the items is manipulated by increasing the number of variables or the number of relationships that the test taker has to deal with.

Scoring of the items reflects the PISA 2012 framework, which defines four processes that are components of problem solving: (1) information retrieval, (2) model building, (3) forecasting, and (4) monitoring and reflecting. Points are awarded for information retrieval, based on whether the test taker recognizes the need to collect baseline data and uses the method of manipulating one variable at a time. Scoring for the process of model building reflects whether the test taker generates a correct model of the problem. Scoring of forecasting is based on the extent to which responses to the items indicate that the test taker has set and achieved target goals. Finally, points are awarded for monitoring and reflecting, which includes checking the goal at each stage, detecting unexpected events, and taking remedial action if necessary.

Another promising example of assessment of complex cognitive competencies, created by the National Council of Bar Examiners, consists of three multistate examinations that jurisdictions may use as one step in the process of licensing lawyers.[1] The three examinations are the Multistate Bar Examination (MBE), the Multistate Essay Examination (MEE), and the Multistate Performance Test (MPT). All are paper-and-pencil tests that are designed to measure the knowledge and skills necessary to be licensed in the profession and to ensure that the newly licensed professional knows what he or she needs to know in order to practice. These overarching goals—as well as the goals of the individual components summarized briefly below—reflect an assumption that law students need to have developed transferable knowledge that they will be able to apply when they become lawyers.

The purpose of the MBE is to assess the extent to which an examinee can apply fundamental legal principles and legal reasoning to analyze a given pattern of facts. The questions focus on the understanding of legal principles rather than on memorization of local case or statutory law. The MBE consists of 60 multiple-choice questions and is administered over an entire day.

The purpose of the MEE is to assess the examinee's ability to (1) identify legal issues raised by a hypothetical factual situation; (2) separate material that is relevant from that which is not; (3) present a reasoned analysis of the relevant issues in a clear, concise, and well-organized composition; and (4) demonstrate an understanding of the fundamental legal principles relevant to the probable resolution of the issues raised by the factual situation. This test lasts for 6 hours and consists of nine 30-minute questions.

The goal of the MPT is to assess the fundamental skills of lawyers in realistic situations by asking the candidate to complete a task that a beginning lawyer should be able to accomplish. It requires applicants to sort detailed factual materials; separate relevant from irrelevant facts; analyze statutory, case, and administrative materials for relevant principles of law; apply relevant law to the facts in a manner likely to resolve a client's problem; identify and resolve ethical dilemmas; communicate effectively in writing; and complete a task within time constraints. Examinees are given 90 minutes to complete each task.

These and other promising examples each start with a strong model of the competencies to be assessed; use simulated cases and scenarios to pose problems that require extended analysis, evaluation, and problem solving; and apply sophisticated scoring models to support inferences about student learning. The PISA example, in addition, demonstrates the dynamic and interactive potential of technology to simulate authentic problem-solving situations.

The PISA problem-solving test is one of a growing set of examples that use technology to simultaneously engage students in problem solving and assess their problem-solving skills. Another example is SimScientists, a

---

[1]The following description of the three examinations relies heavily on Case (2001).

simulation-based curriculum unit that includes a sequence of assessments designed to measure student understanding of ecosystems (Quellmalz, Timms, and Buckley, 2010). The SimScientists summative assessment is designed to measure middle school students' understanding of ecosystems and scientific inquiry. Students are presented with the overarching task of describing an Australian grassland ecosystem for an interpretive center and respond by drawing food webs and conducting investigations with the simulation. Finally, they are asked to present their findings about the grasslands ecosystem.

SimScientists also includes elements focusing on transfer of learning, as described in a previous NRC report (National Research Council, 2011b, p. 94):

> To assess transfer of learning, the curriculum unit engages students with a companion simulation focusing on a different ecosystem (a mountain lake). Formative assessment tasks embedded in both simulations identify the types of errors individual students make, and the system follows up with graduated feedback and coaching. The levels of feedback and coaching progress from notifying the student that an error has occurred and asking him or her to try again, to showing the results of investigations that met the specifications.

Students use this targeted, individual feedback to engage with the tasks in ways that improve their performance. As noted in Chapter 4, practice is essential for deeper learning, but knowledge is acquired much more rapidly if learners receive information about the correctness of their results and the nature of their mistakes.

Combining expertise in content, measurement, learning, and technology, these assessment examples employ evidence-centered design and are developing full validity arguments. They reflect the emerging consensus that problem solving must be assessed as well as developed within specific content domains (as discussed in the previous chapter; also see National Research Council, 2011a). In contrast to these examples, many other current technology-based projects designed to impact student learning lack a firm assessment or measurement basis (National Research Council, 2011b).

Project- and problem-based learning and performance assessments that require students to engage with novel, authentic problems and to create complex, extended responses in a variety of media would seem to be prime vehicles for measuring important cognitive competencies that may transfer. What remains to be seen, however, is whether the assessments are valid for their intended use and if the reliability of scoring and the generalizability of results can achieve acceptable levels of rigor, thereby avoiding validity and reliability problems of complex performance assessments developed in the past (e.g., Shavelson, Baxter, and Gao, 1993; Linn et al., 1995).

Measures of Intrapersonal and Interpersonal Competence

As is the case with interpersonal skills, many of the existing instruments for the measurement of intrapersonal skills have been designed for research and theory development purposes and thus have the same limitations for large-scale educational uses as the instruments for measuring interpersonal skills. These instruments include surveys (self-reports and informant reports), situational judgment tests, and behavioral observations. As with the assessment of interpersonal competencies, it is possible that evidence of intrapersonal competencies could be elicited from the process and products of student work on suitably designed complex tasks. For example, project- or problem-based performance assessments theoretically could be designed to include opportunities for students to demonstrate metacognitive strategies or persistence in the face of obstacles. Student products could be systematically observed or scored for evidence of the targeted competencies, and then these scores could be counted in student grades or scores on end-of-year accountability assessment. To date, however, strong design methodologies, interpretive frameworks and approaches to assuring the score reliability, validity, and fairness have not been developed for such project- or problem-based performance assessments.

There are few well-established practical assessments for interpersonal competencies that are suitable for use in schools, with the exception of tests designed to measure those skills related to formal written and oral communication. Some large-scale measures of collaboration were developed as part of performance assessments during the 1990s, but the technical quality of such measures was never firmly established. The development of those assessments revealed an essential tension between the nature of group work and the need to assign valid scores to individual students. Today there are examples of teacher-developed assessments of teamwork and collaboration being used in classrooms, but technical details are sketchy.

Most well-established instruments for measuring interpersonal competencies have been developed for research and theory-building or for employee selection purposes, rather than for use in schools. These instruments tend to be one of four types: surveys (self-reports and informant reports), social network analysis, situational judgment tests, or behavioral observations (Bedwell, Salas, and Fiore, 2011). Potential problems arise when applying any of these methods for large-scale educational assessment, to which stakes are often attached. Stakes are high when significant positive or negative consequences are applied to individuals or organizations based on their test performance, consequences such as high school graduation, grade-to-grade promotion, specific rewards or penalties, or placement into special programs.

Stakes attached to large-scale assessment results heighten the need for the reliability and validity of scores, particularly in terms of being resistant to fakeability. Cost and feasibility also are dominant issues for large-scale assessments. Each of the instrument types has limitations relative to these criteria. Self-report, social network analysis, and situational judgment tests, which can provide relatively efficient, reliable, and cost-effective measures, are all subject to social desirability bias—the tendency to give socially desirable and socially rewarded rather than honest responses to assessment items or tasks. While careful design can help to minimize or correct for social desirability bias, if any of these three types of assessment instruments were used for high-stakes educational testing, social desirability bias would likely be heightened.

Behavioral ratings, in contrast, present challenges in assuring reliability and cost feasibility. For example, if students' interpersonal skills are assessed based on self, peer, or teacher ratings of student presentations of portfolios of their past work (including work as part of a team), a number of factors may limit the reliability and validity of the scores. These include differences in the nature of the interactions reflected in the portfolios for different students or at different times; differences in raters' application of the scoring rubric; and differences in the groups with whom individual students have interacted. This lack of uniformity in the sample of interpersonal skills included in the portfolio poses a threat to both validity and reliability (National Research Council, 2011a). Dealing with these threats to reliability takes additional time and money beyond that required for simply presenting and scoring student presentations.

Collaborative problem-solving tasks currently under development by PISA offer one of the few examples today of a direct, large-scale assessment targeting social and collaboration competencies; other prototypes are under development by the ATC21S project and by the military. The quality and practical feasibility of any of these measures are not yet fully documented. However, like many of the promising cognitive measures, these rely on the abilities of technology to engage students in interaction, to simulate others with whom students can interact, to track students' ongoing responses, and to draw inferences from those responses.

Summary

In summary, there are a variety of constructs and definitions of cognitive, intrapersonal, and interpersonal competencies and a paucity of high-quality measures for assessing them. All of the examples discussed above are measures of maximum performance rather than of typical performance (see Cronbach, 1970). They measure what students *can do* rather than what they *are likely to do* in a given situation or class of situations. While measures of maximum performance are usually the focus in the cognitive domain, typical performance may be the primary focus of measures for some intrapersonal and interpersonal competencies. For example, measures of dispositions and attitudes related to conscientiousness, multicultural sensitivity, and persistence could be designed to assess what students are likely to do (typical performance). In comparison to measures of maximum performance, measures of typical performance require more complex designs and tend to be less stable and reliable (Patry, 2011).

Both the variety of definitions of constructs across the three domains and the lack of high-quality measures pose challenges for teaching, assessment, and learning of 21st century competencies. They also pose challenges to research on interventions designed to impact student learning and performance, as we discuss below.

EMERGING EVIDENCE OF INSTRUCTION THAT PROMOTES DEEPER LEARNING

Despite the challenges posed by a lack of uniform definitions and high-quality measures of the intended performance outcomes, there is emerging evidence that cognitive, intrapersonal, and interpersonal competencies can be developed in ways that promote transfer. The most extensive and strongest evidence comes from studies of interventions targeting cognitive competencies, but there is also evidence of development of intrapersonal and interpersonal competencies. The research includes studies encompassing how people learn in formal, informal, and workplace learning environments, as discussed further below.

Evidence from Interventions in Formal Learning Environments

As illustrated by the examples in the previous chapter, some classroom-based interventions targeting specific cognitive competencies have also, through changes in teaching practices, fostered development of intrapersonal and interpersonal competencies. The students learn through discourse, reflection, and shared experience in a learning community. For example, Boaler and Staples (2008) note the following:

> The discussions at Railside were often abstract mathematical discussions and the students did not learn mathematics through special materials that were sensitive to issues of gender, culture, or class. But through their mathematical work, the Railside students learned to appreciate the different ways that students saw mathematics problems and learned to value the contribution of different methods, perspectives, representations, partial ideas and even incorrect ideas as they worked to solve problems. (p. 640)

Both the mathematics knowledge and skills and the positive dispositions toward mathematics and feelings of self-efficacy in mathematics developed by these students appear to be durable and transferable, as nearly half of the students enrolled later in calculus classes and all indicated plans to continue study of mathematics.

In the domain of English language arts, Guthrie, Wigfield, and their colleagues developed an instructional system designed to improve young students' reading by improving their motivation and self-regulation as well as their use of cognitive and metacognitive strategies (Guthrie et al., 1996, 2004; Guthrie, McRae, and Klauda, 2007; Wigfield et al., 2008; Taboada et al., 2009). Several empirical studies found this intervention to be successful in improving the performance of young readers, reflecting gains in the cognitive knowledge and skills that were the primary targets of the intervention (Guthrie et al., 2004). The young students involved in the intervention showed greater engagement in reading both in school and outside of school (Wigfield et al., 2008). These findings suggest that the students not only developed the intrapersonal competencies of motivation and self-regulation but also transferred these competencies to their reading in the contexts of both school and home.

There is also some evidence that intrapersonal and interpersonal competencies can be effectively taught and learned in the classroom. In the past, interventions often focused on reducing or preventing undesirable behaviors, such as antisocial behavior, drug use, and criminal activities. Increasingly, however, intervention programs are designed instead to build positive capacities, including resilience, interpersonal skills, and intrapersonal skills, in both children and families. In a recent review of the research on these new skill-building approaches—including meta-analyses and numerous randomized trials—a National Research Council committee (2009b) concluded that effectiveness has been demonstrated for interventions that focus on strengthening families, strengthening individuals, and promoting mental health in schools and in healthcare and community programs.

Durlak et al. (2011) recently conducted a meta-analysis of school-based instructional programs designed to foster social and emotional learning. They located 213 studies that targeted students aged 5 to 18 without any identified adjustment or learning problems, that included a control group, and that reported sufficient data to allow calculation of effect sizes. Almost half of the studies employed randomized designs. More than half (56 percent) were implemented in elementary school, 31 percent in middle school, and the remainder in high school. The majority were classroom based, delivered either by teachers (53 percent) or by personnel from outside the school (21 percent). Most of the programs (77 percent) lasted less than a year, 11 percent lasted 1 to 2 years, and 12 percent lasted more than 2 years.

The authors analyzed the effectiveness of these school-based programs in terms of six student outcomes in the cognitive, intrapersonal, and interpersonal domains: social and emotional skills, attitudes toward self and others, positive social behaviors, conduct problems, emotional distress, and academic performance. Measures of these outcomes included student self-reports; reports and ratings from a teacher, parent, or independent rater; and school records (including suspensions, grades, and achievement test scores). Overall, the meta-analysis showed statistically significant, positive effect sizes for each of the six outcomes, with the strongest effects ($d = 0.57$) in social and emotional skills.[2] These positive effects across the different outcomes suggest that students transferred what they learned about positive social and emotional skills in the instructional programs, displaying improved behavior throughout the school day.

Among the smaller group of 33 interventions that included follow-up data (with an average follow-up period of 92 weeks), the effects at the time of follow up remained statistically significant, although the effect sizes were smaller. These findings suggest that the learning of social and emotional skills was at least somewhat durable.

An even smaller subset of the reviewed studies included measures of academic performance. Among these studies the mean effect size was 0.27, reinforcing the interconnectedness of learning across the cognitive, intrapersonal, and interpersonal domains.

One promising example showing that interventions can develop transferable intrapersonal competencies is Tools of the Mind, a curriculum used in preschool and early primary school to develop self-regulation, improve working memory, and increase adaptability (Diamond et al., 2007). It includes activities such as telling oneself aloud what one should do, dramatic play, and aids to facilitate memory and attention (such as an activity in which a preschooler is asked to hold a picture of an ear as a reminder to listen when another preschooler is speaking). A randomized controlled trial in 18 classrooms in a low-income urban school district indicated that the curriculum was effective in improving self-regulation, classroom behavior, and attention. The documented improvement in classroom behavior suggests that the young children transferred the self-regulation competencies they learned through the activities to their daily routines. The intervention also improved working memory and cognitive flexibility, further illustrating

---

[2]In research on educational interventions, the standardized effect size, symbolized by d, is calculated as the difference in means between treatment and control groups, divided by the pooled standard deviation of the two groups. Following rules of thumb suggested by Cohen (1988), an effect size of approximately 0.20 is considered "small," approximately 0.50 is considered "medium," and approximately 0.80 is considered "large." Thus, the effect size of 0.57 on social and emotional skills is considered "large" or "strong."

the links across the cognitive, intrapersonal, and interpersonal domains (Barnett et al., 2008).

Because of the closely intertwined nature of cognitive, intrapersonal, and interpersonal competencies an intervention targeting learning and skill development in one domain can influence other domains, as illustrated by a study included in the Durlak et al. (2011) meta-analysis. Flay et al. (2006) conducted a randomized controlled trial of the Positive Action Program—a drug education and conflict resolution curriculum with parent and community outreach—in 20 elementary schools in Hawaii. Although the intervention was focused on social and emotional competencies, it had large, statistically significant effects on mathematics (an effect size of 0.34) and reading achievement (0.74).

Evidence from Interventions in Informal Learning Environments

Studies of informal learning environments provide more limited evidence that cognitive, intrapersonal, and interpersonal competencies can be taught in ways that promote deeper learning and transfer. Informal learning takes place in a variety of settings, including after-school clubs, museums, science centers, and homes, and it includes a variety of experiences, from completely unstructured to highly structured workshops and educational programs. Informal learning activities may target a range of different learning goals, including goals determined by the interests of individual learners (National Research Council, 2011b). These characteristics of informal learning pose challenges both to clearly identifying the goals of a particular informal learning activity and to a careful assessment of learners' progress toward those goals—essential components of any rigorous evaluation (National Research Council, 2009a). Despite these challenges, research and evaluation studies have shown, for example, that visitors to museums and science centers can develop a deeper understanding of a targeted scientific concept through the direct sensory or immersive experience provided by the exhibits (National Research Council, 2009a).

Somewhat stronger evidence that informal learning environments can develop important competencies emerges from evaluations of structured after-school programs with clearly defined learning goals. Durlak, Weissberg, and Pachan (2010) conducted a meta-analysis of after-school programs designed to promote social and emotional learning among children and youth. They located 68 studies of social and emotional learning programs that included both a control group and measures of postintervention competencies, and they analyzed data on three categories of outcomes:

1. feelings and attitudes (child self-perception and school bonding);
2. indicators of behavioral adjustment (positive social behaviors, problem behaviors, and drug use); and
3. school performance (achievement test scores, school grades, and school attendance).

Overall, the programs had a positive and statistically significant impact on participants' competencies, with the largest mean effects in self-confidence and self-esteem, increases in positive social behaviors and decreases in problem behaviors, and increases in achievement test scores. The only outcomes for which effects were not statistically significant were school attendance and drug use.

In structured after-school settings, as in the in-school environment, a few examples illustrate the potential of technology- and game-based approaches to develop transferable knowledge and skills. For example, an evaluation of the Fifth Dimension—an informal after-school computer club that incorporates games—showed positive effects on students' computer literacy, comprehension, problem solving, and strategic efficiency (Mayer et al., 1999). However, the use of technology must be carefully structured to support transferable learning, as we discuss further below.

Parenting Interventions

Because informal learning and skill development begins at birth, and because parents strongly influence this process, some interventions target parents' cognitive, intrapersonal, and interpersonal competencies as a route to helping children develop these competencies. Parenting interventions are a route to boosting the competencies and improving the behavior of struggling children (Magnuson and Duncan, 2004). When considering interventions to develop parenting competencies:

> It is useful to distinguish between parenting education and parenting management training. Parenting education programs seek to boost parents' general knowledge about parenting and child development. Information is provided in conjunction with instrumental and emotional support. Home visitation programs for new mothers and parent-teacher programs are perhaps the most familiar examples. Management training programs are designed for parents of children with diagnosed problem behavior, usually conduct disorders. Clinical therapists teach parents concrete behavioral strategies designed to improve their children's behavior. Typically, parents are taught how to reinforce their child's positive behavior and punish negative behavior appropriately. Evaluation evidence on parenting management programs is much more positive than the evidence on parent education programs. (Magnuson and Duncan, 2004, p. 206)

There is a substantial experimental literature on the efficacy of home visitation programs. The most successful (and expensive) of these programs is the nurse/family partnership model developed by David Olds (Olds, Sadler, and Kitzman, 2007). Meta-analyses of its evaluations show some positive effects on certain parent and child outcomes, such as reductions in child maltreatment and visits to emergency rooms, but it is less clear whether such programs affect school readiness skills (Sweet and Appelbaum, 2004). The long-term impacts on school readiness are inconsistent, but the evidence suggests that there could be very modest effects on children's social adjustment and cognitive competencies.

Evidence from Workplace Learning Environments

Another area yielding emerging evidence that interventions can develop transferable competencies is the body of literature in industrial and organizational psychology that focuses on the transfer of learning from organizational training programs to the workplace. This research has been summarized in a number of recent reviews and meta-analyses (e.g., Ford and Weissbein, 1997; Burke and Hutchins, 2008; Cheng and Hampson, 2008; Baldwin, Ford, and Blume, 2009; Blume et al., 2010; Grossman and Salas, 2011).

U.S. employers invest heavily in employee training, spending an estimated $46 billion to $54 billion per year when employee salaries during training time are included (Mikelson and Nightingale, 2004).[3] This investment reflects a belief that training will transfer to improvements in job performance. Although Georgenson (1982) is often cited as estimating that only 10 percent of training experiences transfer from the training classroom to the work site, he did not, in fact, make such an estimate (Fitzpatrick, 2001). In recent years, a number of researchers have sought to measure the actual extent of transfer from training to on-the-job performance, to characterize what is transferred, and to identify the conditions promoting transfer. To measure the extent of transfer, researchers often turn to the Kirkpatrick model for evaluating the effectiveness of training (Kirkpatrick and Kirkpatrick, 2006). This model includes four levels of effectiveness: (1) trainees' immediate reactions after a training session, (2) learning, (3) changes in on-the-job behavior, and (4) results (return on training investment).

---

[3]It is difficult to estimate total employer training investments, partly because most employers do not carefully account for training costs (Mikelson and Nightingale, 2004). In addition, there have been no systematic national surveys since those conducted by the U.S. Census Bureau in 1994 and 1997. More recent surveys, such as those conducted by the American Society for Training and Development (2009), include the most training-intensive firms, causing an upward bias in the results.

In a meta-analysis of the effects of organizational training, Arthur et al. (2003) proposed that transfer takes place if the training is found to be effective at any or all of the levels from (2) through (4) of the framework, such that:

(a) learning is demonstrated through pretraining and posttraining tests of trainees' knowledge and skills (which may include cognitive, intrapersonal, and interpersonal competencies);
(b) improvements in on-the-job behavior are demonstrated through changes in pre- and post-training performance measures; or
(c) results are demonstrated through calculations of organizational return on investment.

The authors found that the training had significant, positive effects for each of these three levels of the evaluation framework: d = .63, .62, and .62 for learning, behavior, and results, respectively. They concluded that training does indeed transfer.

Attention has shifted recently from whether training transfers to which conditions specifically enhance the transfer of training. A convenient framework for characterizing those conditions is Baldwin and Ford's model of transfer (Baldwin and Ford, 1988; Ford and Weissbein, 1997; Baldwin, Ford, and Blume, 2009). The model proposes that three categories of factors influence transfer: trainee characteristics, training design, and work environment. Baldwin and Ford (1988) proposed that the key trainee characteristics promoting transfer are cognitive ability, personality, and motivation, while the key training design features include following the principles of learning, correctly sequencing the training, and providing appropriate training content. The key work environment features that promote transfer include supervisor and peer support for the training and opportunities to use the training on the job (see Figure 6-1).

A meta-analysis of 89 studies conducted by Blume et al. (2010) examined these various factors and found positive relationships between transfer and several of them, including the trainee characteristics of cognitive ability and motivation (as well as conscientiousness) and support within the work environment. The authors also examined moderators of these relationships and found that the above factors predicted transfer more strongly when the training content focused on "open" skills, such as leadership development, rather than on "closed" skills, such as how to use a particular type of computer software. Transfer was also promoted to the extent that the training environment and the transfer environment (the job) were similar. This latter finding reflects the research from learning sciences discussed in Chapter 4, which found that transfer is enhanced when the original learning

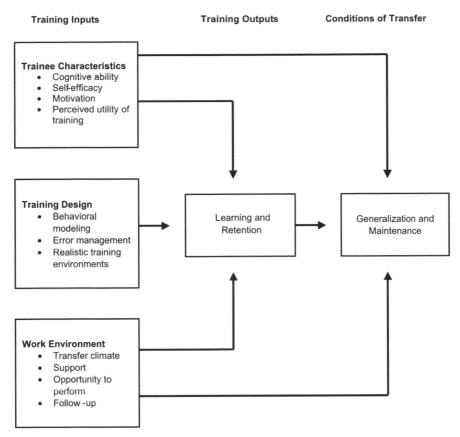

FIGURE 6-1 A model of the transfer process.
SOURCE: Grossman and Salas (2011). Reprinted with permission from John Wiley and Sons.

situation and the new learning situation have similar underlying principles (e.g., Singley and Anderson, 1989).

Because the Blume et al. (2010) meta-analysis included studies that varied in terms of the content of the training being evaluated, the research design, and the evaluation methods, it is informative to supplement that report's findings with information obtained using other methodologies. Burke and Hutchins (2008) surveyed training professionals about best practices and identified several factors thought to contribute to effective transfer. The most important were supervisory support, coaching, opportunities to perform what was learned in training, interactive training, measurement of transfer, and job-relevant training. These survey findings are consistent with the empirical studies of the predictors of transfer.

Grossman and Salas (2011) conducted a comprehensive review of the meta-analyses and other research reviews with the purpose of extracting

> the strongest, most consistent findings from the literature in order to help organizations, and even researchers, identify the "bottom line" . . . [and to] serve as a valuable complement to Burke and Hutchins's (2008) practice-based paper. (p. 117)

Within the category of trainee characteristics, Grossman and Salas confirmed the importance of cognitive ability, self-efficacy, and motivation for facilitating transfer of training to the job. They suggested that goal-setting was well established as a means to increase motivation and that transfer was facilitated when learners understood the relevance of the training to the job. These findings reinforce the findings from cognitive research and the studies of educational interventions showing that intrapersonal competencies, including motivation, enhance learning and transfer.

Grossman and Salas also discussed training design and concluded that the elements that most strongly facilitate transfer include behavior modeling, error management (an increasingly popular training strategy of allowing trainees to make errors and providing error management instructions), and realistic training environments (e.g., on-the-job training and the use of low- and high-fidelity simulations).

Concerning the work environment, the authors found that the transfer climate was the most important factor influencing transfer (Grossman and Salas, 2011). This finding is supported by the meta-analyses from Colquitt, LePine, and Noe (2000) and Blume et al. (2010). Specifically, Grossman and Salas found that transfer is facilitated when the trainee's workplace prompts the use of the new competencies learned in training and when trainees are given goals, incentives, feedback, and the opportunity to practice the competencies. Two other features of the work environment shown to play an important role in facilitating transfer were supervisor support (which included such things as recognition, encouragement, rewards, and modeling) and peer support. These findings were similar to those of Blume et al. (2010). Still other features of the work environment that were found to play a role in facilitating transfer were the opportunity to perform the learned competencies with minimal delay, posttraining follow-up, and feedback. Figure 6-1 presents a summary of the factors affecting transfer that was originally developed by Baldwin and Ford (1988) and later modified by Grossman and Salas to reflect their findings.

Research on Team Training. Evidence that cognitive, intrapersonal, and interpersonal skills can be taught and learned also emerges from research on team training in organizations, although this research does not focus specifically on questions of transfer. In a recent meta-analysis of the research on team training, Salas et al. (2008) analyzed data from 45 studies of team training, focusing on four types of outcomes that cut across the three domains: (1) cognitive outcomes, such as declarative and procedural knowledge of work tasks; (2) affective outcomes, such as feelings of trust and confidence in team members' ability; (3) team processes, such as communication, coordination, strategy development, self-correction, and assertiveness; and (4) team performance, such as quantity, quality, accuracy, and efficiency. This variety of outcome measures reflects the variety of goals of team training interventions, which often target multiple cognitive, intrapersonal, and interpersonal competencies. These goals are based on the assumption that team training transfers within and across domains so that knowledge of work tasks, for example, is applied in ways that improve task (and team) performance. Salas and his colleagues found statistically significant, positive correlations between the training interventions and each of the four outcomes, with the highest correlation being for team processes (i.e., training targeting development of intrapersonal and interpersonal competencies).

INSTRUCTIONAL DESIGN PRINCIPLES FOR TRANSFER—COGNITIVE DOMAIN

While the evidence discussed above and in Chapters 4 and 5 indicates that various cognitive competencies are teachable and learnable in ways that promote transfer, we noted in Chapter 5 that such instruction remains rare in U.S. classrooms; few effective strategies and programs to foster deeper learning exist. Research and theory suggest a set of principles that can guide the development of such strategies and programs, as discussed below. It is important to note that the principles are derived from research that has focused primarily on transfer of knowledge and skills within a single topic area or domain of knowledge (see Box 6-1).

How can instructors teach in ways that promote transfer? Addressing this seemingly simple question has been a central task of researchers in learning and instruction for more than a century, and within the past several decades, a number of useful advances have been made toward providing evidence-based answers (Mayer, 2008; Mayer and Alexander, 2011). Evidence-based guidelines for promoting deeper learning (i.e., learning of transferable knowledge) have been offered by a recent task force report from the Association for Psychological Science (Graesser, Hakel, and Halpern, 2007), a guidebook published by the Institute of Education

BOX 6-1
Deeper Learning Across Topics or Disciplines

Most of the research to date on deeper learning has focused on learning within a single discipline, often investigating how children learn a specific topic, procedure, or strategy. This focus reflects the limited success of earlier efforts to develop generic knowledge or skills that could be widely transferred or applied across disciplines, topics, or knowledge domains. In science, for example, early research sought to clarify children's understanding of scientific experimentation by presenting them with "knowledge-lean" tasks about causes and effects that required no prior knowledge of relevant science concepts. However, such methods were criticized, and further research clearly demonstrated that children's prior knowledge plays an important role in their ability to formulate a scientific question about a topic and design an experiment to test the question (National Research Council, 2007). Current research presents children with "knowledge-rich" tasks, recognizing that their causal reasoning is closely related to their prior knowledge of the question or concept to be investigated.

Only a few studies have examined transfer across disciplines, topics, or contexts. For example, Bassok and Holyoak (1989) studied transfer of learning in algebra and physics, focusing on problems with identical underlying structures but different surface features—arithmetic-progression problems in algebra and constant-acceleration problems in physics. High school and college students were first trained to solve such problems, either in algebra or physics, and then were presented with word problems that used either content from the domain in which they were trained or content based on an unfamiliar domain. The algebra students, whose training included the information that the problems were broadly applicable, were very likely to spontaneously recognize that physics problems involving velocity and distance could be addressed using the same equations. These students recognized the applicability to physics, regardless of whether they had learned arithmetic-progression problems using word problems focusing on several different types of content (e.g., growth of savings accounts, height of a human pyramid) or had learned using word problems focusing on a single type of content—i.e., money problems. In contrast, students who had learned to solve constant-acceleration problems in physics almost never recognized or transferred this approach to solve the algebra problems. The authors note that the algebra-focused students were able to "screen out" the domain-specific content of the word problems, while the physics-focused students had been taught that the physical concepts involved in word problems were critical to the applicability of the equations. Bassok and Holyoak concluded that although expertise is generally based on content-specific knowledge, it may be possible to teach some mathematical procedures in a way that enables students to transfer these procedures across content domains; they called for further research to explore such possibilities.

Studies such as these provide some clues about how to support transfer of learning across specific knowledge domains, but much further research is needed to clarify whether, and to what extent, it may be possible to teach students in ways that promote deeper learning and transfer across disciplines or broad content domains.

SOURCE: Created by the committee.

Sciences (Pashler et al., 2007), and a review of problem-solving transfer in the *Handbook of Educational Psychology* (Mayer and Wittrock, 2006).

Before describing various research-based principles for instructional design, it is worth noting that recent research on teaching and learning reveals that young children are capable of surprisingly sophisticated thinking and reasoning in science, mathematics, and other domains (National Research Council and Institute of Medicine, 2009; National Research Council, 2012). With carefully designed guidance and instruction, they can begin the process of deeper learning and development of transferable knowledge as early as preschool. As noted in Chapters 4 and 5, this process takes time and extensive practice over many years, suggesting that instruction for transfer should be introduced in the earliest grades and should be sustained throughout the K-12 years as well as in postsecondary education. Thus, the principles discussed below should be seen as broadly applicable to the design of instruction across a wide array of subject matter areas and across grade levels spanning K-16 and beyond.

Research-Based Methods for Developing Transferable Knowledge

Using Multiple and Varied Representations of Concepts and Tasks

Mayer (2009, 2011b) has shown, based on 11 experimental comparisons, that adding diagrams to a text (or adding animation to a narration) that describes how a mechanical or biological system works can increase student performance on a subsequent problem-solving transfer test by an average of more than one standard deviation. Allowing students to use concrete manipulatives to represent arithmetic procedures has been shown to increase transfer test performance both in classic studies in which bundles of sticks are used to represent two-column subtraction (Brownell and Moser, 1949) and in an interactive, computer-based lesson in which students move a bunny along a number line to represent addition and subtraction of signed numbers (Moreno and Mayer, 1999).

Research suggests that the use of multiple and varied representations is also effective in informal learning environments. For example, a recent National Research Council (2009a) study found that visitors to museums and science centers commonly report developing a deeper understanding of a concept through the concrete, sensory, or immersive experiences provided by the exhibits. One investigation reported in this study found that children who interacted purposefully with exhibits about magnetism gained conceptual understanding of the concept of magnetism (Rennie and McClafferty, 2002).

While adding diagrams or animations to text can enhance learning and transfer, researchers have found that how multimedia learning environments are designed strongly influences their effectiveness. Based on dozens of experiments leading to his theory of multimedia learning, Mayer (2009) has identified 12 principles of multimedia design that can enhance transfer (see Box 6-2).

Encouraging Elaboration, Questioning, and Self-Explanation

Chi and colleagues have shown that, in both book-based and computer-based learning environments, students learn more deeply from reading a science text if they are prompted to explain the material to themselves aloud as they read (Roy and Chi, 2005; Fonseca and Chi, 2011). Research has investigated how different types of questioning techniques promote deeper learning (Graesser and Person, 1984; Graesser, D'Mello, and Cade, 2011), indicating that some successful tutoring techniques include asking why, how, what if, what if not, and so what. As noted in the previous chapter, carefully designed questions posed by teachers and fellow students, such as asking students to justify their answers, have been shown to support deeper learning in mathematics (Griffin, 2005; Boaler and Staples, 2008) and science (Herrenkohl et al., 1999). Asking the learner to summarize the material in a text can also lead to deeper learning (Pressley and Woloshyn, 1995; Mayer and Wittrock, 1996). Finally, research on the testing effect shows that students learn better when they test themselves (without feedback) on material that they have just read than when they study it again; this is true both with paper-based materials (Roediger and Karpicke, 2006) and with online multimedia lessons (Johnson and Mayer, 2009).

There is evidence that this method also supports learning for transfer in designed informal science learning centers (e.g., zoos, museums, and aquariums). Exhibits can be designed to encourage learners to pose questions to themselves and others, helping them think abstractly about scientific phenomena (National Research Council, 2009a). When parents provide explanations of science exhibits to their children, they may help them link the new information to their previous knowledge. How exhibits are designed appears to influence the number and kinds of questions visitors ask.

Engaging Learners in Challenging Tasks, with Supportive Guidance and Feedback

For more than 40 years, research has repeatedly shown that asking students to solve challenging problems in science and other disciplines without appropriate guidance and support (i.e., pure discovery) is ineffective in promoting deep learning (Shulman and Keislar, 1966; Mayer, 2004; de Jong, 2005; Kirchner, Sweller, and Clark, 2006). In contrast, asking students to solve challenging problems while providing appropriate and specific cognitive guidance along the way (i.e., guided discovery) can be a useful

BOX 6-2
Principles of Multimedia Design for Deeper Learning

Principles for Reducing Extraneous Processing (thinking unrelated to the learning goal)

- *Coherence principle:* Exclude extraneous words, pictures, and sounds.
- *Signaling principle:* Add cues to highlight the organization of essential material.
- *Redundancy principle:* Graphics with narration are more effective than graphics with narration and on-screen text.
- *Spatial contiguity principle:* Place corresponding words and pictures close together on the page or screen.
- *Temporal contiguity principle:* Present corresponding words and pictures simultaneously rather than successively.

Principles for Managing Essential Processing (thinking related to the learning goal)

- *Segmenting principle:* Present lesson in user-paced segments.
- *Pretraining principle:* Present names and characteristics of key concepts in advance of the main lesson.
- *Modality principle:* Use graphics and narration, rather than animation and on-screen text.

Principles for Managing Generative Processing (thinking that enables deeper learning)

- *Multimedia principle:* Use words and pictures, rather than words alone.
- *Personalization principle:* Use words in a conversational style.
- *Voice principle:* Narration should be spoken with a friendly human voice rather than a voice produced by a machine.
- *Image principle:* Adding a speaker's image does not necessarily enhance learning.

Boundary Conditions

The series of experiments also indicated that the effectiveness of these design principles for supporting deeper learning are limited by two boundary conditions. First, some design effects are stronger for low-experience learners than for high-experience learners, which Mayer (2009) refers to as the individual-differences condition. Second, the effects of applying the principles are stronger for multimedia lessons with highly complex content than for those with less complex content and are also stronger for fast-paced presentations than for slow-paced presentations.

SOURCE: Adapted from Mayer (2009).

technique for promoting deep learning (de Jong, 2005; Tobias and Duffy, 2009). For example, there is no compelling evidence that beginners deeply learn science concepts or processes by freely exploring a science simulation or game (National Research Council, 2011b), but including guidance in the form of advice, feedback, prompts, and scaffolding (i.e., completing part of the task for the learner) can promote deeper learning in beginners (de Jong, 2005; Azevedo and Aleven, 2010).

Providing guided exploration and metacognitive support also enhances learning for transfer in informal settings. Based on its review of the research on informal science learning, a National Research Council committee (2009a) recommended that science exhibits and programs be designed with specific learning goals in mind and that they provide support to sustain learners' engagement and learning. For example, exhibits and programs should "prompt and support participants to interpret their learning experiences in light of relevant prior knowledge, experiences, and interests" (p. 307). There is emerging evidence that designing simulations to enable guided exploration, with support, enhances deeper learning of science (National Research Council, 2011b).

Teaching with Examples and Cases

A worked-out example is a step-by-step modeling and explanation of how to carry out a procedure, such as how to solve probability problems (Renkl, 2005, 2011). Under appropriate conditions, students gain deep understanding when they receive worked-out examples as they begin to learn a new procedural skill, both in paper-based and computer-based venues (Sweller and Cooper, 1985; Renkl, 2005, 2011). In particular, deep learning is facilitated when the problem is broken into conceptually meaningful steps which are clearly explained and when the explanations are gradually taken away with increasing practice (Renkl, 2005, 2011).

Priming Student Motivation

Deep learning occurs when students are motivated to exert the effort to learn, so another way to promote deep learning is to prime student motivation (Schunk, Pintrich, and Meece, 2008; Summers, 2008; Wentzel and Wigfield, 2009). Research on academic motivation shows that students learn more deeply when they attribute their performance to effort rather than to ability (Graham and Williams, 2009), when they have the goal of mastering the material rather than the goal of performing well or not performing poorly (Anderman and Wolters, 2006; Maehr and Zusho, 2009), when they expect to succeed on a learning task and value the learning task (Wigfield, Tonks, and Klauda, 2009), when they have the belief that they are capable of achieving the task at hand (Schunk and Zimmerman, 2006; Schunk and Pajares, 2009), when they believe that intelligence is changeable rather than fixed (Dweck and Master, 2009), and when they are interested in the learning task (Schiefele, 2009). There is promising evidence that these kinds of beliefs, expectancies, goals, and interests can be fostered in learners by, for example, peer modeling techniques (Schunk, Pintrich, and Meece, 2008) and through the interventions described in Chapter 4 (Yaeger and Walton, 2011). Elementary school students showed increased self-efficacy for solving subtraction problems and increased test performance after watching a peer demonstrate how to solve subtraction problems while exhibiting high self-efficacy (such as saying, "I can do that one" or "I like doing these") versus control conditions (Schunk and Hanson, 1985). As discussed in Chapter 4, research has shown that, in a responsive social setting, learners can adopt the criteria for competence they see in others and then use this information to judge and perfect the adequacy of their own performance (National Research Council, 2001).

Although informal learning environments are often designed to tap into learners' own, intrinsic motivations for learning, they can also prime and extend this motivation. For example, to prime motivation and support deeper learning in structured informal science learning environments (e.g., zoos, aquariums, museums, and science centers), research suggests that science programs and exhibits should

- be interactive;
- provide multiple ways for learners to engage with concepts, practices, and phenomena within a particular setting; and
- prompt and support participants to interpret their learning experiences in light of relevant prior knowledge, experiences, and interests (National Research Council, 2009a, p. 307).

Similarly, research suggests that to prime learners' motivation for the difficult task of learning science through inquiry, simulations and games should provide explanatory guidance, feedback, and scaffolding; incorporate an element of narrative or fantasy; and allow a degree of user control without allowing pure, open-ended discovery (National Research Council, 2011b).

Using Formative Assessment

The formative assessment concept (discussed further below) emphasizes the dynamic process of *using* assessment evidence to continually improve student learning; this is in contrast to the concept of summative assessment, which focuses on development and implementation of an instrument to measure what a student has learned up to a particular point in time (National Research Council, 2001; Shepard, 2005; Heritage, 2010). Deeper learning is enhanced when formative assessment is used to: (1) make learning goals clear to students; (2) continuously monitor, provide feedback, and respond to students' learning progress; and (3) involve students in self- and peer assessment. These uses of formative assessment are grounded in research showing that practice is essential for deeper learning and skill development but that practice without feedback yields little learning (Thorndike, 1927; see also Chapter 4).

Research on each of the six major instructional approaches to teaching for transfer discussed above helps to pinpoint the boundary conditions for each instructional method, including for whom, for which learning contexts, and for which instructional objectives.

Promoting Deeper Learning Through Problem-Based Learning: An Example

One curriculum model that incorporates several of the methods described above is problem-based learning (PBL). PBL approaches represent learning tasks in the form of rich extended problems that, if carefully designed and implemented, can engage learners in challenging tasks (problems) while providing guidance and feedback. They can encourage elaboration, questioning, and self-explanation and can prime motivation by presenting problems that are relevant and interesting to the learners. While a variety of different approaches to PBL have been developed, such instruction often follows six key principles (Barrows, 1996):

1. Student-centered learning
2. Small groups
3. Tutor as a facilitator or guide
4. Problems first
5. The problem is the tool to achieve knowledge and problem-solving skills
6. Self-directed learning

Two recent meta-analyses of the research on interventions following these principles suggest that PBL approaches can support deeper learning and transfer. Gijbels et al. (2005) focused on empirical studies that compared PBL with lecture-based instruction in higher education in Europe (with most of the studies coming from medical education). The meta-analysis identified no significant difference in the understanding of concepts between students engaged in PBL and those receiving lecture-based instruction. However, students in the PBL environments demonstrated deeper understanding of the underlying principles that linked the concepts together. In addition, students in the PBL environments demonstrated a slightly better ability to apply their knowledge than students in the lecture-based classes. As noted in the previous chapter, two hallmarks of deeper learning are that it develops understanding of underlying principles and that it supports the application of knowledge—i.e., transfer.

More recently, Strobel and van Barneveld (2009) conducted a meta-synthesis of eight previous meta-analyses and research reviews that had compared PBL approaches with traditional lecture-based instruction. They found that how learning goals were defined and assessed in the various individual studies affected the findings about the comparative effectiveness of the two different approaches. When the learning goal was knowledge, and assessments were focused on short-term retention, traditional approaches were more effective than PBL, but when knowledge assessments focused on longer-term retention (12 weeks to 2 years following the initial instruction), PBL approaches were more effective. Furthermore, when learning goals were related to transfer or application of knowledge, PBL approaches were more effective. Two particular learning goals were identified by the authors as showing such advantages: performance, as measured by supervisor ratings of medical students' clinical practice, and mixed knowledge and skill (including application of knowledge). Although PBL appears promising, more extensive and rigorous research is needed to determine its effectiveness in supporting deeper learning.

Design Principles for Teaching Problem-Solving and Metacognitive Strategies

Problem solving and metacognition are important competencies that are often included in lists of 21st century skills. Problem-solving and metacognitive strategies differ in several respects. Problem solving typically involves applying sets of procedures organized as strategies that allow persons to tackle a range of new tasks and situations within some performance domain such as how to simplify an algebraic equation or summarize a text, and they represent one of the five types of transferable knowledge discussed in Chapter 4 (see Table 4-3). Metacognition refers to a person's ability to select, monitor, manage, and evaluate cognitive processing during the learning or performance of a cognitive task. Metacognitive strategies are higher-level methods for managing one's thinking and reasoning while learning or performing a task. Metacognitive strategies may play a central role in people's ability to transfer—that is, in people's ability to solve new problems and learn new things. The ability to apply metacognitive strategies when learning is a key dimension of self-regulated learning, as discussed in Chapter 4. Recent research advances have specified metacognitive strategies, determined their role in solving problems in mathematics (e.g., Griffin, 2005) and other disciplines, and illuminated how to teach them. These advances reflect the central role of metacognition in the development of transferable 21st century competencies.

There are five main issues to consider in developing transferable strategies for effective problem solving and metacognition: determining what to teach, how to teach, where to teach, when to teach, and how long to teach (Mayer, 2008).

What to Teach

In determining what to teach, the first question one must answer is whether competency in problem solving or metacognition is based on improving the mind in general as a single monolithic ability or on acquiring a collection of smaller component skills. Early in the history of psychology and education the varying beliefs about the nature of cognitive ability were epitomized by the opposing approaches of Galton (1883) and Binet (1962). Galton proposed that cognitive ability was a unitary construct best measured by reaction time tasks and perceptual discrimination tasks. Later research showed that Galton's battery of cognitive measures did not correlate strongly with such measures of intellectual ability as school grades (Sternberg, 1990). In contrast, when Binet was charged with developing a test to predict academic success in the Paris school system, he conceptualized cognitive ability as a collection of small component skills and pieces of knowledge that could be learned, and his test was successful in predicting school success.

Similarly, modern psychometric approaches to human cognitive ability that are based on factor analyses of large batteries of cognitive tests reveal that there are many small component factors to cognitive ability rather than a single general ability factor (Carroll, 1993; Willis, Dumont, and Kaufman, 2011). And research-based cognitive theories of intelligence are based on the idea that cognitive performance on academic tasks depends on a collection of smaller cognitive and metacognitive processes rather than on a single mental ability (Mayer, 2010; Hunt, 2011). Although conventional wisdom among laypeople may hold that intellectual ability is a single monolithic ability, research on testing and individual differences in information processing suggests that intellectual ability is best seen as a collection of smaller component skills. It follows that cognitive strategy instruction should focus on helping students develop a collection of clearly defined component skills and learning how to assemble and integrate them rather than on improving their minds in general.

How to Teach

On the issue of how to teach, a key question is whether instruction should focus on the product of problem solving (i.e., getting the right answer) or on the process of problem solving (i.e., the thinking that goes into getting the right answer). Three research-based instructional techniques for the teaching of problem-solving and metacognitive strategies are modeling, prompting, and apprenticeship. In modeling the learner observes an expert perform the task, usually with commentary so that the learner receives a step-by-step explanation for why each step is taken. Modeling generally takes the form of worked-out examples that can be printed in books, presented on computer screens, or presented live by an expert. In prompting, the learner is given a problem to solve along with questions and hints about the reasons for carrying out various actions. For example, in self-explanation methods, the learner is asked to explain aspects of his or her cognitive processing while solving a problem. Because such explanations require reflection on one's own thinking and learning, these methods help learners develop metacognitive strategies.

In a classic study, Bloom and Broder (1950) taught college students how to solve problems on exams in college subjects such as economics by asking them to think aloud as they solved a problem, watch a model think aloud as he solved the problem, and then compare their thought processes with that of the model problem solver. Several hours of training based on this modeling of effective problem-solving processes resulted in significant improvements in exam scores as compared to a control group that did not receive this training. Modeling of the cognitive processes of successful problem solvers has been a component in the development of several successful problem-solving programs, as indicated in assessments of the Productive Thinking Program (Olton and Crutchfield, 1969; Mansfield, Busse, and Krepelka, 1978), Instrumental Enrichment (Feuerstein, 1980), and Project Intelligence (Hernstein et al., 1986; Nickerson, 2011).

Apprenticeship teaching and learning methods can help learners understand and apply the process of problem solving. In apprenticeship, a mentor or teacher models problem solving by describing how he or she approaches the process, coaches by providing guidance and tips to the learner who is carrying out a task, and scaffolds by directly performing or eliminating difficult parts of the task that the learner is unable to perform (Mayer and Wittrock, 2006). One example of apprenticeship methods is reciprocal teaching, as when students and a teacher took turns discussing strategies for increasing reading comprehension (Palincsar and Brown, 1984; Brown and Palincsar, 1989). Students who engaged in reciprocal teaching demonstrated a much larger gain in reading comprehension scores than students who learned reading with conventional methods, as the reciprocal teaching method helped them to solve problems they encountered while reading text.

Azevedo and Cromley (2004) identified several metacognitive strategies that are commonly used in the learning of new material, including planning, monitoring, using strategies, managing, and enjoying. Planning refers to the development of a plan for learning, and it includes activating relevant prior knowledge. Monitoring refers to recognizing when one does or does not comprehend something and figuring out what needs to be clarified. Using strategies involves determining when to use various learning strategies, such as taking notes, writing summaries, and generating drawings. Managing involves using time wisely, such as seeking help when needed. Enjoying involves expressing interest in the material. In short, a reasonable conclusion is that instructional methods should focus on the processes of problem solving and metacognition rather than solely on the final products of those processes.

Where to Teach

On the issue of where to teach, the key issue is whether problem-solving and metacognitive strategies should be learned in a specific domain or in a general way. Early in the history of educational psychology Thorndike sought to test the conventional wisdom of the day, which held that certain school subjects such as Latin and geometry helped to develop proper habits of mind—general ways of thinking that applied across disciplines (Thorndike and Woodworth, 1901; Thorndike, 1932). For example, in a classic study, Thorndike (1923) found that students who had learned Latin and students who had not learned Latin showed no differences in their ability to learn a new school subject: English. Combined with numerous other studies showing a lack of general transfer, these results led Thorndike to conclude that transfer is always specific—that is, the elements and relations in the learned material must be the same as the elements and relations in the to-be-learned material. Research on problem-solving and metacognitive expertise supports the idea that competency tends to be domain specific, as discussed in Chapter 4. People who are experts in solving problems in one domain are not able to transfer their problem-solving skill to other domains (de Groot, 1965; Ericsson et al., 2006). As noted above, research has shown that children's ability to solve problems in science is dependent on their prior knowledge of the topic or concept under study (National Research Council, 2007). These findings suggest that strategy instruction should be conducted within the specific context in which the problems will be solved (i.e., embedded within specific disciplines) rather than as a general stand-alone course.

When to Teach

On the subject of when to teach, the key question is whether problem-solving strategies should be taught before or after lower-level skills are mastered. Although the research base is less developed on this question, there is converging evidence that novices can benefit from training in high-level strategies. For example, in writing instruction students can be taught how to communicate with words—by dictating to an adult, for example, or by giving an oral presentation or being allowed to write with misspelled words and improper grammar—before they have mastered lower-level skills such as spelling and punctuation (Bereiter and Scardamalia, 1987; De La Paz and Graham, 1995). In observational studies of cognitive apprenticeship, beginners successfully learn high-level skills through a process of *assisted performance* (Tharp and Gallimore, 1988) in which they are allowed to attempt parts of complex tasks before than have mastered basic skills. These findings suggest that higher-order thinking skills can be learned along with lower-order ones early in the instructional process.

How Long to Teach

On the fifth issue, how long to teach, the main question is what the role should be of prolonged, deliberate practice in learning problem-solving strategies. Research on the development of expertise indicates that "high degrees of competence only come through extensive practice" (Anderson and Schunn, 2000, p. 17) and that learners need feedback that explains how to improve (Shute, 2008; Hattie and Gin, 2011). For example, students were found to develop expert-like performance in troubleshooting electronic and mechanical equipment if they spent 20-25 hours with a computer simulation in which they received immediate and focused feedback (Lesgold, 2001). In case studies, Ericsson and colleagues have found a close relationship between the development of professional expertise and the amount of *deliberate practice*—intensive practice at increasingly more challenging levels—even among learners with equivalent talent (see, e.g., Ericsson, 2003). Although programs that require only a few hours of work can produce improvements in problem-solving skill, the development of expert problem-solving skill requires years of deliberate practice.

Research indicates that extended time and practice also enhances learning in informal settings. For example, the National Research Council (2009a) recommends that designers of science exhibits and programs support and encourage learners to extend their learning over time, noting that "learning experiences in informal settings can be sporadic and . . . without support, learners may not find ways to sustain their engagement with science or a given topic."

BOX 6-3
Issues in Teaching Cognitive and Metacognitive Skills

1. What to teach: Focus on a collection of small component skills rather than trying to improve the mind as a single monolithic ability.
2. How to teach: Focus on the learning process (through modeling, prompting, or apprenticeship) rather than on the product.
3. Where to teach: Focus on learning to use the skill in a specific domain rather than in general.
4. When to teach: Focus on teaching higher skills even before lower skills are mastered.
5. How long to teach: Focus on deliberate practice to develop expertise.

SOURCE: Adapted from Mayer (2008).

Summary

Research and theory to date suggest answers to each of the five questions posed above (see Box 6-3). They suggest that instructors should teach component skills and their integration rather trying to improve the mind in general; should focus on the processes of problem solving and metacognition (through modeling or prompting) rather than solely on product; should focus on using the strategies in a specific context rather than in general; should focus on learning problem-solving and metacognitive strategies before or while lower-level skills are mastered; and should focus on prolonged, deliberate practice and application rather than one-shot deals.

Summary: Developing Transferable Cognitive Competencies

A persistent theme in research on learning and teaching for transfer concerns the situated nature of learning. That is, it is not fruitful to try to teach high-level thinking skills in general; rather, transferable knowledge is best learned within the disciplinary situations or sets of topics within which the knowledge will be used. In the previous chapter, we explored learning and teaching for transfer within three disciplines—English language arts, mathematics, and science. Within each discipline, the kinds of teaching techniques for transferable knowledge are adapted to the particular subject matter by such means as using multiple representations, encouraging questioning and self-explanation, providing guidance and support during exploration, teaching with examples, and priming motivation. The examples included in that chapter (Herrenkohl et al., 1999; Griffin, 2005) provide straightforward evidence that pure discovery (or unassisted inquiry) is not a particularly effective instructional method and that a more effective approach involves a combination of explicit instruction and guided exploration with metacognitive support.

Similarly, the disciplinary goals discussed in the previous chapter vary in how they approach the teaching of cognitive competencies. On the topic of what to teach, each discipline focuses on competencies that are important for the particular subject matter—such as discourse structures for argumentation and the interpretation of evidence in science, problem solving in mathematics, and comprehension of text in English language arts. On the issue of how to teach, each discipline adapts various techniques, including the modeling of thinking processes within discipline-specific tasks. On the subject of where to teach, high-level strategies are taught within discipline-specific situations rather than as general strategies. On the question of when to teach, each discipline teaches high-level content along with more basic, foundational content rather than waiting for basic skills to be mastered first. Finally, on the subject of how long to teach, each discipline views disciplinary learning as a long-term learning progression in which major competencies are learned at increasingly more sophisticated levels over the course of schooling—such as the way in which learning to read or write becomes more sophisticated and adapted for specific purposes.

INSTRUCTIONAL DESIGN PRINCIPLES— INTRAPERSONAL AND INTERPERSONAL DOMAINS

The research on instruction that directly targets intrapersonal and interpersonal learning goals is less extensive and rigorous than the research on instruction targeting cognitive learning goals. Although the limited evidence base poses a challenge to identifying specific principles of instructional design to advance intrapersonal and interpersonal knowledge and skills, there is suggestive evidence that some of the principles for instruction in the cognitive domain may be applicable to instruction in these two other domains.

In their meta-analysis of studies of after-school social and emotional learning programs described above, Durlak, Weissberg, and Pachan (2010) analyzed the studies' findings related to eight outcomes clustered into three categories, as follows:

- Feelings and attitudes (child self-perceptions, bonding to school)
- Behavioral adjustment (positive social behaviors, problem behaviors, drug use)
- School performance (achievement test scores, grades, attendance)

Based on prior research, the authors identified four practices thought to work together in combination to enhance the effectiveness of such programs:

- A sequenced, step-by-step training approach
- Emphasizing active forms of learning, so that youth can practice new skills
- Focusing specific time and attention on skill training
- Clearly defining goals, so that youth know what they are expected to learn

Among the programs evaluated in the studies, 41 followed all four of the research-based practices listed above, while 27 did not follow all four. The group of programs that followed the four practices showed statistically significant mean effects for all outcomes (including drug use and school attendance), while the group of programs that did not follow all four practices did not yield significant mean effects for any of the outcomes. These findings support the authors' hypothesis that the four research-based practices work best in combination to support the development of intrapersonal and interpersonal skills.

In a more recent meta-analysis of school-based social and emotional learning programs, Durlak et al. (2011) reviewed 213 studies, examining findings of effectiveness in terms of six outcomes:

- Social and emotional skills
- Attitudes toward self and others
- Positive social behaviors
- Conduct problems
- Emotional distress
- Academic performance

When the authors considered the findings in terms of the four research-based practices identified in their earlier study (Durlak, Weissberg, and Pachan, 2010), they found that the group of programs that followed all four of these recommended practices showed significant effects for all six outcomes, whereas programs that did not follow all four practices showed significant effects for only three outcomes (attitudes, conduct problems, and academic performance). The authors also found that the quality of implementation mattered. When programs were well conducted and proceeded according to plan, gains across the six outcomes were more likely.

These four practices are similar to some of the research-based methods and design principles described above for supporting deeper learning in the cognitive domain. For example, the earlier discussion identified the method of encouraging elaboration, questioning, and self-explanation as an effective way to support deeper learning of cognitive skills and knowledge. Similarly, the research on teaching social and emotional skills suggests that active forms of learning that include elaboration and questioning—such as role playing and behavioral rehearsal strategies—support deeper learning of intrapersonal and interpersonal skills and knowledge. These active forms of social and emotional learning provide opportunities for learners to practice new strategies and receive feedback.

The research on social and emotional skills indicates that it is important for teachers and school leaders to give sufficient attention to skill development, with a sequential and integrated curriculum providing opportunities for extensive practice. This echoes two findings about teaching cognitive skills: (1) teaching should be conducted within the specific context in which problems will be solved—in this case, social and emotional problems; and (2) the development of expert problem-solving skill requires years of deliberate practice. Providing adequate time and attention for skill development in the school curriculum appears to enhance the learning of intrapersonal and interpersonal skills. Finally, the research on social and emotional learning—like the research on cognitive learning—indicates that establishing explicit learning goals enhances effectiveness (Durlak et al., 2011). Just as the research on instruction for cognitive outcomes has demonstrated that learners need support and guidance to progress toward clearly defined goals (and that pure "discovery" does not lead to deep learning), so, too, has the research on instruction for social and emotional outcomes.

Research on team training also provides suggestive evidence that certain instructional design principles are important for the deeper learning of intrapersonal and interpersonal skills. In their meta-analysis, Salas et al. (2008) analyzed the potential moderating influence that the content of the team-training interventions had on outcomes. They identified three types of content: primarily task work; primarily teamwork (i.e., communication and other interpersonal skills); and both task work and teamwork. Their results suggest that when the goal is performance improvement the content makes little difference. However, for process outcomes (i.e., the development of intrapersonal and interpersonal skills that facilitate effective teamwork) and affective outcomes, teamwork and mixed-content training are associated with larger effect sizes than training focused on task work. The finding that, in situations when the goal is to improve team processes, focusing training content on teamwork skills improves effectiveness provides further support for the design principle that instruction should focus on clearly defined learning goals. The authors caution, however, that this conclusion is based on only a small number of studies.

ASSESSMENT *OF* AND *FOR* DEEPER LEARNING

Earlier in this chapter we discussed the need for clear learning goals and valid measures of important student outcomes, be they cognitive, intrapersonal, or interpersonal. Thus any discussion of issues related to the use of assessment to promote deeper learning presupposes that concerns about what to assess, how to assess, and how to draw valid inferences from the evidence have been addressed. These concerns must be addressed if assessment is to be useful in supporting the processes of teaching and learning. In this section we focus on issues related to how assessment can function in educational settings to accomplish the goal of supporting and promoting deeper learning.

Since its beginning, educational testing has been viewed as a tool for improving teaching and learning (see, for example, Thorndike, 1918), but perspectives on the ways that it can best support such improvement have expanded in recent years. Historically the focus has been on assessments *of* learning—the so-called *summative assessments*—and on the data they can provide to support instructional planning and decision making. More recently, assessment *for* learning—the so-called *formative assessment*—has been the subject of an explosion of interest, spurred largely by Black and Wiliam's 1998 landmark review showing impressive effects of formative assessment on student learning, particularly for low-ability students. A more recent meta-analysis of studies of formative assessment showed more modest, but still significant, effects on learning (Kingston and Nash, 2011).

The formative assessment concept emphasizes the dynamic process of *using* assessment evidence to continually improve student learning, while summative assessment focuses on development and implementation of an assessment instrument to measure what a student has learned up to a particular point in time (National Research Council, 2001; Shepard, 2005; Heritage, 2010).

Both types of assessment have a role in classroom instruction and in the assessment of deeper learning and 21st century skills, as described below. (The role of accountability testing in the development of these skills is treated in Chapter 7.)

Assessments *of* Learning

Assessments of learning look back over a period of time (a unit, a semester, a year, multiple years) in order to measure and make judgments about what students have learned and about how well programs and strategies are working—as well as how they can be improved. Assessments of learning often serve as the starting point for the design of instruction and teaching because they make explicit for both teachers and students what is expected and they provide benchmarks against which success or progress can be judged. For the purpose of instruction aimed at deeper learning and development of 21st century skills, it is essential that such measures (1) fully represent the targeted skills and knowledge and a model of their development; (2) be fair in enabling students to show what they know; and (3) provide reliable, unbiased, and generalizable inferences about student competence (Linn, Baker, and Dunbar, 1991; American Educational Research Association, American Psychological Association, and the National Council for Measurement in Education, 1999). In other words, the intended learning goals, along with their development, the assessment observations, and the interpretative framework (National Research Council, 2001) must be justified and fully synchronized.

When this is the case, the results for individual students can be useful for grading and placing students, for initial diagnoses of learning needs, and, in the case of students who are academically oriented, for motivating performance. Aggregated at the class, school, or higher levels, results may help in the identification of new curriculum and promising practices as well as in the assessment of teaching strategies and the evaluation of personnel and institutions.

Assessment *for* Learning: Formative Assessment

In contrast to assessments *of* learning that look backward over what has been learned, assessments *for* learning—formative assessments—chart the road forward by diagnosing where students are relative to learning goals and by making it possible to take immediate action to close any gaps (see Sadler, 1989). As defined by Black and Wiliam (1998), formative assessment involves both understanding and immediately responding to students' learning status. In other words, it involves both diagnosis and actions to accelerate student progress toward identified goals.

Such actions may be teacher directed and coordinated with a hypothesized model of learning. Actions could include: teachers asking questions to probe, diagnose, and respond to student understanding; teachers asking students to explain and elaborate their thinking; teachers providing feedback to help students transform their misconceptions and transition to more sophisticated understanding; and teachers analyzing student work and using results to plan and deliver appropriate next steps, for example, an alternate learning activity for students who evidence particular difficulties or misconceptions. But the actions are also student centered and student directed. A hallmark of formative assessment is its emphasis on student efficacy, as students are encouraged to be responsible for their learning, and the classroom is turned into a learning community (Gardner, 2006; Harlen, 2006). To assume that responsibility, students must clearly understand what learning is expected of them, including its nature and quality. Students receive feedback that helps them to understand and master performance gaps, and they are involved in assessing and responding to their own work and that of their peers (see also Heritage, 2010).

The importance of the teacher's role in formative assessment was demonstrated by the recent meta-analysis by Kingston and Nash (2011). The authors estimated a weighted mean effect size of 0.20 across the selected studies. However, in those studies investigating the use of formative assessment based on professional development that supported teachers in implementing the strategy, the weighted mean effect size was 0.30. Formative assessment occurs hand in hand with the classroom teaching and learning process and is an integral component of teaching and learning for transfer. It embodies many of the principles of designing instruction for transfer that were discussed in the previous section of this chapter. For example, formative assessment includes questioning, elaboration, and self-explanation, all of which have been shown to improve transfer. Formative assessment can provide the feedback and guidance that learners need when engaged in challenging tasks. Furthermore, by making learning goals explicit, by engaging students in self- and peer assessment, by involving students in a learning community, and by demonstrating student efficacy, formative assessment can promote students as agents in their own learning, which can increase student motivation, autonomy, and metacognition as well as collaboration and academic learning (Gardner, 2006; Shepard, 2006). Thus, formative assessment is conducive to—and may provide direct support for—the development of transferable cognitive, intrapersonal, and interpersonal skills.

A few examples suggest that teachers and students can enhance deeper learning by drawing on the evidence of their learning progress and needs provided by the formative assessment embedded within simulations and games. One such example, SimScientists, was described above. Another example, called Packet Tracer, was developed for use in the Cisco Networking Academy, which helps prepare networking professionals by providing online curricula and assessments to public and private education and training institutions throughout the world. In the early years of the networking academy, assessments were conducted by instructors and consisted of either hands-on exams with real networking equipment or else multiple-choice exams. Now Packet Tracer has been integrated into the online curricula, allowing instructors and students to construct their own activities and students to explore problems on their own. Student-initiated assessments are embedded in the curriculum and include quizzes, interactive activities, and "challenge labs"—structured activities focusing on specific curriculum goals, such as integration of routers within a computer network. Students use the results of these assessments to guide their online learning activities and to improve their performance. A student may, with instructor authorization, access and re-access an assessment repeatedly.

Formative and Summative Assessment: Classroom Systems of Assessment

Assessments of learning and for learning (summative and formative assessments) can work together in a coherent system to support the development of cognitive, intrapersonal, and interpersonal skills. If they are to do so, however, the assessments must be in sync with each other and with the model of how learning develops. Figure 6-2 shows the interrelationships among components of such a model. The model features explicit learning goals for targeted cognitive, intrapersonal, and interpersonal competencies and poses a sequential and integrated approach to their development, as supported by the literature (see, for example, Durlak and Weissburg, 2011).

In Figure 6-2, the benchmarks represent critical juncture points in progress toward the ultimate goals, while the formative assessment represents the interactive process between the teachers and students and continuous data that facilitate student progress toward the junctures and ultimate goals.

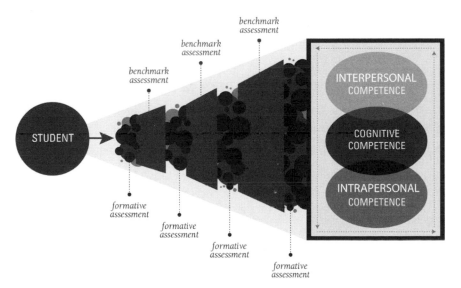

FIGURE 6-2 A coherent assessment system.
SOURCE: Adapted from Herman (2010a).

Formative Assessment: Teacher Roles and Practices

The coherent assessment system depicted in Figure 6-2 depends on formative assessment to facilitate student progress. Herman has described formative assessment as follows (2010b, p. 74):

> Rather than imparting knowledge in a transmission-oriented process, in formative assessment teachers guide students toward significant learning goals and actively engage students as assessors of themselves and their peers. Formative assessment occurs when teachers make their learning goals and success criteria explicit for students, gather evidence of how student learning is progressing, partner with students in a process of reciprocal feedback, and engage the classroom as a community to improve students' learning. The social context of learning is fundamental to the process as is the need for classroom culture and norms that support active learning communities—for example, shared language and understanding of expected performance; relationships of trust and respect; shared responsibility for and power in the learning process. Theorists (Munns and Woodward, 2006) observe that enacting a meaningful process of formative assessment influences what students perceive as valued knowledge, who can learn, who controls and is valued in the learning process.

Yet formative assessment itself involves a change in instructional practice: It is not a regular part of most teachers' practice, and teachers' pedagogical content knowledge may be an impediment to its realization (Heritage et al., 2009; Herman, Osmundson, and Silver, 2010). These and other challenges related to teaching and assessing 21st century competencies are discussed in Chapter 7. In that chapter, we reach conclusions about the challenges and offer recommendations to overcome them.

CONCLUSIONS AND RECOMMENDATIONS

The research literature on teaching and assessment of 21st century competencies has examined a plethora of variously defined cognitive, interpersonal, and interpersonal competencies, Although the lack of uniform definitions makes it difficult to identify and delineate the desired learning outcomes of an educational intervention—an essential first step toward measuring effectiveness—emerging evidence demonstrates that it is possible to develop transferable competencies.

- **Conclusion: Although the absence of common definitions and quality measures poses a challenge to research, emerging evidence indicates that cognitive, intrapersonal, and interpersonal competencies can be taught and learned in ways that promote transfer.**

The emerging evidence on teaching and learning of cognitive, intrapersonal, and interpersonal competencies builds on a larger body of evidence related to teaching for transfer. Researchers have examined the question of how to design instruction for transfer for more than a century. In recent decades, advances in the research have begun to provide evidence-based answers to this question. Although this research has focused on acquisition of cognitive competencies, it indicates that the process of learning for transfer involves the interplay of cognitive, intrapersonal, and interpersonal competencies, as reflected in our recommendations for design of instruction and teaching methods:

- **Recommendation 3: Designers and developers of instruction targeted at deeper learning and development of transferable 21st century competencies should begin with clearly delineated learning goals and a model of how learning is expected to develop, along with assessments to measure student progress toward and attainment of the goals. Such instruction can and should begin with the earliest grades and be sustained throughout students' K-12 careers.**

- **Recommendation 4: Funding agencies should support the development of curriculum and instructional programs that include research-based teaching methods, such as:**

  o **Using multiple and varied representations of concepts and tasks,** such as diagrams, numerical and mathematical representations, and simulations, combined with activities and guidance that support mapping across the varied representations.

  o **Encouraging elaboration, questioning, and explanation**—for example, prompting students who are reading a history text to think about the author's intent and/or to explain specific information and arguments as they read—either silently to themselves or to others.

  o **Engaging learners in challenging tasks,** while also supporting them with guidance, feedback, and encouragement to reflect on their own learning processes and the status of their understanding.

  o **Teaching with examples and cases,** such as modeling step-by-step how students can carry out a procedure to solve a problem and using sets of worked examples.

  o **Priming student motivation** by connecting topics to students' personal lives and interests, engaging students in collaborative problem solving, and drawing attention to the knowledge and skills students are developing, rather than grades or scores.

o   **Using formative assessment** to: (a) make learning goals clear to students; (b) continuously monitor, provide feedback, and respond to students' learning progress; and (c) involve students in self- and peer assessment.

The ability to solve complex problems and metacognition are important cognitive and intrapersonal competencies that are often included in lists of 21st century skills. For instruction aimed at development of problem-solving and metacognitive competencies, we recommend:

- **Recommendation 5: Designers and developers of curriculum, instruction, and assessment in problem solving and metacognition should use modeling and feedback techniques that highlight the processes of thinking rather than focusing exclusively on the products of thinking. Problem-solving and metacognitive competencies should be taught and assessed within a specific discipline or topic area rather than as a stand-alone course. Teaching and learning of problem-solving and metacognitive competencies need not wait until all of the related component competencies have achieved fluency. Finally, sustained instruction and effort are necessary to develop expertise in problem solving and metacognition; there is simply no way to achieve competence without time, effort, motivation, and informative feedback.**

Most of the available research on design and implementation of instruction for transfer has focused on the cognitive domain. We compared the instructional design principles and research-based teaching methods emerging from this research with the instructional design principles and research-based teaching methods that are beginning to emerge from the smaller body of research focusing on development of intrapersonal and interpersonal skills, identifying some areas of overlap and similarities.

- **Conclusion: The instructional features listed above, shown by research to support the acquisition of cognitive competencies that transfer, could plausibly be applied to the design and implementation of instruction that would support the acquisition of transferable intrapersonal and interpersonal competencies.**

The many gaps and weaknesses in the research reviewed here, particularly the lack of common definitions and measures, and the limited research in the intrapersonal and interpersonal domains limit our understanding of how to teach for transfer across the three domains.

- Recommendation 6: Foundations and federal agencies should support research programs designed to fill gaps in the evidence base on teaching and assessment for deeper learning and transfer. One important target for future research is how to design instruction and assessment for transfer in the intrapersonal and interpersonal domains. Investigators should examine whether, and to what extent, instructional design principles and methods shown to increase transfer in the cognitive domain are applicable to instruction targeted to the development of intrapersonal and interpersonal competencies. Such programs of research would benefit from efforts to specify more uniform, clearly defined constructs and to produce associated measures of cognitive, intrapersonal, and interpersonal competencies.

7

Systems to Support Deeper Learning

This chapter discusses elements of the U.S. education system that present both opportunities to advance the process of deeper learning and challenges that may slow such advance. The first section focuses on the role of the larger educational system in hindering or supporting educational interventions that foster deeper learning and development of 21st century competencies, with attention to two critical system elements (1) teacher preparation and professional development, and (2) assessment. The second section briefly summarizes the opportunities that could potentially emerge from wide implementation of educational interventions that foster deeper learning, as well as the challenges to such wide implementation. The chapter ends with conclusions and recommendations.

DESIGNING COHERENT EDUCATIONAL SYSTEMS FOR TRANSFER

The previous chapters presented a vision of the cognitive, intrapersonal, and interpersonal competencies that are valuable for functioning effectively at home, work, and in the community. The vision is one in which students and other learners develop a suite of enduring, transferable competencies in the cognitive, intrapersonal, and interpersonal domains. In Chapter 6, the committee recommended that formal and informal learning environments should include a set of coherent, interrelated features if they are to support development of such competencies. However, unless there is coherence in the larger educational environment, it will be difficult to widely implement instruction that incorporates such features.

In formal education, realizing the vision of deeper, transferable knowledge for all students will require complementary changes across the many elements that make up the public education system. These elements include curriculum, instruction, assessment, and teacher preparation and professional development.

While this report provides preliminary definitions of the kinds of transferable competencies that are valuable and offers general guidelines for use in designing instruction to develop these competencies, further research and development are needed to create more specific instructional materials and strategies—the curriculum. Future curricula inspired by our vision of deeper learning should integrate learning across the cognitive, intrapersonal, and interpersonal domains in whatever ways are appropriate for the targeted learning goals. For example, when targeting cognitive knowledge and thinking strategies, curricula should integrate development of the intrapersonal skills of metacognition, self-efficacy, and positive attitudes toward learning that have been shown to enhance deeper learning in the cognitive domain.

Reflecting our findings about the development of competencies across different ages and stages of development, curricula designed to support the process of deeper learning should incorporate a developmental perspective. They should be offered beginning in preschool and provide repeated opportunities across grade levels and domains (cognitive, intrapersonal, interpersonal) for students to develop and practice transferable competencies.

Teacher Preparation and Professional Development

Current systems of teacher preparation and professional development will require major changes if they are to support teaching that encourages deeper learning and the development of transferable competencies. Changes will need to be made not only in conceptions of what constitutes effective professional practice but also in the purposes, structure, and organization of preservice and professional learning opportunities (Garrick and Rhodes, 2000; Darling-Hammond, 2006; Webster-Wright, 2009; Lampert, 2010).

Ball and Cohen (1999) have called for such major changes, proposing a practice-based theory of professional education that would enable teachers to "support much deeper and more complex learning for their students" (p. 7). The authors identified several types of knowledge and skills teachers would require for such instruction, including:

- understanding of subject matter;
- knowledge of both students' common ideas and misconceptions related to the subject matter and also the thinking of individual students;

- understanding of, and sensitivity to, cultural, ethnic, and gender differences;
- knowledge of how children learn; and
- a repertoire of flexible, adaptable teaching strategies to engage learners.

The authors proposed that teachers could develop these capacities by learning in and from practice. Teachers would learn how to elicit students' thinking on an ongoing basis and use what they find out to improve their teaching practice, framing, guiding, and revising tasks and questions. They would approach teaching from a stance of inquiry. Finally, the authors sketched the outlines of professional education that would develop the knowledge and skills teachers require. Such education would focus on learning professional performance, would cultivate the knowledge and skills outlined above, and would be centered in teachers' professional practice. Teachers' learning would be supported by colleagues in communities of practice, as they reflected together on samples of student work or videotaped lessons.

Building on this theory of practice-based professional education, Windschitl (2009), Wilson (2011), and others have recommended replacing current disjointed teacher learning opportunities with more integrated continuums of teacher preparation, induction, support, and ongoing professional development. Windschitl (2009) proposed that teacher preparation programs within such a continuum should center on a common core curriculum grounded in a substantial knowledge of child or adolescent development, learning, and subject-specific pedagogy; those programs also should provide future teachers with extended opportunities to practice under the guidance of mentors (student teaching), lasting at least 30 weeks, that reflect the program's vision of good teaching and that are interwoven with coursework.

Research to date has identified other characteristics of effective teacher preparation programs, including extensive use of case study methods, teacher research, performance assessments, and portfolio examinations that are used to relate teachers' learning to classroom practice (Darling-Hammond, 1999). Deeper learning and the acquisition of 21st century competencies—for both teachers and their students—might also be supported through induction programs that help new teachers make effective use of study groups, peer learning, managed classroom discussions, and disciplined discourse routines (Monk and King, 1994; Ghousseini, 2009). Wilson (2011) and others have noted that one of the most promising practices for both induction and professional development involves bringing teachers together to analyze samples of student work, such as drawings, explanations, or essays, or to observe videotaped classroom dialogues. Working from principled analyses of how the students are responding to the instruction, the teachers can then change their instructional practices accordingly.

Windschitl (2009) identified a number of features of professional development that could help science teachers implement new teaching approaches to cultivate students' 21st century competencies in the context of science. These features are as follows:

- Active learning opportunities focusing on science content, scientific practice, and evidence of student learning (Desimone et al., 2002).
- Coherence of the professional development with teachers' existing knowledge, with other development activities, with existing curriculum, and with standards in local contexts (Garet et al., 2001; Desimone et al., 2002).
- The collective development of an evidence-based "inquiry stance" by participants toward their practice (Blumenfeld et al., 1991; Kubitskey and Fishman, 2006).
- The collective participation by teachers from same school, grade, or subject area (Desimone et al., 2002).
- Adequate time both for planning and for enacting new teaching practices.

More broadly across the disciplines, preservice teachers and inservice teachers will need opportunities to engage in the kinds of teaching and learning environments envisioned in this report. Experiencing instruction designed to support transfer will help them to design and implement such instruction in their own classrooms. Teachers will also need opportunities to learn about different approaches to assessment and the purposes of these different approaches. For example, as noted in the previous chapter, formative assessment can play a key role in fostering deeper learning and the development of 21st century competencies. However, most teachers are not familiar with formative assessment and do not regularly incorporate it in their teaching practice (Heritage et al., 2009; Herman, Osmundson, and Silver, 2010).

Assessment

Research has shown that assessment and feedback play an essential role in the deeper learning of cognitive competencies. In particular, as noted in Chapter 6, ongoing formative assessment by teachers can provide guidance to students which supports and extends their learning, encouraging deeper learning and development of transferable competencies. Current educational policies, however, focus on summative assessments that measure mastery of content and often hold schools and districts accountable for improving student scores on such assessments. Although this focus on summative assessment poses a challenge to the wider teaching and learning of 21st century competencies, recent policy developments do appear to open the window for a wider diffusion of interventions to develop these competencies. For example, the previous chapter noted that the new Common Core State Standards and *A Framework for K-12 Science Education: Practices, Crosscutting Concepts, and Core Ideas* (hereafter referred to as the NRC science framework) include facets of 21st century competencies.

While the new English language arts and mathematics standards and the science framework articulate goals for deeper learning and the development of facets of 21st century competencies, the extent to which these goals are realized in schools will be strongly influenced by their inclusion in district, state, and national assessments. Because educational policy remains focused on outcomes from summative assessments that are part of accountability systems, teachers and administrators will focus instruction on whatever is included in state assessments. Thus, as new assessment systems are developed to reflect the new standards in English language arts, mathematics, and science, significant attention will need to be given to the design of tasks and situations that call upon a range of important 21st century competencies as applied in each of the major content areas.

Although improved assessments would facilitate a wider focus on teaching approaches that support the development of 21st century competencies, there are a number of challenges to developing such assessments. First, research to date has focused on a wide variety of different constructs in the cognitive, intrapersonal, and interpersonal domains. Although our taxonomy offers a useful starting point, further research is needed to more carefully organize, align, and define these constructs. There are also psychometric challenges. Progress has been made in assessing cognitive competencies, but much further research is needed to develop assessments of intrapersonal and interpersonal competencies that are suitable for both formative and summative assessment uses in educational settings. Experiences during the 1980s and 1990s in the development and implementation of performance assessments, including assessments with open-ended tasks, can offer valuable insights, but assessments must be reliable, valid, and fair if they are to be widely used in formal and informal learning environments.

A third challenge involves political and economic forces influencing assessment development and use. Traditionally, policy makers have favored the use of standardized, on-demand, end-of-year tests for purposes of accountability. Composed largely of selected response items, these tests are relatively cheap to develop, administer, and score; have sound psychometric properties; and provide easily quantifiable and comparable scores for assessing individuals and institutions. Yet, as discussed in Chapter 6, such standardized tests have not been conducive to measuring or supporting the process of deeper learning nor to the development of 21st century competencies. In the face of current fiscal constraints at the federal and state levels, policy makers may seek to minimize assessment costs by maintaining lower cost, traditional test formats, rather than incorporating into their systems relatively more expensive, richer performance- and curriculum-based assessments that may better measure 21st century competencies.

The fourth challenge involves teacher and administrator capacity to understand and interpret the new assessments. The features of instruction and assessment discussed in Chapter 6 are not well known to teachers, students, or school administrators.

With support from the U.S. Department of Education, two large consortia of states are currently developing new assessment frameworks and methods aligned with the Common Core State Standards in English language arts and mathematics. If these assessment and frameworks include the facets of 21st century competencies included in the Common Core State Standards, this will provide a strong incentive for states, districts, schools, and teachers to emphasize those facets of 21st century competencies in English language arts and science instruction. Next Generation Science Standards based on the NRC science framework are under development, and the NRC has begun a study to develop an assessment framework based on the NRC science framework. When new science assessments are created, the inclusion of facets of 21st century competencies will, as is the case with English language arts and mathematics, provide a strong incentive for states, districts, schools, and teachers to emphasize those facets in the context of science lessons.

OPPORTUNITIES AND CHALLENGES

The development of 21st century competencies in K-12 education and informal learning environments opens up many new opportunities. Because these competencies support the learning of school subjects, more attention to them in school programs and also in informal learning environments could potentially reduce disparities in educational attainment. Reducing these disparities would prepare a broader swathe of young people to enjoy the positive outcomes of increased educational attainment, including greater success in the workplace, improved health, and greater civic participation relative to people with fewer years of schooling. At the same time, developing these competencies in K-12 education could also lead to positive adult outcomes for more young people, independent of any increases in their years of schooling.

Important challenges do remain, however. For educational interventions capable of developing transferable knowledge and skills to move beyond isolated promising examples and flourish more widely in the educational system, larger systemic issues involving curriculum, instruction, assessment, and professional development will need to be addressed. In particular, as noted above, new types of assessment systems are needed that are capable of accurately measuring and supporting the acquisition of these skills. A sustained program of research and development will be required to create assessments that are capable of measuring cognitive, intrapersonal, and interpersonal competencies. As noted in Chapter 3, such assessments are needed first for research purposes, to increase our understanding of the extent to which these competencies affect later life outcomes. In addition, improved assessments of the competencies would be valuable for formative assessment purposes and might ultimately be used for summative purposes.

It will be important for researchers and publishers to develop new curricula that incorporate the research-based design principles and instructional methods described in Chapter 6. Finally, as noted briefly above, new approaches to teacher preparation and professional development will be needed to help current and prospective teachers understand the instructional principles for the teaching and assessment of 21st century competencies and the role of these competencies in the learning of core academic content. If teachers are not only to understand these ideas but also to translate them into their daily instructional practice, they will need support from school and district administrators, including time for learning, shared lesson planning and review, and reflection.

CONCLUSIONS AND RECOMMENDATIONS

While new national goals that encompass 21st century competencies have been articulated in the Common Core State Standards for English language arts and mathematics and in the NRC science education framework, the extent to which these goals are realized in educational settings will be strongly influenced by the nature of their inclusion in district, state, and national assessments. Because educational policy remains focused on outcomes from summative assessments that are part of accountability systems, teachers and administrators will focus instruction on whatever is included in state assessments. Thus as new assessment systems are developed to reflect the new standards in English language arts, mathematics, and science, it will be necessary to give significant attention to the design of tasks and situations that call upon a range of important 21st century competencies as applied in each of the major content areas. A sustained program of research and development will be required to create assessments that are capable of measuring cognitive, intrapersonal, and interpersonal skills.

- Recommendation 7: Foundations and federal agencies should support research to more clearly define and develop assessments of 21st century competencies. In particular, they should provide sustained support for the development of valid, reliable, and fair assessments of intrapersonal and interpersonal competencies, initially for research purposes and, later, for formative assessment. Pending the results of these efforts, foundations and agencies should consider support for development of summative assessments of these competencies.

Two large consortia of states, with support from the U.S. Department of Education, are currently developing new assessment frameworks and methods aligned with the Common Core State Standards in English language arts and mathematics. If these assessment frameworks include the facets of 21st century competencies represented in the Common Core State Standards, they will provide a strong incentive for states, districts, schools, and teachers to emphasize these critical facets of 21st century competencies as part of disciplinary instruction.

- Recommendation 8: As the state consortia develop new assessment systems to reflect the Common Core State Standards in English language arts and mathematics, they should devote significant attention to the design of tasks and situations that call upon a range of important 21st century competencies as applied in each of the major content areas.

Next Generation Science Standards are at an early stage of development, and assessments aligned with these standards have not yet been created. When new science assessments are developed, the inclusion of facets of 21st century competencies will provide a similarly strong incentive for states, districts, schools, and teachers to emphasize those facets in classroom science instruction.

- Recommendation 9: As states and test developers begin to create new assessment systems aligned with new science standards, they should devote significant attention to designing measures of 21st century competencies properly reflecting a blend of science practices, crosscutting concepts, and core ideas.

Because 21st century competencies support learning of school subjects in particular and educational attainment more generally, more attention to the development of these skills in the K-12 curriculum could potentially reduce disparities in educational attainment and allow a broader swathe of young people to enjoy the fruits of workplace success, improved health, and greater civic participation. However, important challenges to achieving this outcome remain. For educational interventions focused on developing transferable competencies to move beyond isolated promising examples and flourish more widely in formal educational settings, larger systemic issues and policies involving curriculum, instruction, assessment and professional development will need to be addressed. Addressing these systemic issues will require supportive state and federal policies and programs, to facilitate the development of new types of assessment systems, new curricula that incorporate the instructional design guidelines and research-based features described above, and new approaches to teacher preparation and professional development.

- Recommendation 10: The states and the federal government should establish policies and programs—in the areas of assessment, accountability, curriculum and materials, and teacher education—to support students' acquisition of transferable 21st century competencies. For example, when reauthorizing the Elementary and Secondary Education Act, the Congress should facilitate the systemic development, implementation, and evaluation of educational interventions targeting deeper learning processes and the development of transferable competencies.

References

Abramowitz, A.I. (1983). Social determinism, rationality, and partisanship among college students. *Political Behavior, 5*, 353-362.

Achen, C. (2002). Parental socialization and rational party identification. *Political Behavior, 24*(2), 151-170.

Allport, G.W., and Odbert, H.S. (1936). Trait names: A psycho-lexical study. *Psychological Monographs, 47*(1), whole no. 171.

Almlund, M., Duckworth, A., Heckman, J., and Kautz, T. (2011). Personality psychology and economics. In E.A. Hanushek, S. Machin, and L. Wossmann (Eds.), *Handbook of the economics of education* (pp. 1-181). Amsterdam: Elsevier.

Altonji, J. G., Blom, E., and Maghir, C. (2012). *Heterogeneity in human capital investments: High school curriculum, college major, and careers*. NBER Working Paper No. 17985. Cambridge, MA: National Bureau of Economic Research. Available: http://www.nber.org/papers/w17985 [June 2012].

American Association for the Advancement of Science. (1989). *Science for all Americans: A project 2061 report on literacy goals in science, mathematics, and technology*. Washington, DC: Author.

American Association for the Advancement of Science. (1993). *Benchmarks for science literacy*. Washington, DC: Author.

American Association of School Librarians and Association for Educational Communications and Technology. (1998). *Information literacy standards for student learning*. Chicago, IL: American Library Association. Available: http://www.ala.org/ala/mgrps/divs/aasl/aaslarchive/pubsarchive/informationpower/InformationLiteracyStandards_final.pdf [November 2011].

American Educational Research Association, American Psychological Association, and the National Council for Measurement in Education. (1999). *Standards for educational and psychological testing*. Washington, DC: American Educational Research Association.

American Psychological Association. (2007). *APA dictionary of psychology*. Washington, DC: Author.

American Society for Training and Development. (2009). *The 2009 state of the industry report.* Summary available: http://www.astd.org/Publications/Research-Reports/2009-State-of-Industry-Report.aspx [March 2012].

Ananiadou, K., and Claro, M. (2009). *21st century skills and competences for new millennium learners in OECD countries.* Paris: OECD. Available: http://www.oecd-ilibrary.org/education/21st-century-skills-and-competences-for-new-millennium-learners-in-oecd-countries_218525261154 [April 2011].

Anderman, E.M. (2011). *The teaching and learning 21st century skills.* Paper presented at the NRC Workshop on Assessment of 21st Century Skills, National Research Council, Irvine, CA, January 12-13. Available: http://www7.nationalacademies.org/bota/21st_Century_Workshop_Anderman_Paper.pdf [September 2011].

Anderman, E.M., and Wolters, C. (2006). Goals, values, and affect. In P. Alexander and P. Winne (Eds.), *Handbook of educational psychology* (2nd ed., pp. 369-390). Mahwah, NJ: Erlbaum.

Anderson, J.R. (1982). Acquisition of cognitive skill. *Psychological Review, 89,* 369-406.

Anderson, J.R. (1990). *Cognitive psychology and its implications.* New York: W.H. Freeman.

Anderson, J.R., and Schunn, C.D. (2000). Implications of the ACT-R learning theory: No magic bullets. In R. Glaser (Ed.), *Advances in instructional psychology* (vol. 5, pp. 1-33). Mahwah, NJ: Erlbaum.

Anderson, L.W., Krathwohl, D.R., Airasian, P.W., Cruikshank, K.A., Mayer, R.A., Pintrich, P.R., Raths, J., and Wittrock, M.C. (2001). *A taxonomy for learning, teaching, and assessing: A revision of Bloom's taxonomy of educational objectives.* Boston, MA: Allyn & Bacon.

Arseneault, L., Moffitt, T.E., Caspi, A., Taylor, P.J., and Silva, P.A. (2000). Mental disorders and violence in a total birth cohort: Results from the Dunedin study. *Archives of General Psychiatry, 57,* 979-986.

Arthur, W., Jr., Bennett, W., Jr., Edens, P.S., and Bell, S.T. (2003). Effectiveness of training in organizations: A Meta-analysis of design and evaluation features. *Journal of Applied Psychology, 88*(2), 234-245.

Ashton, M.C., Lee, K., and Son, C. (2000). Honesty as the sixth factor of personality: Correlations with Machiavellianism, primary psychopathy, and social adroitness. *European Journal of Personality, 14,* 359-368.

Autor, D. (2007). *Discussion: High-tech and here to stay: Future skill demands in low-wage service occupations.* Presentation to the NRC Workshop on Future Skill Demands. Available: http://www7.nationalacademies.org/cfe/Discussion_about_High_Touch_Here-to-Stay_Presentation_PDF.pdf [September 2011].

Autor, D., Levy, F., and Murnane, R. (2003). The skill content of recent technological change: An empirical exploration. *Quarterly Journal of Economics, 118*(4), 1,279-1,333.

Autor, D.H., Katz, L.F., and Kearney, M.S. (2008). Trends in U.S. wage inequality: Revisiting the revisionists. *Review of Economics and Statistics, 90*(2), 300-323.

Azevedo, R., and Aleven, V. (Eds.). (2010). *International handbook of metacognition and learning technologies.* Amsterdam: Springer.

Azevedo, R., and Cromley, J.G. (2004). Does training on self-regulated learning facilitate students' learning with hypermedia? *Journal of Educational Psychology, 96*(3), 523-535.

Baddeley, A. D. (1986). *Working memory.* Oxford: Oxford University Press.

Baldwin, T.T., and Ford, K.J. (1988). Transfer of training: A review and directions for future research. *Personnel Psychology, 41,* 63-105.

Baldwin, T.T., Ford, K.J., and Blume, B.D. (2009). Transfer of training 1988-2009: An updated review and agenda for future research. *International Review of Industrial and Organizational Psychology, 24,* 41-70.

Balfanz, R., Mac Ivar, D., and Byrnes, V. (2006). The implementation and impact of evidence-based mathematics reforms in high-poverty middle schools: A multi-site, multi-year study. *Journal for Research in Mathematics Education, 37,* 33-64.

Ball, D.L., and Cohen, D.K. (1999). Developing practice, developing practitioners: Toward a practice-based theory of professional education. In G. Sykes and L. Darling-Hammond (Eds.), *Teaching as the learning profession: Handbook of policy and practice* (pp. 3-32). San Francisco: Jossey Bass.

Barnett, W.S., Jung, K., Yarosz, D.J., Thomas, J., Hornbeck, A., Stechuk, R., and Burns, M.S. (2008). Educational effects of the tools of the mind curriculum: A randomized trial. *Early Childhood Research Quarterly, 23*(3), 299-313.

Barr, R., Kamil, M.L., Mosenthal, P., and Pearson, P.D. (Eds.). (1991). *Handbook of reading research* (vol. 2). New York: Longman.

Barrick, M.R., Mount, M.K., and Judge, T.A. (2001). Personality and performance at the beginning of the new millennium: What do we know and where do we go next? *International Journal of Selection & Assessment, 9,* 9-30.

Barrow, L., and Rouse, C. (2005). Do returns to schooling differ by race and ethnicity? *American Economic Review, 95*(2), 83-87.

Barrows, H.S. (1996). Problem-based learning in medicine and beyond. In L. Wilkerson and W.H. Gijselaers (Eds.), *Bringing problem-based learning to higher education: Theory and practice. New directions for teaching and learning* (no. 68, pp. 3-13). San Francisco: Jossey-Bass.

Bartlett, F. (1932). *Remembering.* London: Cambridge University Press.

Bassok, M., and Holyoak, K. (1989). Interdomain transfer between isomorphic topics in algebra and physics. *Journal of Experimental Psychology: Learning, 15*(1), 153-166.

Becker, G. (1964). *Human capital.* New York: Columbia University Press.

Bedwell, W.L., Salas, E., and Fiore, S.M. (2011). *Developing the 21st century (and beyond) workforce: A review of interpersonal skills and measurement strategies.* Paper prepared for the NRC Workshop on Assessing 21st Century Skills. Available: http://www7.national academies.org/bota/21st_Century_Workshop_Salas_Fiore_Paper.pdf [October 2011].

Bereiter, C., and Scardamalia, M. (1987). *The psychology of written composition.* Hillsdale, NJ: Erlbaum.

Binet, A. (1962). The nature and measurement of intelligence. In L. Postman (Ed.), *Psychology in the making: Histories of selected research programs* (pp. 469- 525). New York: Knopf. [Originally published in French, Paris, France: Flammarion, 1911.]

Binkley, M., Erstad, O., Herman, J., Raizen, S., Ripley, M., and Rumble, M. (2010). *Defining 21st century skills.* White paper commissioned for the Assessment and Teaching of 21st Century Skills Project (ATC21S). Available on request: http://atc21s.org/index.php/resources/white-papers/#item1 [August 2012].

Black, P., and Wiliam, D. (1998). Assessment and classroom learning. *Assessment in Education, 5*(1), 7-74.

Blackwell, L.A., Trzesniewski, K.H., and Dweck, C.S. (2007). Theories of intelligence and achievement across the junior high school transition: A longitudinal study and an intervention. *Child Development, 78,* 246-263.

Blaug, M. (1975). *The Cambridge revolution: Success or failure? A critical analysis of Cambridge theories of value and distribution, revised edition.* London: Institute of Economic Affairs.

Bloom, B.S. (1956). *Taxonomy of educational objectives, handbook I: The cognitive domain.* New York: David McKay.

Bloom, B.S., and Broder, L.J. (1950). *Problem-solving processes of college students.* Chicago: University of Chicago Press.

Blume, B.D., Ford, J.K., Baldwin, T.T., and Huang, J.L. (2010). Transfer of training: A meta-analytic review. *Journal of Management, 39,* 1,065-1,105.

Blumenfeld, P., Soloway, E., Marx, R.W., Guzdial, M., and Palincsar, A. (1991). Motivating project-based learning: Sustaining the doing, supporting the learning. *Educational Psychologist, 26*(3/4), 369-398.

Blundell, R., Dearden, L., Meghir, C., and Sianesi, B. (1999). Human capital investment: The returns from education to the individual, the firm, and the economy. *Fiscal Studies, 20*(1), 1-23.

Boaler, J. (1998). Open and closed mathematics: Student experiences and understandings. *Journal for Research in Mathematics Education, 29,* 41-62.

Boaler, J., and Staples, M. (2008). Creating mathematical futures through an equitable teaching approach: The case of Railside school. *Teachers College Record, 110*(3), 608-645.

Bollen, K.A., and Lennox, R. (1991). Conventional wisdom on measurement: A structural equation perspective. *Psychological Bulletin, 110*(2), 305-314.

Bongers, I.L., Koot, H.M., van der Ende, J., and Verhulst, F.C. (2003). The normative development of child and adolescent problem behavior. *Journal of Abnormal Psychology, 112*(5), 179-192.

Borghans, L., ter Weel, B., and Weinberg, B.A. (2005). *People people: Social capital and the labor-market outcomes of underrepresented groups.* IZA Discussion Paper No. 1494. Available: http://papers.ssrn.com/sol3/papers.cfm?abstract_id=670207 [April 2012].

Borghans, L., ter Weel, B., and Weinberg, B. (2008). Interpersonal styles and labor market outcomes. *Journal of Human Resources, 43*(4), 815-858.

Bowles, S., Gintis, H., and Osborne, M. (2001). The determinants of earnings: A behavioral approach. *Journal of Economic Literature, 39*(4), 137-176.

Brown, A.L., and Palincsar, A.S. (1989). Guided, cooperative learning and individual knowledge acquisition. In L.B. Resnick (Ed.), *Knowing, learning, and instruction: Essays in honor of Robert Glaser* (pp. 393-451). Hillsdale, NJ: Erlbaum.

Brownell, W.A., and Moser, H.E. (1949). Meaningful vs. mechanical learning: A study on grade 3 subtraction. In *Duke University Research Studies in Education,* No. 8. Durham, NC: Duke University Press.

Brownell, W.A., and Sims, V.M. (1946). The nature of understanding. In N.B. Henry (Ed.), *The measurement of understanding: Forty-fifth yearbook of the National Society for the Study of Education. Part I* (pp. 27-43). Chicago: University of Chicago Press.

Brunello, G., and Schlotter, M. (2010). *The effect of non-cognitive skills and personality traits on labour market outcomes.* Analytical Report for the European Commission prepared by the European Expert Network on Economics of Education. Available: http://www.epis.pt/downloads/dest_15_10_2010.pdf [April 2012].

Burke, L.A., and Hutchins, H.M. (2008). Training transfer: An integrative literature review. *Human Resource Development Review, 6,* 263-296.

Campbell, S.B., Shaw, D.S., and Gilliom, M. (2000). Early externalizing behavior problems: Toddlers and preschoolers at risk for later adjustment. *Development and Psychopathology, 12*(3), 467-488.

Card, D. (1999). The causal effect of education on earnings. In O. Ashenfelter and D. Card (Eds.), *Handbook of labor economics* (vol. 3A, Chapter 30, 1,801-1,863). Netherlands: North Holland.

Carneiro, P., Crawford, C., and Goodman, A. (2007). *The impact of early cognitive and non-cognitive skills on later outcomes.* London: Centre for the Economics of Education, London School of Economics.

Carpenter, T.P., Fennema, E., Peterson, P.L., Chiang, C.P., and Loef, M. (1989). Using knowledge of children's mathematical thinking in classroom teaching: An experimental study. *American Educational Research Journal, 26,* 499-531.

Carpenter, T.P., Fennema, E., and Franke, M. (1996). Cognitively guided instruction: A knowledge base for reform in primary mathematics instruction. *Elementary School Journal,* 97(1), 3-20.

Carroll, J.B. (1993). *Human cognitive abilities.* New York: Cambridge University Press.

Case, S. (2001). *Assessment of cirtical thinking and problem solving on the multistate bar exam.* Presentation at the NRC Workshop on Assessment of 21st Century Skills. Available: http://www7.nationalacademies.org/bota/21st_century_workshop_case.pdf [April 2012].

Cervetti, G.N., Barber, J., Dorph, R., Pearson, P.D., and Goldschmidt, P.G. (2012). The impact of an integrated approach to science and literacy in elementary school classrooms. *Journal of Research in Science Teaching, 49*(5), 631-658.

Charles, R., and Silver, E.A. (Eds.). (1988). *Research agenda for mathematics education: Teaching and assessing mathematical problem solving.* Reston, VA: National Council of Teachers of Mathematics (Co-published with Erlbaum, Hillsdale, NJ).

Chase, W.G., and Simon, H.A. (1973). The mind's eye in chess. In W.G. Chase (Ed.), *Visual information processing* (pp. 215-281). New York: Academic Press.

Cheng, E.W.L., and Hampson, I. (2008). Transfer of training: A review and new insights. *Journal of Management, 10,* 327-341.

Chi, M.T.H., and Koeske, R.D. (1983). Network representation of a child's dinosaur knowledge. *Developmental Psychology, 19,* 29-39.

Chi, M.T.H., and VanLehn, K.A. (1991). The content of physics self-explanations. *The Journal of the Learning Sciences, 1*(1), 69-105.

Chi, M.T.H., Glaser, R., and Rees, E. (1982). Expertise in problem solving. In R.J. Sternberg (Ed.), *Advances in the psychology of human intelligence: Volume 1* (pp. 7-75). Hillsdale, NJ: Erlbaum.

Chi, M.T.H., Bassok, M., Lewis, M.W., Reimann, P., and Glaser, R. (1989). Self-explanations: How students study and use examples to solve problems. *Cognitive Science, 13,* 145-182.

Chung, Y.P. (1990). Educated mis-employment in Hong Kong: Earnings effects of employment in unmatched fields of work. *Economics of Education Review, 9,* 343-350.

Ciccone, A., and Peri, G. (2005). Long-run substitutability between more and less educated workers: Evidence from U.S. states, 1950-1990. *The Review of Economics and Statistics, 87*(4), 652-663.

Cobern, W.W., Schuster, D.G., Adams, B., Undreiu, A., Skjold, B.A., Applegate, B., Loving, C.C., and Gobert, J.D. (2010). Experimental comparison of inquiry and direct instruction in science. *Research in Science & Technological Education, 28*(1), 81-96.

Cohen, D.K. (1990). A revolution in one classroom: The case of Mrs. Oublier. *Educational Evaluation and Policy Analysis, 12,* 327-345.

Cohen, D.K., McLaughlin, M., and Talbert, J. (Eds.). (1993). *Teaching for understanding: Challenges for policy and practice.* San Francisco: Jossey-Bass.

Cohen, G.L., Garcia, J., Apfel, N., and Master, A. (2006). Reducing the racial achievement gap: A social-psychological intervention. *Science, 313,* 1,307-1,310.

Cohen, G.L., Garcia, J., Purdie-Vaughns, V., Apfel, N., and Brzustoski, P. (2009). Recursive processes in self-affirmation: Intervening to close the minority achievement gap. *Science, 324,* 400-403.

Cohen, J. (1988). *Statistical power analysis for the behavioral sciences* (2nd ed.). Hillsdale, NJ: Erlbaum.

Cohen, J., and Cohen, P. (1988). *Applied multiple regression/correlation analysis for the behavioral sciences* (2nd ed). Hillsdale, NJ: Erlbaum.

Coleman, W.C., and Cureton, E.E. (1954). Intelligence and achievement: The "Jangle Fallacy"again. *Educational and Psychological Measurement, 14,* 347-351.

Colquitt, J.A., LePine, J.A., and Noe, R.A. (2000). Toward an integrative theory of training motivation: A meta-analytic path analysis of 20 years of research. *Journal of Applied Psychology, 85,* 678-707.

Common Core State Standards Initiative. (2010a). *English language arts standards.* Washington, DC: National Governors Association and Council of Chief State School Officers. Available: http://www.corestandards.org/the-standards/english-language-arts-standards [February 2012].

Common Core State Standards Initiative. (2010b). *Mathematics standards.* Washington, DC: National Governors Association and Council of Chief State School Officers. Available: http://www.corestandards.org/assets/CCSSI_Math%20Standards.pdf [April 2012].

Conley, D.T. (2007). *Redefining college readiness.* Eugene, OR: Educational Policy Improvement Center. Available: https://www.epiconline.org/files/pdf/RedefiningCollegeReadiness.pdf [October 2011].

Conley, D. (2011). *Crosswalk analysis of deeper learning skills to common core state standards.* Prepared for the William H. and Flora Hewlett Foundation by the Educational Policy Improvement Center (EPIC). Unpublished manuscript.

Conti, G., Heckman, J., and Urzua, S. (2010a). The education-health gradient. *American Economic Review, 100*(2), 234.

Conti, G., Heckman, J., and Urzua, S. (2010b). Understanding the early origins of the education-health gradient: A framework that can also be applied to analyze gene-environment interactions. *Perspectives on Psychological Science, 5*(5), 585-605.

Costa, P.T., and McCrae, R.R. (1992). *Revised NEO personality inventory (NEO-PI-R) and NEO five-factor inventory (NEO-FFI) professional manual.* Odessa, FL: Psychological Assessment Resources.

Cronbach, L.J. (1970). *Essentials of psychological testing* (3rd ed.). New York: Harper & Row.

Cunha, F., and Heckman, J.J. (2008). Formulating, identifying, and estimating the technology of cognitive and noncognitive skill formation. *The Journal of Human Resources, 43*(4), 738-782.

Currie, J., and Stabile, M. (2007). Child mental health and human capital accumulation: The case of ADHD. *Journal of Health Economics, 25*(6), 1,094-1,118.

Currie, J., and Thomas, D. (1999). *Early test scores, socioeconomic status and future outcomes.* NBER Working Paper No. 6943. Cambridge, MA: National Bureau of Economic Research.

Cutler, D.M., and Lleras-Muney, A. (2010a). Education and health: Evaluating theories and evidence. In R. Schoeni, J.S. House, G.A. Kaplan, and H. Pollack (Eds.), *Making Americans healthier* (pp. 29-60). New York: Russell Sage Foundation.

Cutler, D.M., and Lleras-Muney, A. (2010b). Understanding differences in health behavior by education. *Journal of Health Economics, 29*(1), 1-28.

Darling-Hammond, L. (1999). Target time toward teachers. *Journal of Staff Development, 20,* 31-36.

Darling-Hammond, L. (2006). Constructing 21st-century teacher education. *Journal of Teacher Education, 57*(X), 1-15.

Davila, J., and Bradbury, T. (2001). Attachment insecurity and the distinction between unhappy spouses who do and do not divorce. *Journal of Family Psychology, 15*(3), 371-393.

De Groot, A.D. (1965). *Thought and choice in chess.* The Hague: Mouton.

de Jong, T. (2005). The guided discovery principle in multimedia learning. In R.E. Mayer (Ed.), *The Cambridge handbook of multimedia learning* (pp. 215-228). New York: Cambridge University Press.

De La Paz, S. (2005). Effects of historical reasoning instruction and writing strategy mastery in culturally and academically diverse middle school classrooms. *Journal of Educational Psychology, 97*(2), 139-156.

De La Paz, S., and Graham, S. (1995). Dictation: Applications to writing for students with disabilities. In T. Scruggs and M. Mastropieri (Eds.), *Advances in learning and behavioral disabilities* (vol. 9, pp. 227-247). Greenwich, CT: JAI Press.

Delli Carpini, M.X., and Keeter, S. (1997). *What Americans know about politics and why it matters.* New Haven: Yale University Press.

DeSimone, L.M., Porter, A.S., Garet, M.S., Yoon, K.S., and Birman, B. (2002). Effects of professional development on teachers' instruction: Results from a three-year longitudinal study. *Educational Evaluation and Policy Analysis, 24*(2), 81-112.

Diamond, A., Barnett, W.S., Thomas, J., and Munro, S. (2007). Preschool program improves cognitive control. *Science, 318,* 1,387-1,388.

Dunbar, K. (2000). How scientists think in the real world: Implications for science education. *Journal of Applied Developmental Psychology, 21*(1), 49-58.

Duncan, G., and Magnuson, K. (2011). The nature and impact of early achievement skills, attention skills, and behavior problems. In G.J. Duncan and R.J. Murnane (Eds.), *Whither opportunity: Rising inequality, schools, and children's life chances* (pp. 47-70). New York: Russell Sage Foundation.

Duncan, G.J., and Murnane, R.J. (Eds.). (2011). *Whither opportunity: Rising inequality, schools, and children's life chances.* New York: Russell Sage Foundation.

Duncan, G., Dowsett, C., Classens, A., Magnuson, K., Huston, A., Klebanov, P., Pagani, L., et al. (2007). School readiness and later achievement. *Developmental Psychology, 43*(6), 1,428-1,446.

Duncker, K. (1945). On problem solving. *Psychological Monographs, 58*(5), whole no. 270.

Durlak, J.A., Weissberg, R.P., and Pachan, M. (2010). A meta-analysis of after-school programs that seek to promote personal and social skills in children and adolescents. *American Journal of Community Psychology, 45,* 294-309.

Durlak, J.A., Dymnicki, A.B., Taylor, R.D., Weissberg, R.P., and Schellinger, K.B. (2011). The impact of enhancing students' social and emotional learning: A meta-analysis of school-based universal interventions. *Child Development, 82*(1), 405-432.

Dweck, C.S., and Leggett, E.L. (1988). A social-cognitive approach to motivation and personality. *Psychological Review, 95,* 256-273.

Dweck, C.S., and Master, A. (2009). Self-theories and motivation: Students' beliefs about intelligence. In K.R. Wentzel and A. Wigfield (Eds.), *Handbook of motivation at school* (pp. 123-140). New York: Routledge.

Eisenberg, N., Sadovsky, A., Spinrad, T.L., Fabes, R.A., Losoya, S.H., Valiente, C., Reiser, M., Cumberland, A., and Shepard, S.A. (2005). The relations of problem behavior status to children's negative emotionality, effortful control, and impulsivity: Concurrent relations and prediction of change. *Developmental Psychology, 41*(1), 193-211.

Entwisle, D.R., Alexander, K.L., and Olson, L.S. (2005). First grade and educational attainment by age 22: A new story. *American Journal of Sociology, 110*(5), 1,458-1,502.

Ericsson, A. (2003). The search for general abilities and basic capabilities: Theoretical implications for the modifiability and complexity of mechanisms mediating expert performance. In R.J. Sternberg and E.L. Grigorenko (Eds.), *The psychology of abilities, competencies, and expertise* (pp. 93-125). New York: Cambridge University Press.

Ericsson, K.A., Charness, N., Feltovich, P.J., and Hoffman, R.R. (Eds.). (2006). *The Cambridge handbook of expertise and expert performance.* New York: Cambridge University Press.

Fantuzzo, J., Bulotsky, R., McDermott, P., Mosca, S., and Lutz, M.N. (2003). A multivariate analysis of emotional and behavioral adjustment and preschool educational outcomes. *School Psychology Review, 32*(2), 185-203.

Fawcett, H.P. (1938). *The nature of proof: A description and evaluation of certain procedures used in a senior high school to develop an understanding of the nature of proof.* New York: Teachers College, Columbia University.

Fennema, E., and Romberg, T.A. (Eds.). (1999). *Mathematics classrooms that promote understanding.* Mahwah, NJ: Erlbaum.

Feuerstein, R. (1980). *Instrumental enrichment: An intervention program for cognitive modifiability.* Baltimore, MD: University Park Press.

Finegold, D., and Notabartolo, A.S. (2010). *21st century competencies and their impact: An interdisciplinary literature review.* Paper commissioned for the NRC Project on Research on 21st Century Competencies: A Planning Process on behalf of the Hewlett Foundation. Available: http://www7.nationalacademies.org/bota/Finegold_Notabartolo_Impact_Paper.pdf [October 2011].

Fitzpatrick, R. (2001). The strange case of the transfer of training estimate. *The Industrial-Organizational Psychologist, 39*(2), 18-19.

Flay, B., Acock, A., Vuchinich, S., and Beets, M. (2006). *Progress report of the randomized trial of positive action in Hawaii: End of third year of intervention.* Unpublished manuscript, Oregon State University. Available: http://www.positiveaction.net/content/PDFs/research/3rd_Year_Progress_Report_with_Academic_and_Behavior_Results.pdf [April 2012].

Fonseca, B.A., and Chi, M.T.H. (2011). Instruction based on self-explanation. In R.E. Mayer and P.A. Alexander (Eds), *Handbook of research on learning and instruction* (pp. 296-321). New York: Routledge.

Ford, J.K., and Weissbein, D.A. (1997). Transfer of training: An update review and analysis. *Performance Improvement Quarterly, 10*, 22-41.

Freebody, P., and Luke, A. (1990). Literacies programs: Debates and demands in cultural context. *Prospect: Australian Journal of TESOL, 5*(7), 7-16.

Fuson, K.C., and Briars, D.J. (1990). Using a base-ten blocks learning/teaching approach for first- and second-grade place-value and multidigit addition and subtraction. *Journal for Research in Mathematics Education, 21*, 180-206.

Galton, F. (1883). *Inquiry into human faculty and its development.* London: Macmillan.

Garcia Bedolla, L. (2010). *21st century competencies and civic participation.* Paper prepared for the NRC Meeting on 21st Century Competencies: A Planning Process on Behalf of the Hewlett Foundation. Available: http://nrc51/xpedio/groups/dbasse/documents/webpage/056891.pdf [September 2011].

Gardner, J. (Ed.). (2006). *Assessment and learning.* London: Sage.

Garet, M.S., Porter, A.C., Desimone, L., Birman, B.F., and Yoon, K.S. (2001). What makes professional development effective? Results from a national sample of teachers. *American Educational Research Journal, 38*(4), 915-945.

Garrick, J., and Rhodes, C. (2000). *Research and knowledge at work: Perspectives, case studies, and innovative strategies.* London: Routledge.

Gathmann, C., and Schonberg, U. (2010). How general is human capital? A task-based approach. *Journal of Labor Economics, 28*(1), 1-49.

Gatta, M., Boushey, H., and Appelbaum, E. (2007). *High-touch and here to stay: Future skill demands in low-wage service occupations.* Paper presented at the NRC Workshop on Future Skill Demands. Available: http://www7.nationalacademies.org/cfe/Future_Skill_Demands_Mary_Gatta_Paper.pdf [September 2011].

Georgenson, D.L. (1982). The problem of transfer calls for partnership. *Training and Development Journal, 36*(10), 75-78.

Ghousseini, H. (2009). Designing opportunities to learn to lead classroom mathematics discussions in pre-service teacher education: Focusing on enactment. In D. Mewborn and H. Lee (Eds.), *Scholarly practices and inquiry in the preparation of mathematics teachers* (pp. 147-158). San Diego, CA: Association of Mathematics Teacher Educators.

Gijbels, D., Dochy, F., Van den Bossche, P., and Segers, M. (2005). Effects of problem-based learning: A meta-analysis from the angle of assessment. *Review of Educational Research, 75*(1), 27-61.

Glaser, R. (1992). Expert knowledge and processes of thinking. In D.F. Halpern (Ed.), *Enhancing thinking skills in the sciences and mathematics* (pp. 63-75). Hillsdale, NJ: Erlbaum.

Glaser, R., and Baxter, G. (1999). *Assessing active knowledge.* Paper presented at the CRESST Conference, Benchmarks for Accountability: Are We There Yet? UCLA, Los Angeles.

Goldberg, L.R. (1992). The development of markers for the big-five factor structure. *Psychological Assessment, 4,* 26-42.

Goldberg, L.R. (1993). The structure of phenotypic personality traits. *American Psychologist, 48,* 26-34.

Goldberg, L.R., Sweeney, D., Merenda, P.F., and Hughes, J.E. (1998). Demographic variables and personality: The effects of gender, age, education, and ethnic/racial status on self-descriptions of personality attributes. *Personality and Individual Differences, 24*(3), 393-403.

Goldin, C.D. (1991). The role of World War II in the rise of women's employment. *American Economic Review, 81*(4), 741-756.

Gonzaga, G.C., Campos, B., and Bradbury, T. (2007). Similarity, convergence, and relationship satisfaction in dating and married couples. *Journal of Personality and Social Psychology, 93*(1), 34-48.

Good, T.L., Grouws, D.A., and Ebmeier, H. (1983). *Active mathematics teaching.* New York: Longman.

Goos, M., Manning, M., and Salomons, A. (2009). The polarization of the European labor market. *American Economic Review Papers and Proceedings, 99*(2), 58-63. Available: http://www.econ.kuleuven.be/public/n06022/aerpp09.pdf [September 2011].

Gottman, J.M. (1994). *What predicts divorce? The relationship between marital processes and marital outcomes.* Hillsdale, NJ: Erlbaum.

Graesser, A.C., and Person, N.K. (1994). Question asking during learning. *American Educational Research Journal, 31,* 104-137.

Graesser, A., Hakel, M., and Halpern, D.F. (2007). Life long learning at work and at home. *APS Observer, 20,* 17-21.

Graesser, A.C., D'Mello, S., and Cade, W. (2011). Instruction based on tutoring. In R.E. Mayer and P.A. Alexander (Eds.), *Handbook of research on learning and instruction* (pp. 408-426). New York: Routledge.

Graham, S. (2006). Strategy instruction and the teaching of writing: A meta-analysis. In C. MacArthur, S. Graham, and J. Fitzgerald (Eds). *Handbook of writing research* (pp. 187-207). New York: Guilford.

Graham, S., and Williams, C. (2009). An attributional approach to motivation in school. In K.R. Wentzel and A. Wigfield (Eds.), *Handbook of motivation at school* (pp. 11-34). New York: Routledge.

Greeno, J.G., Pearson, P.D., and Schoenfeld, A.H. (1996). *Implications for NAEP of research on learning and cognition. Report of a study commissioned by the National Academy of Education.* Panel on the NAEP Trial State Assessment, Conducted by the Institute for Research on Learning. Stanford, CA: National Academy of Education.

Griffin, S. (2005). Fostering the development of whole-number sense: Teaching mathematics in the primary grades. In National Research Council, M.S. Donovan, and J.D. Bransford (Eds.), *How students learn: History, mathematics and science in the classroom* (pp. 257-308). Washington, DC: The National Academies Press.

Grissmer, D., Grimm, K.J., Aiyer, S.M., Murrah, W.M., and Steele, J.S. (2010). Fine motor skills and early comprehension of the world: Two new school readiness indicators. *Developmental Psychology, 46*(5), 1,008-1,017.

Grossman, R., and Salas, E. (2011). The transfer of training: What really matters. *International Journal of Training and Development, 15*(2), 103-120.

Grouws, D.A., Smith, M.S., and Sztajn, P. (2004). The preparation and teaching practices of United States mathematics teachers: Grades 4 and 8. In P. Kloosterman and F.K. Lester (Eds.), *Results and interpretations of the 1990-2000 mathematics assessments of the National Assessment of Educational Progress* (pp. 221-267). Reston, VA: National Council of Teachers of Mathematics.

Guthrie, J., Van Meter, P., McCann, A., Wigfield, A., Bennett, L., Poundstone, C., Rice, M. Faibisch, F., Hunt, B., and Mitchell, A. (1996). Growth of literacy engagement: Changes in motivations and strategies during concept-oriented reading instruction. *Reading Research Quarterly, 31*, 306-332.

Guthrie, J., Wigfield, A., Barbosa, P., Perencevich, K., Taboada, A., Davis, M., Scafiddi, N., and Tonks, S. (2004). Increasing reading comprehension and engagement through concept-oriented reading instruction. *Journal of Educational Research, 96*, 403-423.

Guthrie, J., McRae, A., and Klauda, S. (2007). Contributions of concept-oriented reading instruction to knowledge about interventions for motivations in reading. *Educational Psychologist, 42*, 237-250.

Guthrie, J., Wigfield, A., and You, W. (2012). Instructional contexts for engagement and achievement in reading. In S. Christensen, C. Wylie, and A. Reschly (Eds.), *Handbook of research on student engagement* (part 4, pp. 601-634). New York: Springer.

Halford, W.K., Markman, H.J., Kling, G.H., and Stanley, S.M. (2003). Best practices in couple relationship education. *Journal of Marital and Family Therapy, 29*, 385-406.

Handel, M.J. (2010). *What do people do at work: A profile of U.S. jobs from the survey of workplace skills, technology, and management practices (STAMP)*. Unpublished. Data Tables. Available at: http://www.cedefop.europa.eu/EN/Files/4217-att1-9._A_profile_of_US_jobs_from_the_STAMP_survey_Michael_J._Handel.pdf [September 2011].

Hanushek, E.A., and Woessmann, L. (2008). The role of cognitive skills in economic development. *Journal of Economic Literature, 46*(3), 607-668.

Harlen, W. (2006). *Teaching, learning, and assessing science 5-12* (4th ed.). London: Sage.

Hatano, G. (1990). The nature of everyday science: A brief introduction. *British Journal of Developmental Psychology, 8*, 245-250.

Hatano, G., and Inagaki, K. (1986). Two courses of expertise. In H.A.H. Stevenson, H. Azuma, and K. Hakuta (Eds.), *Child development and education in Japan* (pp. 262-272). New York: Freeman.

Hattie, J., and Gin, M. (2011). Instruction based on feedback. In R.E. Mayer and P.A. Alexander (Eds.), *Handbook of research on learning and instruction* (pp. 249-271). New York: Routledge.

Hauser, R.M., and Palloni, A. (2011). Adolescent IQ and survival in the Wisconsin longitudinal study. *The Journals of Gerontology, Series B: Psychological Sciences and Social Sciences, 66B*(Sl), i90-i100.

Heckman, J.J., and Rubinstein, Y. (2001). The importance of noncognitive skills: Lessons from the GED testing program. *American Economic Review, 91*(2), 145-149.

Heckman, J., Stixrud, J., and Urzua, S. (2006). The effects of cognitive and noncognitive abilities on labor market outcomes and social behavior. *Journal of Labor Economics 24*(3), 411-482.

Henningsen, M., and Stein, M.K. (1997). Mathematical tasks and student cognition: Classroom-based factors that support and inhibit high-level mathematical thinking and reasoning. *Journal for Research in Mathematics Education, 29*, 514-549.

Heritage, M. (2010). *Formative assessment: Making it happen in the classroom.* Corwin Press: Thousand Oaks, CA.

Heritage, M., Kim, J., Vendlinski, T., and Herman, J. (2009). From evidence to action: A seamless process in formative assessment? *Educational Measurement: Issues and Practice, 28*(3), 24-31.

Herman, J.L. (2008). Accountability and assessment in the service of learning: Is public interest in K-12 education being served? In L. Shepard and K. Ryan (Eds.), *The future of test-based educational accountability* (pp. 211-232). New York: Taylor and Francis.

Herman, J.L. (2010a). *Coherence: Key to next generation assessment success.* Los Angeles, CA: CRESST. Available: http://www.cse.ucla.edu/products/policy/coherence_v6.pdf [April 2012].

Herman, J.L. (2010b). Impact of assessment on classroom practice. In P. Peterson, E. Baker, and B. McGraw (Eds.), *International encyclopedia of education* (3rd ed., pp. 69-74). London: Elsevier.

Herman, J.L., Osmundson, E., and Silver, D. (2010). *Capturing quality in formative assessment practice: Measurement challenges.* CRESST Technical Report #770. Los Angeles, CA: CRESST.

Hernstein, R.J., Nickerson, R.S., Sanchez, M., and Swets, J.A. (1986). Teaching thinking skills. *American Psychologist, 41*, 1,279-1,289.

Herrenkohl, L.R., Palincsar, A.S., DeWater, L.S., and Kawasaki, K. (1999). Developing scientific communities in classrooms: A sociocognitive approach. *The Journal of the Learning Sciences, 8*(3&4), 451-493.

Hiebert, J., and Carpenter, T.P. (1992). Learning and teaching with understanding. In D.A. Grouws (Ed.), *Handbook of research on mathematics teaching and learning* (pp. 65-97). New York: Macmillan.

Hiebert, J., and Grouws, D.A. (2007). The effects of classroom mathematics teaching on students' learning. In F.K. Lester (Ed.), *Second handbook of research on mathematics teaching and learning* (pp. 371-404). Charlotte, NC: Information Age.

Hiebert, J., and Wearne, D. (1993). Instructional tasks, classroom discourse, and students' learning in second-grade arithmetic. *American Educational Research Journal, 30*, 393-425.

Hiebert, J., Carpenter, T.P., Fennema, E., Fuson, K., Human, P., Murray, H., et al. (1996). Problem solving as a basis for reform in curriculum and instruction: The case of mathematics. *Educational Researcher, 25*(4), 12-21.

Hiebert, J., Stigler, J., Jacobs, J., Givvin, K., Garnier, H., Smith, M., et al. (2005). Mathematics teaching in the United States today (and tomorrow): Results from the TIMSS 1999 video study. *Educational Evaluation and Policy Analysis, 27*, 111-132.

Horn, J.L. (1970). Organization of data on life-span development of human abilities. In L.R. Goulet and P. B. Baltes (Eds.). *Life-span developmental psychology: Research and theory.* New York: Academic Press.

Hoyle, R.H., and Davisson, E.K. (2011). *Assessment of self-regulation and related constructs: Prospects and challenges.* Paper prepared for the NRC Workshop on Assessment of 21st Century Skills. Available: http://www7.nationalacademies.org/bota/21st_Century_Workshop_Hoyle_Paper.pdf [October 2011].

Hunt, E. (2011). *Human intelligence.* New York: Cambridge University Press.

Jarvis, C.B., MacKenzie, S.B., and Podsakoff, P.M. (2003). A critical review of construct indicators and measurement model misspecification in marketing and consumer research.
Journal of Consumer Research, 30, 199-218.

Jockin, V., McGue, M., and Lykken, D.T. (1996). Personality and divorce: A genetic analysis.
Journal of Personality and Social Psychology, 71, 288-299.

Johnson, C.I., and Mayer, R.E. (2009). A testing effect in multimedia learning. *Journal of
Educational Psychology, 101,* 621-629.

Judd, C.H. (1908). The relation of special training to general intelligence. *Educational Review
36,* 28-42.

Judge, T.A., and Bono, J.E. (2001). A rose by any other name: Are self-esteem, generalized
self-efficacy, neuroticism, and locus of control indicators of a common construct? In B.W.
Roberts and R. Hogan (Eds.), *Personality psychology in the workplace* (pp. 93-118).
Washington, DC: American Psychological Association.

Judge, T.A., Erez, A., Bono, J.E., and Thoreson, J.E. (2002). Are measures of self-esteem,
neuroticism, locus of control, and generalized self-efficacy indicators of a common core
construct? *Journal of Personality and Social Psychology, 83*(3), 693-710.

Kahne, J., and Sporte, S.E. (2008). Developing citizens: the impact of civic learning opportunities on students: Commitment to civic participation. *American Educational Research
Journal, 45*(3), 738-766.

Kamil, M., Mosenthal, P., Pearson, P.D., and Barr, R. (Eds.). (2000). *Handbook of reading
research, Vol 111.* Hillsdale, NJ: Erlbaum.

Kamil, M.L., Pearson, P.D., Moje, E., and Afflerbach, P. (Eds.). (2011). *Handbook of reading
research, Vol IV.* London: Routledge.

Karmiloff-Smith, A. (1979, reprinted 1981). *A functional approach to child language.* Cambridge: Cambridge University Press.

Karney, B.R., and Bradbury, T.N. (1995). The longitudinal course of marital quality and
stability: A review of theory, method and research. *Psychological Bulletin, 118,* 3-34.

Karney, B.R., and Bradbury, T.N. (1997). Neuroticism, marital interaction, and the trajectory
of marital satisfaction. *Journal of Personality and Social Psychology, 72,* 1,075-1,092.

Karney, B.R., Beckett, M., Collins, R., and Shaw, R. (2007). *Adolescent romantic relationships
as precursors of healthy adult marriages: A review of theory, research, and programs.*
Santa Monica, CA: RAND.

Katona, G. (1940). *Organizing and memorizing: Studies in the psychology of learning and
teaching.* New York: Columbia University Press.

Katona, G. (1942). *War without inflation, the psychological approach to problems of war
economy.* New York: Columbia University Press.

Kelley, T.A. (1927). *Interpretation of educational measurements.* Yonkers, NY: World.

Kingston, N., and Nash, B. (2011). Formative assessment: A meta-analysis and a call for
research. *Educational Measurement: Issues and Practice, 30,* 28-37.

Kintsch, W. (1998). *Comprehension: A paradigm for cognition.* London: Cambridge University Press.

Kirkpatrick, D.L., and Kirkpatrick, J.D. (2006). *Evaluating training programs: The four levels*
(3rd ed.). San Francisco: Berrett-Koehler.

Kirschner, P., Sweller, J., and Clark, R. (2006). Why minimal guidance during instruction does
not work: An analysis of the failure of constructivist, discovery, problem-based, experi-
ential, and inquiry-based teaching. *Educational Psychologist, 41,* 75-86.

Klahr, D., and Nigam, M. (2004). The equivalence of learning paths in early science instruction: Effects of direct instruction and discovery learning. *Psychological Science, 15*(10),
661-667.

Klahr, D., and Simon, H.A. (1999). Studies of scientific discovery: Complementary approaches
and convergent findings. *Psychological Bulletin, 125,* 524-543.

Kolodner, J.L., Camp, P.J., Crismond, D., Fasse, B.B., Gray, J., Holbrook, J., Puntambekar, S., and Ryan, M. (2003). Problem-based learning meets case-based reasoning in the middle-school science classroom: Putting Learning by Design™ into practice. *The Journal of the Learning Sciences, 12*(4), 495-547.

Krajcik, J., Slotta, J., McNeill, K.L., and Reiser, B. (2008). Designing learning environments to support students constructing coherent understandings. In Y. Kali, M.C. Linn, and J.E. Roseman (Eds.), *Designing coherent science education: Implications of curriculum, instruction, and policy* (pp. 39-64). New York: Teachers College Press.

Kubitskey, B., and Fishman, B.J. (2006). A role for professional development in sustainability: Linking the written curriculum to enactment. In S.A. Barab, K.E. Hay, and D.T. Hickey, (Eds.), *Proceedings of the 7th International Conference of the Learning Sciences, 1*(363-369). Mahwah, NJ: Erlbaum.

Lacey, T.A., and Wright, B. (2009). Occupational employment projections to 2018. *Monthly labor review* (November), 82-123. Available: http://www.bls.gov/opub/mlr/2009/11/art5full.pdf [September 2011].

Lampert, M. (2010). Learning teaching in, from, and for practice: What do we mean? *Journal of Teacher Education, 61*(1-2).

Lave, J. (1988). *Cognition in practice: Mind, mathematics, and culture in everyday life.* Cambridge, England: Cambridge University Press.

Lave, J., and Wenger, E. (1991). *Situated learning: Legitimate peripheral participation.* Cambridge, England: Cambridge University Press.

Lesgold, A.M. (2001). The nature and methods of learning by doing. *American Psychologist, 56,* 964-973.

Leuven, E., and Oosterbeek, H. (1997). Demand and supply of work-related training: Evidence from four countries. *Research in Labor Economics, 18,* 303-330.

Levy, F., and Murnane, R.J. (2004). The new division of labor: How computers are creating the next job market. Princeton, NJ: Princeton University Press.

Lindqvist, E., and Vestman, R. (2011). The labor market returns to cognitive and noncognitive ability: Evidence from the Swedish enlistment. *American Economic Journal: Applied Economics, 3,* 101-128.

Linn, M., Davis, E., and Bell, P. (Eds.). (2004). *Internet environments for science education.* Mahwah, NJ: Erlbaum.

Linn, R.L., Baker, E.L., and Dunbar, S.B. (1991). Complex, performance-based assessment: Expectations and validation criteria. *Educational Researcher, 20*(8), 15-21.

Linn, R., Burton, E., DeStefano, L., and Hanson, M. (1995). *Generalizability of New Standards Project 1993 pilot study tasks in mathematics CSE Technical Report 392.* Los Angeles, CA: CRESST.

Lochner, L. (2011). *Non-production benefits of education: Crime, health, & good citizenship.* Working Paper 167222. Cambridge, MA: National Bureau of Economic Research.

Lopez, M.H., Levine, P., Both, D., Kiesa, A., Kirby, E., and Marcelo, K. (2006). *The 2006 civic and political health of the nation: A detailed look at how youth participate in politics and communities.* College Park, MD: Center for Information and Research on Civic Learning and Engagement.

Luke, A., and Freebody, P. (1997). The social practices of reading. In S. Muspratt, A. Luke, and P. Freebody (Eds.), *Constructing critical literacies: Teaching and learning textual practices* (pp. 185-226). St Leonards, New South Wales: Allen and Unwin.

Lynch, L. (1992). Private sector training and earnings. *American Economic Review, 82*(1), 299-312.

Lynch, L.M. (Ed.). (1994). *Training and the private sector: International comparisons.* Chicago: University of Chicago Press, National Bureau of Economic Research.

Maehr, M.L., and Zusho, A. (2009). Achievement goal theory: The past, present, and future. In K.R. Wentzel and A. Wigfield (Eds.), *Handbook of motivation at school* (pp. 77-104). New York: Routledge.

Magnuson, K., and Duncan, G. (2004). Parent- vs. child-based intervention strategies for promoting children's well-being. In A. Kalil and T. De Leire (Eds.), *Family investments in children: Resources and behaviors that promote success* (pp. 209-235). Mahwah, NJ: Erlbaum.

Mansfield, R.S., Busse, T.V., and Krepelka, E.J. (1978). The effectiveness of creativity training. *Review of Educational Research, 48,* 517-536.

Marche, S. (2012). Is Facebook making us lonely? *The Atlantic,* May.

Mayer, R.E. (1995). *Conflict management: The courage to confront* (2nd ed.). Columbus, OH: Battelle Press.

Mayer, R.E. (2004). Should there be a three-strikes rule against pure discovery learning? The case for guided methods of instruction. *American Psychologist, 59,* 14-19.

Mayer, R.E. (2008). *Learning and instruction* (2nd ed.). Upper Saddle River, NJ: Pearson.

Mayer, R.E. (2009). *Multimedia learning* (2nd ed.). New York: Cambridge University Press.

Mayer, R.E. (2010). *Applying the science of learning.* Upper Saddle River, NJ: Pearson.

Mayer, R.E. (2011a). Instruction based on visualizations. In R.E. Mayer and P.A. Alexander (Eds.), *Handbook of research on learning and instruction* (pp. 427-445). New York: Routledge.

Mayer, R.E. (2011b). Intelligence and achievement. In R.J. Sternberg and S.B. Kaufman (Eds.), *The Cambridge handbook of intelligence* (pp. 738-747). New York: Cambridge University Press.

Mayer, R.E., and Alexander, P.A. (Eds.). (2011). *Handbook of research on learning and instruction.* New York: Routledge.

Mayer, R.E., and Wittrock, M.C. (1996). Problem-solving transfer. In D.C. Berliner and R.C. Calfee (Eds.), *Handbook of educational psychology* (pp. 47-62). New York: Macmillan.

Mayer, R.E., and Wittrock, M.C. (2006). Problem solving. In P.A. Alexander and P.H. Winne (Eds.), *Handbook of educational psychology* (2nd ed., pp. 287-304). Mahwah, NJ: Erlbaum.

Mayer, R.E., Lanton, B., Duran, R., and Schustrack, M. (1999). *Using new information technologies in the creation of sustainable afterschool literacy activities: Evaluation of cognitive outcomes.* Final report to the Andrew W. Mellon Foundation. Available: http://www.psych.ucsb.edu/~mayer/fifth_dim_website/HTML/res_reports/final_report.html [September 2011].

Mayer, R.E., Heiser, J., and Lonn, S. (2001). Cognitive constraints on multimedia learning: When presenting more material results in less understanding. *Journal of Educational Psychology, 93,* 187-198.

McArdle, J.J., Hamagami, F., Meredith, W., and Bradway, K.P. (2000). Modeling the dynamic hypotheses of gf-gc theory using longitudinal life-span data. *Learning and Individual Differences, 12*(1), 53-79.

McCrae, R.R., and Costa, P.T. (1987). Validation of the five-factor model of personality across instruments and observers. *Journal of Personality and Social Psychology, 52,* 81-90.

McGue, M., and Lykken, D.T. (1992). Genetic influence on risk of divorce. *Psychological Science, 3,* 368-373.

McLeod, D.B. (1992). Research on affect in mathematics education: A reconceptualization. In D.A. Grouws (Ed.), *Handbook of research on mathematics teaching and learning* (pp. 575-596). New York: Macmillan.

McLeod, D.B., and Adams, V.M. (Eds.). (1989). *Affect and mathematical problem solving: A new perspective.* New York, NY: Springer-Verlag.

Mikelson, K.S., and Nightingale, D.S. (2004). *Estimating public and private expenditures on occupational training in the United States.* Prepared for the U.S. Department of Labor Employment and Training Administration under Contract No. AF-12536-02-30. Available: http://wdr.doleta.gov/research/FullText_Documents/Estimating%20Public%20 and%20Private%20Expenditures%20on%20Occupational%20Training%20in%20 the%20United%20States.pdf [January 2012].

Mincer, J. (1974). *Schooling, experience, & earnings.* New York: Columbia University Press.

Mischel, W. (1968). *Personality and assessment.* New York: Wiley.

Mischel, W., Shoda, Y., and Peake, P.K. (1988). The nature of adolescent competencies predicted by preschool delay of gratification. *Journal of Personality and Social Psychology, 54,* 687-696.

Moffitt, T.E. (1993). Adolescence-limited and life-course-persistent antisocial behavior: A developmental taxonomy. *Psychological Review, 100,* 674-701.

Moffitt, T.E., Arseneault, L., Belsky, D., Dickson, N., Hancox, R.J., et al. (2011). A gradient of childhood self-control predicts health, wealth, and public safety. *Proceedings of the National Academy of Sciences, 108*(7), 2,693-2,698. Available: http://www.pnas.org/content/108/7/2693.full.pdf+html?sid=fa66ea3e-274e-41f0-b586-8e-671f9c150d [April 2012].

Moje, E.B. (2008). Foregrounding the disciplines in secondary literacy teaching and learning: A call for change. *Journal of Adolescent and Adult Literacy, 52*(2), 96-107.

Monk, D.H., and King, J. (1994). Multi-level teacher resource effects on pupil performance in secondary mathematics and science: The role of teacher subject matter preparation in contemporary policy issues: Choices and consequences in education. In R. Ehrenberg (Ed.), *Contemporary policy issues: Choices and consequences in education* (pp. 29-58). Ithaca, NY: ILR Press.

Moreno, R., and Mayer, R.E. (1999). Multimedia-supported metaphors for meaning making in mathematics. *Cognition & Instruction, 17,* 215-248.

Moreno, R., and Mayer, R.E. (2005). Role of guidance, reflection, and interactivity in an agent-based multimedia game. *Journal of Educational Psychology, 97,* 117-128.

Moretti, E. (2004). Workers' education, spillovers, and productivity: Evidence from plant-level production functions. *American Economic Review, 94*(3), 656-690.

Munns, G., and Woodward, H. (2006). Student engagement and student self-assessment: The REAL framework. *Assessment in Education: Principles, Policy & Practice, 13*(2), 193-213.

Murnane, R.J., Willett, J.B., and Levy, F. (1995). The growing importance of cognitive skills in wage determination. *The Review of Economics and Statistics, 77*(2), 251-266.

Murphy, P.K., Wilkinson, I.A.G., Soter, A.O., Hennessey, M.N., and Alexander, J.F. (2009). Examining the effects of classroom discussion on students' comprehension of text: A meta-analysis. *Journal of Educational Psychology, 101,* 740-764.

National Council of Teachers of Mathematics. (1989). *Curriculum and evaluation standards for school mathematics.* Reston, VA: Author.

National Council of Teachers of Mathematics. (1991). *Professional standards for teaching mathematics.* Reston, VA: Author.

National Council of Teachers of Mathematics. (2000). *Principles and standards for school mathematics.* Reston, VA: Author.

National Institute of Child Health and Human Development. (2000). Report of the National Reading Panel. *Teaching children to read: An evidence-based assessment of the scientific research literature on reading and its implications for reading instruction* (NIH Publication No. 00-4769). Washington, DC: U.S. Government Printing Office.

National Research Council. (1989). *Fairness in employment testing: Validity generalization; minority issues, and the general aptitude test battery.* J.A. Hartigan and A.K. Wigdor (Eds.). Committee on the General Aptitude Test Battery, Commission on Behavioral and Social Sciences and Education. Washington, DC: National Academy Press.

National Research Council. (1996). *National science education standards.* National Committee on Science Education Standards and Assessment. Center for Science, Mathematics, and Engineering Education. Washington, DC: National Academy Press.

National Research Council. (1998). *Preventing reading difficulties in young children.* C.E. Snow, M.S. Burns, and P. Griffin (Eds.), Committee on the Prevention of Reading Difficulties in Young Children. Commission on Behavioral and Social Sciences and Education. Washington, DC: National Academy Press.

National Research Council. (1999). *How people learn: Brain, mind, experience, and school.* J.D. Bransford, A.L. Brown, and R.R. Cocking (Eds.), Committee on Developments in the Science of Learning. Commission on Behavioral and Social Sciences and Education. Washington, DC: National Academy Press.

National Research Council. (2000). *Forecasting demand and supply of doctoral scientists and engineers: Report of a workshop on methodology.* Office of Scientific and Engineering Personnel, Policy and Global Affairs. Washington, DC: National Academy Press.

National Research Council. (2001). *Knowing what students know: The science and design of educational assessment.* J.W. Pellegrino, N. Chudowsky, and R. Glaser (Eds.), Committee on the Foundations of Assessment. Board on Testing and Assessment, Center for Education. Division of Behavioral and Social Sciences and Education. Washington, DC: National Academy Press.

National Research Council. (2005). *How students learn: History, mathematics, and science in the classroom.* M.S. Donovan and J.D. Bransford (Eds.), Committee on *How People Learn*, A Targeted Report for Teachers. Division of Behavioral and Social Sciences and Education. Washington, DC: The National Academies Press.

National Research Council. (2006). *America's lab report: Investigations in high school science.* S.R. Singer, M.L. Hilton, and H.A. Schweingruber (Eds.), Committee on High School Science Laboratories: Role and Vision. Board on Science Education, Center for Education. Division of Behavioral and Social Sciences and Education. Washington, DC: The National Academies Press.

National Research Council. (2007). *Taking science to school: Learning and teaching science in grades K-8.* R.A. Duschl, H.A. Schweingruber, and A.W. Shouse (Eds.), Committee on Science Learning, Kindergarten through Eighth Grade. Board on Science Education, Center for Education. Division of Behavioral and Social Sciences and Education. Washington, DC: The National Academies Press.

National Research Council. (2008). *Research on future skill demands: A workshop summary.* M.L. Hilton, Rapporteur, Planning Committee on Research Evidence Related to Future Skill Demands. Center for Education. Division of Behavioral and Social Sciences and Education. Washington, DC: The National Academies Press.

National Research Council. (2009a). *Learning science in informal environments: People, places and pursuits.* P. Bell, B. Lewenstein, A.W. Shouse, and M.A. Feder (Eds.), Committee on Learning Science in Informal Environments. Board on Science Education, Center for Education. Division of Behavioral and Social Sciences and Education. Washington, DC: The National Academies Press.

National Research Council. (2009b). *Mathematics learning in early childhood: Paths toward excellence and equity.* C.T. Cross, T.A. Woods, and H. Schweingruber (Eds.), Committee on Early Childhood Mathematics. Center for Education. Division of Behavioral and Social Sciences and Education. Washington, DC: The National Academies Press.

National Research Council. (2010). *Exploring the intersection of science education and 21st century skills: A workshop summary.* M. Hilton, Rapporteur. Board on Science Education, Center for Education, Division of Behavioral and Social Sciences and Education. Washington, DC: The National Academies Press.

National Research Council. (2011a). *Assessing 21st century skills: Summary of a workshop.* J.A. Koenig, Rapporteur. Committee on the Assessment of 21st Century Skills. Board on Testing and Assessment, Division of Behavioral and Social Sciences and Education. Washington, DC: The National Academies Press.

National Research Council. (2011b). *Learning science through computer games and simulations.* Committee on Science Learning: Computer Games, Simulations, and Education. M.A. Honey and M.L. Hilton (Eds.). Board on Science Education, Division of Behavioral and Social Sciences and Education. Washington, DC: The National Academies Press.

National Research Council. (2012). *A framework for K-12 science education: Practices, crosscutting concepts, and core ideas.* Committee on a Conceptual Framework for New K-12 Science Education Standards. Board on Science Education, Division of Behavioral and Social Sciences and Education. Washington, DC: The National Academies Press.

National Research Council and Institute of Medicine. (2004). *Engaging schools: Fostering high school students' motivation to learn.* Committee on Increasing High School Students' Engagement and Motivation to Learn. Board on Children, Youth, and Families, Division of Behavioral and Social Sciences and Education. Washington, DC: The National Academies Press.

National Research Council and Institute of Medicine. (2009). *Preventing mental, emotional, and behavioral disorders among young people: Progress and possibilities.* Committee on the Prevention of Mental Disorders and Substance Abuse Among Children, Youth, and Young Adults: Research Advances and Promising Interventions. M.E. O'Connell, T. Boat, and K.E. Warner (Eds.). Board on Children, Youth, and Families, Division of Behavioral and Social Sciences and Education. Washington, DC: The National Academies Press.

Neal, D., and Johnson, W. (1996). The role of premarket factors in black-white wage differences. *The Journal of Political Economy, 104*(5), 869-895.

Nelson, R.R., and Phelps, E.S. (1966). Investment in humans, technological diffusion, and economic growth. *The American Economic Review, 56*(1/2), 69-75.

Nelson, T.O. (1996). Consciousness and metacognition. *American Psychologist, 51,* 102-116.

Newell, A. (1990). *Unified theories of cognition.* Cambridge, MA: Harvard University Press.

Newell, A., and Simon, H.A. (1972). *Human problem solving.* Englewood Cliffs, NJ: Prentice-Hall.

Newman, D.L., Caspi, A., Moffitt, T.E., and Silva, P.A. (1997). Antecedents of adult interpersonal functioning: Effects of individual differences in age 3 temperament. *Developmental Psychology, 33,* 206-217.

Newman, R. (2008). Adaptive and nonadaptive help seeking with peer harassment: An integrative perspective of coping and self-regulation. *Educational Psychologist, 43,* 1-15.

Newmann, F.M., and Associates. (1996). *Authentic achievement: Restructuring schools for intellectual quality.* San Francisco, CA: Jossey-Bass

Nickerson, R.S. (2011). Developing intelligence through instruction. In R.J. Sternberg and S.B. Kaufman (Eds.), *The Cambridge handbook of intelligence* (pp. 107-129). New York: Cambridge University Press.

Niemi, R.G., and J. Junn. (1998). *Civic education.* New Haven, CT: Yale University Press.

Ochs, E., Jacoby, S., and Gonzales, P. (1994). Interpretative journeys: How physicists talk and travel through graphic space. *Configurations 2*(1), 151-172.

OECD. (2005). *Definition and selection of key competencies: Executive summary.* Paris: Author. Available: http://www.oecd.org/dataoecd/47/61/35070367.pdf [June 2012].

OECD. (2010). *PISA 2009 results: What students know and can do: Student performance in reading, mathematics, and science.* Paris: Author. Available: http://www.oecd.org/document/61/0,3746,en_32252351_32235731_46567613_1_1_1_1,00.html [January 2012].

Olds, D., Sadler, L., and Kitzman, H. (2007). Programs for parents of infants and toddlers: Recent evidence from a randomized trial. *Journal of Child Psychology and Psychiatry, 48,* 355-391.

Olton, R.M., and Crutchfield, R.S. (1969). Developing the skills of productive thinking. In P. Mussen, J. Langer, and M.V. Covington (Eds.), *New directions in developmental psychology.* New York: Holt, Reinehart, and Winston.

Oreopoulos, P., and Salvanes, K.G. (2011). Priceless: The nonpecuniary benefits of schooling. *Journal of Economic Perspectives, 25*(1), 159-184.

Oswald, F.L., Schmitt, N., Kim, B.H., Ramsay, L.J., and Gillespie, M.A. (2004). Developing a biodata measure and situational judgment inventory as predictors of college student performance. *Journal of Applied Psychology, 89,* 187-207.

Palincsar, A., and Brown, A. (1984). Reciprocal teaching of comprehension-fostering and comprehension-monitoring activities. *Cognition and Instruction, 1,* 117-175.

Partnership for 21st Century Skills. (2010). *21st century readiness for every student: A policymaker's guide.* Tucson, AZ: Author. Available: http://www.p21.org/documents/policymakersguide_final.pdf [April 2011].

Partnership for 21st Century Skills. (2011). *Overview of state leadership initiative.* Available: http://www.p21.org/index.php?option=com_content&task=view&id=505&Itemid=189 [April 2011].

Pashler, H., Cepeda, J.T., Wixted, J.T., and Rohrer, D. (2005).When does feedback facilitate learning of words? *Journal of Experimental Psychology: Learning, Memory, and Cognition, 31,* 3-8.

Pashler, H., Bain, P.M., Bottge, B.A., Graesser, A., Koedinger, K., McDaniel, M., et al. (2007). *Organizing instruction and study to improve student learning. IES practice guide* (NCER 2007-2004). Washington, DC: National Center for Education Research.

Patry, J.L. (2011). Methodological consequences of situation specificity: Biases in assessments. *Frontiers in Psychology, 2*(18). Available: http://www.frontiersin.org/Quantitative_Psychology_and_Measurement/10.3389/fpsyg.2011.00018/full [June 2012].

Paunonen, S.V., and Ashton, M.C. (2001). Big five factors and facets and the prediction of behavior. *Journal of Personality and Social Psychology, 81*(3), 524-539.

Pearson, P.D., Barr, R., Kamil, M.L., and Mosenthal, P. (Eds.). (1984). *Handbook of reading research.* New York: Longman.

Peterson, N.G., Mumford, M.D., Borman, W.C., Jeanneret, P.R., Fleishman, E.A., and Levin, K.Y. (Eds.). (1997). *O*NET final technical report* (vols. 1-3). Salt Lake City: Utah Department of Employment Security, on behalf of the U.S. Department of Labor Employment and Training Administration.

Peterson, N.G., Mumford, M.D., Borman, W.C., Jeanneret, P.R, and Fleishman, E.A. (Eds.). (1999). *An occupational information system for the 21st century: The development of O*NET.* Washington, DC: American Psychological Association.

Piaget, J. (1963). *The origins of intelligence in children.* New York: W.W. Norton. [Originally published in French, 1936.]

Pianta, R., and Stuhlman, M. (2004). Teacher-child relationships and children's success in the first years of school. *School Psychology Review, 33*(3), 444-458.

Pintrich, P. (2000). The role of goal orientation in self-regulated learning. In M. Boekaerts, P. Pintrich, and M. Zeidner (Eds.), *Handbook of self-regulation* (pp. 451-502). San Diego, CA: Academic Press.

Pintrich, P. (2004). A conceptual framework for assessing motivation and self-regulated learning in college students. *Educational Psychology Review, 16*, 385-407.

Plass, J., Moreno, R., and Brünken, R. (Eds.). (2010). *Cognitive load theory.* New York: Cambridge University Press.

Polanyi, M. (1958). *Personal knowledge: Towards a post-critical philosophy.* Chicago: University of Chicago Press.

Poropat, A.E. (2009). A meta-analysis of the five-factor model of personality and academic performance. *Psychological Bulletin, 135*(2), 322-338. Available: http://edci6300intro research.pbworks.com/f/poropat+2009+metaanalysis+FFM.pdf [July 2011].

Porter, A. (1989). A curriculum out of balance: The case of elementary school mathematics. *Educational Researcher, 18*(5), 9-15.

Pressley, M., and Woloshyn, V. (1995). *Cognitive strategy instruction.* Cambridge, MA: Brookline Books.

Psacharopoulos, G., and Patrinos, H. (2004). Returns to investment in education: A further update. *Education Economics, 12*(2), 111-134.

Putnam, R.D. (2000). *Bowling alone: The collapse and revival of American community.* New York: Simon and Schuster.

Quellmalz, E.S., Timms, M.J., and Buckley, B.C. (2010). The promise of simulation-based science assessment: The Calipers Project. *International Journal of Learning Technologies, 5*(3), 243-263.

Ramani, G.B., and Siegler, R.S. (2008). Promoting broad and stable inprovements in low-income children's numerical knowledge through playing number board games. *Child Development, 79*, 375-394.

Ramani, G.B., and Siegler, R.S. (2011). Reducing the gap in numerical knowledge between low- and middle-income preschoolers. *Journal of Applied Developmental Psychology, 32*, 146-159.

Raver, C.C. (2004). Placing emotional self-regulation in sociocultural and socioeconomic contexts. *Child Development, 75*(2), 346-353.

Raver, C.C., Smith-Donald, R., Hayes, T., and Jones, S.M. (2005). *Self-regulation across differing risk and sociocultural contexts: Preliminary findings from the Chicago school readiness project.* Biennial meeting of the Society for Research in Child Development, Atlanta, GA.

Renkl, A. (2005). The worked-out example principle in multimedia learning. In R.E. Mayer (Ed.), *The Cambridge handbook of multimedia learning* (pp. 229-245). New York: Cambridge University Press.

Renkl, A. (2011). Instruction based on examples. In R.E. Mayer and P.A. Alexander (Eds.), *Handbook of research on learning and instruction* (pp. 272-295). New York: Routledge.

Rennie, L.J., and McClafferty, T.P. (2002). Objects and learning: Understanding young children's interaction with science exhibits. In S.G. Paris (Ed.), *Perspectives on object-centered learning in museums* (pp. 191-213). Mahwah, NJ: Erlbaum.

Resnick, L., and Resnick, D. (1992). Assessing the thinking curriculum: New tools for educational reform. In B.R. Gifford and M.C. O'Connor (Eds.), *Changing assessments: Alternative views of aptitude, achievement and instruction* (pp. 37-75). Boston, MA: Kluwer Academic.

Roberts, B.W., Walton, K.E., and Viechtbauer, W. (2006). Patterns of mean-level change in personality traits across the life course: A meta-analysis of longitudinal studies. *Psychological Bulletin, 132*(1), 1-25.

Roberts, B., Kuncel, N., Shiner, R., Caspi, A., and Goldberg, L. (2007). The power of personality: The comparative validity of personality traits, socioeconomic status, and cognitive ability for predicting important life outcomes. *Perspectives on Psychological Science, 2*, 313.

Roediger, H.L., III., and Karpicke, J.D. (2006). The power of testing memory: Basic research and implications for educational practice. *Perspectives on Psychological Science, 1,* 181-210.

Roscoe, R.D., and Chi, M.T.H. (2007). Understanding tutor learning: Knowledge-building and knowledge-telling in peer tutors' explanations and questions. *Review of Educational Research, 77,* 534-574.

Rosenbloom, P.S., and Newell, A. (1987). Learning by chunking: A production-system model of practice. In D. Klahr, P. Langley, and R. Neches (Eds.), *Production system models of learning and development* (pp. 221-286). Cambridge, MA: Bradford Books/MIT Press.

Rotter, J.B. (1990). Internal versus external control of reinforcement: A case history of a variable. *American Psychologist, 45,* 489-493.

Roy, M., and Chi, M.T.H. (2005). The self-explanation principle in multimedia learning. In R.E. Mayer (Ed.), *The Cambridge handbook of multimedia learning* (pp. 271-286). New York: Cambridge University Press.

Sackett, P.R., Schmitt, N., Ellingson, J.E., and Kabin, M.B. (2001). High stakes testing in employment, credentialing, and higher education: Prospects in a post-affirmative action world. *American Psychologist, 56*(4), 302-318.

Sadler, D.R. (1989). Formative assessment and the design of instructional systems. *Instructional Science, 18,* 119-144.

Salas, E., DiazGranados, D., Klein, C., Burke, C.S., Stagl, K.C., Goodwin, G.F., and Halpin, S.M. (2008). Does team training improve team performance? A meta-analysis. *Human Factors, 50*(6), 903-933.

Schiefele, U. (2009). Situational and individual interest. In K.R. Wentzel and A. Wigfield (Eds.), *Handbook of motivation at school* (pp. 197-222). New York: Routledge.

Schmidt, F.L., and Hunter, J. (1998). The validity and utility of selection methods in personnel psychology: Practical and theoretical implications of 85 years of research findings. *Psychological Bulletin, 124*(2), 262-274.

Schmidt, F.L., and Hunter, J. (2004). General mental ability in the world of work: Occupational attainment and job performance. *Journal of Personality and Social Psychology, 86*(1), 162-173.

Schoenfeld, A. (1985). Metacognitive and epistemological issues in mathematical problem solving. In E.A. Silver (Ed.), *Teaching and learning mathematical problem solving: Multiple research perspectives* (pp. 361-379). Hillsdale, NJ: Erlbaum.

Schoenfeld, A. (1992). Learning to think mathematically: Problem solving, metacognition, and sense making in mathematics. In D.A. Grouws (Ed.), *Handbook of research on mathematics teaching and learning* (pp. 334-370). New York: Macmillan.

Schultz, T.W. (1961). Investment in human capital. *American Economic Review, 51*(1), 1-17.

Schultz, T.W. (1975). The value of the ability to deal with disequilibria. *American Economic Review, 13*(3), 827-846.

Schunk, D.H., and Hanson, A.R. (1985). Peer models: Influences on children's self-efficacy and achievement. *Journal of Educational Psychology, 77,* 313-322.

Schunk, D.H., and Pajares, F. (2009). Self-efficacy theory. In K.R. Wentzel and A. Wigfield (Eds.), *Handbook of motivation at school* (pp. 35-54). New York: Routledge.

Schunk, D.H., and Zimmerman, B.J. (2006). Competence and control beliefs: Distinguishing the ends and means. In P.A. Alexander and P.H. Winne (Eds.), *Handbook of educational psychology* (2nd ed., pp. 349-367). Mahwah, NJ: Erlbaum.

Schunk, D.H., Pintrich, P.R., and Meece, J.L. (2008). *Motivation in education* (3rd ed.). Upper Saddle River, NJ: Pearson.

Schwartz, D.L., Bransford, J.D., and Sears, D. (2005). Efficiency and innovation in transfer. In J.P. Mestre (Ed.), *Transfer of learning from a modern multidisciplinary perspective* (pp. 1-51). Greenwich, CT: Information Age.

Scribner, S. (1984). Studying working intelligence. In B. Rogoff and J. Lave (Eds.), *Everyday cognition: Its development in social context*, (pp. 9-40). Cambridge, MA: Harvard University Press.

Secretary's Commission on Achieving Necessary Skills. (1991). *What work requires of schools: A SCANS report for America 2000*. Washington, DC: U.S. Department of Labor. Available: http://wdr.doleta.gov/SCANS/whatwork/ [April 2012].

Shavelson, R.J., Baxter, G.P., and Gao, X. (1993). Sampling variability of performance assessments. *Journal of Educational Measurement, 33*(3), 215-232.

Shepard, L.A. (2005). *Linking formative assessment to scaffolding. Educational Leadership, 63*(3), 66-70.

Shepard, L.A. (2006). Classroom assessment. In R.L. Brennan (Ed.), *Educational measurement* (pp. 623-646). Washington, DC: National Council on Measurement in Education and American Council on Education/Praeger.

Shoda, Y., Mischel, W., and Peake, P.K. (1990). Predicting adolescent cognitive and self-regulatory competencies from preschool delay of gratification: Identifying diagnostic conditions. *Developmental Psychology, 26,* 978-986.

Shulman, L.S., and Keislar, E.R. (Eds.). (1966). *Learning by discovery: A critical appraisal.* Chicago: Rand McNally.

Shute, V.J. (2008). Focus on formative feedback. *Review of Educational Research, 78,* 153-189.

Siegler, R.S., and Ramani, G.B. (2009). Playing linear number board games—but not circular ones—improves low-income preschoolers' numerical understanding. *Journal of Educational Psychology, 101,* 545-560.

Silver, E.A. (Ed.). (1985). *Teaching and learning mathematical problem solving: Multiple research perspectives.* Hillsdale, NJ: Erlbaum.

Silver, E.A. (1994). Mathematical thinking and reasoning for all students: Moving from rhetoric to reality. In D.F. Robitaille, D.H. Wheeler, and C. Kieran (Eds.), *Selected lectures from the 7th international congress on mathematical education* (pp. 311-326). Sainte-Foy, Quebec: Les Presses De L'Université Laval.

Silver, E.A., and Mesa, V. (2011). Coordination characterizations of high-quality mathematics teaching: Probing the intersection. In Y. Li and G. Kaiser (Eds.), *Expertise in mathematics instruction: An international perspective* (pp. 63-84). New York: Springer.

Simon, H.A. (1979). *Models of thought.* New Haven, CT: Yale University Press.

Singley, M.K., and Anderson, J.R. (1989). *The transfer of cognitive skill.* Cambridge, MA: Harvard University Press.

Sirin, S.R. (2005). Socioeconomic status and academic achievement: A meta-analytic review of research 1990-2000. *Review of Educational Research, 75*(3), 417-453.

Smith, C., Snir, J., and Grosslight, L. (1992). Using conceptual models to facilitate conceptual change: The case of weight-density differentiation. *Cognition and Instruction, 9,* 221-283.

Smith, C.L., Grosslight, L., Davis, H., Maclin, D., Unger, C., and Snir, J. (1994). *Archimedes and beyond: Helping middle school students to construct an understanding of density and matter.* Cambridge, MA: Weight and Density Research Group, Harvard University.

Smith, E.S. (1999). The effects of investments in the social capital of youth on political and civic behavior in young adulthood: A longitudinal analysis. *Political Psychology, 20*(3), 553-580.

Snow, C.E. (2002). *Reading for understanding: Toward an R&D program in reading comprehension.* Santa Monica, CA: RAND. Available: http://www.rand.org/pubs/monograph_reports/MR1465.html [February 2012].

Son, J.Y., and Goldstone, R.L. (2009). Fostering general transfer with specific simulations. *Pragmatics and Cognition, 17,* 1-42.

Spearman, C. (1904). General intelligence: Objectively determined and measured. *American Journal of Psychology, 15,* 201-292.

Spearman, C. (1927). *The abilities of man: Their nature and measurement.* New York: Macmillan.

Srivastava, S., John, O.P., Gosling, S.D., and Potter, J. (2003). Development of personality in early and middle adulthood: Set like plaster or persistent change? *Journal of Personality and Social Psychology, 84*(5), 1,041-1,053.

Stake, R.E., and Easley, J. (1978). *Case studies in science education.* Urbana, IL: University of Illinois.

Stein, M.K., and Lane, S. (1996). Instructional tasks and the development of student capacity to think and reason: An analysis of the relationship between teaching and learning in a reform mathematics project. *Educational Research and Evaluation, 2*(1), 50-80.

Stein, M.K., Grover, B.W., and Henningsen, M. (1996). Building capacity for mathematical thinking and reasoning: An analysis of mathematical tasks used in reform classrooms. *American Educational Research Journal, 33,* 455-488.

Stenner, A.J., Burdick, D.S., and Stone, M.H. (2008). Formative and reflective models: Can a Rasch analysis tell the difference? *Rasch Measurement Transacation, 22*(1), 1,152-1,153.

Sternberg, R.J. (1990). *Metaphors of mind: Conceptions of the nature of human intelligence.* New York: Cambridge University Press.

Stigler, J.W., and Hiebert, J. (1999). *The teaching gap.* New York: The Free Press.

Stigler, J.W., Gonzalez, P., Kawanaka, T., Knoll, S., and Serrano, A. (1999). *The TIMSS videotape classroom study: Methods and findings from an exploratory research project on eighth-grade mathematics instruction in Germany, Japan, and the United States* (NCES 1999-074). Washington, DC: U.S. Department of Education: National Center for Education Statistics.

Stodolsky, S.S. (1988). *The subject matters: Classroom activities in math and social sciences.* Chicago: University of Chicago.

Storms, M.D., and Nisbett, R.E. (1970). Insomnia and the attribution process. *Journal of Personality and Social Psychology, 16,* 319-328.

Strobel, J., and van Barneveld, A. (2009). When is PBL more effective? A meta-synthesis of meta-analyses comparing PBL to conventional classrooms. *Interdisciplinary Journal of Problem-based Learning, 3*(1), 43-58. Available: http://docs.lib.purdue.edu/cgi/view content.cgi?article=1046&context=ijpbl [December 2011].

Summers, J.J. (2008). Cognitive approaches to motivation in education. In T.L. Good (Ed.), *21st century education: A reference handbook* (vol. 1, pp. 113-120). Thousand Oaks, CA: Sage.

Sweet, M.A., and Appelbaum, M.I. (2004). Is home visiting an effective strategy? A meta-analytic review of home visiting programs for families with young children. *Child Development, 75,* 1,435-1,456.

Sweller, J. (1999). *Instructional design in technical areas.* Melbourne: ACER Press.

Sweller, J., and Cooper, G.A. (1985). The use of worked examples as a substitute for problem solving in learning algebra. *Cognition & Instruction, 2,* 59-89.

Taboada, A., Tonks, S., Wigfield, A., and Guthrie, J. (2009). Effects of motivational and cognitive variables on reading comprehension. *Reading and Writing, 22,* 85-106.

Tharp, R.G., and Gallimore, R. (1988). *Rousing minds to life.* Cambridge, UK: Cambridge University Press.

Thorndike, E.L. (1903). *Educational psychology.* New York: Lemchke and Buechner.

Thorndike, E.L. (1918). The nature, purposes, and general methods of measurements of educational products. In G.M. Whipple (Ed.), *The measurement of educational products. The seventeenth yearbook of the National Society for the Study of Education, Part II.* (pp. 16-24). Bloomington, Indiana: Public School.

Thorndike, E.L. (1923). The influence of first-year Latin upon the ability to read English. *School Sociology, 17,* 165-168.

Thorndike, E.L. (1927). The law of effect. *American Journal of Psychology, 39,* 212-222.

Thorndike, E.L. (1932). *The fundamentals of learning.* New York: Teachers College Press.

Thorndike, E.L., and Woodworth, R.S. (1901). The influence of improvement in one mental function upon the efficiency of other functions. *Psychological Review, 8,* 247-261.

Thurow, L. (1975). *Generating inequality: Mechanisms of distribution in the U.S. economy.* New York: Basic Books.

Tobias, S., and Duffy, T.M. (Eds.). (2009). *Constructivist instruction: Success or failure?* New York: Routledge.

U.S. Department of Labor. (1983). *Test validation for 12,000 jobs: An application of job classification and validity generalization analysis to the general aptitude test battery.* USES Test Research Report No. 45. Division of Counseling and Test Development, Employment and Training Administration. Washington, D.C: Author.

van Eijck, K., and de Graaf, P.M. (2004). The big five at school: The impact of personality on educational attainment. *Netherlands' Journal of Social Sciences, 40*(1), 24-40.

Vitaro, F., Brendengen, M., Larose, S., and Tremblay, R.E. (2005). Kindergarten disruptive behaviors, protective factors, and educational achievement by early adulthood. *Journal of Educational Psychology, 97,* 617-629.

Voogt, J., and Parcja Roblin, N. (2010). *21st century skills discussion paper.* Report prepared for Kennisnet, University of Twente, the Netherlands. Available: http://www.international symposiumoneducationalreform.com/storage/21st%20Century%20Skills.pdf [October 2011].

Webb, N.L. (1999). *Alignment of science and mathematics standards and assessments in four states.* Research monograph #18, National Institute for Science Education and Council of Chief State School Officers. Madison: Wisconsin Center for Education Research. Available: http://www.wcer.wisc.edu/archive/nise/publications/Research_Monographs/vol18.pdf [February 2012].

Webster-Wright, A. (2009). Reframing professional development through understanding authentic professional learning. *Review of Educational Research, 79*(2), 702-739.

Weiss, I.R., and Pasley, J.D. (2004). What is high-quality instruction? *Educational Leadership, 61*(5), 24.

Weiss, I.R., Banilower, E.R., McMahon, K.C., and Smith, P.S. (2001). *Report of the 2000 National Survey of Science and Mathematics Education.* Chapel Hill, NC: Horizon Research.

Weiss, I.R., Pasley, J.D., Smith, P.S., Banilower, E.R., and Heck, D.J. (2003). *Looking inside the classroom: A study of K-12 mathematics and science education in the United States.* Chapel Hill, NC: Horizon Research.

Welch, F. (1970). Education in production. *Journal of Political Economy, 78*(1), 35-59.

Wentzel, K.R., and Wigfield, A. (Eds.). (2009). *Handbook of motivation at school.* New York: Routledge.

Wertheimer, M. (1959). *Productive thinking.* NY: Harper & Rowe.

Wigfield, A., Guthrie, J., Perencevich, K., Taboada, A., Klauda, S., McRae, A., and Barbosa, P. (2008). Role of reading engagement in mediating effects of reading comprehension instruction on reading outcomes. *Psychology in the Schools, 45,* 432-445.

Wigfield, A., Tonks, S., and Klauda, S.L. (2009). Expectancy-value theory. In K.R. Wentzel and A. Wigfield (Eds.), *Handbook of motivation at school* (pp. 55-76). New York: Routledge.

Willis, J.O., Dumont, R., and Kaufman, A.S. (2011). Factor-analytic models of intelligence. In R.J. Sternberg and S.B. Kaufman (Eds.), *The Cambridge handbook of intelligence* (pp. 39-57). New York: Cambridge University Press.

Wilson, S. (2011). *Effective STEM teacher preparation, induction, and professional development*. Paper presented at the NRC Workshop on Highly Successful STEM Schools or Programs. Available: http://www7.nationalacademies.org/bose/Successful_STEM_Schools_Homepage.html [May 2011].

Wilson, T.D., and Linville, P.W. (1982). Improving the academic performance of college freshmen: Attribution therapy revisited. *Journal of Personality and Social Psychology, 42,* 367-376.

Wilson, T.D., and Linville, P.W. (1985). Improving the performance of college freshmen with attributional techniques. *Journal of Personality and Social Psychology, 49,* 287-293.

Windschitl, M. (2009). *Cultivating 21st century skills in science learners: How systems of teacher preparation and professional development will have to evolve*. Paper commissioned for the NRC Workshop on Exploring the Intersection between Science Education and the Development of 21st Century Skills. Available: http://www7.nationalacademies.org/bose/WindschitlPresentation.pdf [June 2011].

Wolters, C. (2010). *Self-regulated learning and the 21st century competencies*. Paper prepared for the NRC Planning Meeting on 21st Century Competencies. Available: http://www7.nationalacademies.org/BOTA/Wolters_Self_Regulated_Learning_Paper.pdf [December 2011].

Yaeger, D.S., and Walton, G.M. (2011). Social-psychological interventions in education: They're not magic. *Review of Educational Research, 81,* 267-301.

Zuckerman, E. (2012). A small world after all? *The Wilson Quarterly, XXXVI(2),* 44-47.

Zukin, C., Ketter, S., Andolina, M., Jenkins, K., and Delli Carpini, M.X. (2006). *A new engagement? Political participation, civic life, and the changing American citizen*. New York: Oxford University Press.

Appendix A

21st Century Skills and Competencies Included in the OECD Survey

1. Creativity/innovation
2. Critical thinking
3. Problem solving
4. Decision making
5. Communication
6. Collaboration
7. Information literacy
8. Research and inquiry
9. Media literacy
10. Digital citizenship
11. Information and communications technology operations and concepts
12. Flexibility and adaptability
13. Initiative and self-direction
14. Productivity
15. Leadership and responsibility
16. Other (please specify)

SOURCE: Adapted from Ananiadou and Claro (2009).

Appendix B

Reports on 21st Century Skills Used in Aligning and Clustering Competencies

Report	Skills
Association for Career and Technical Education. (2010). *What Is Career Ready?* Alexandria, VA: Author. Available: http://dpi.wi.gove/oea/pdf/crpaper.pdf [October 2011].	• Critical thinking • Problem solving • Oral/written communication • Creativity • Adaptability • Diversity • Continuous learning • Collaboration • Teamwork • Responsibility • Professionalism/ethics
Bedwell, W.L., Salas, E., and Fiore, S.M. (2011). *Developing the 21st Century (and Beyond) Workforce: A Review of Interpersonal Skills and Measurement Strategies.* Paper prepared for the NRC Workshop on Assessing 21st Century Skills. Available: http://www7.nationalacademies.org/bota/21st_Century_Workshop_Salas_Fiore_Paper.pdf [October 2011].	• Active listening • Oral communication • Written communication • Cooperation • Coordination • Trust • Service orientation • Conflict resolution • Negotiation • Assertive communication • Self-presentation • Social influence

Report	Skills
Binkley, M., Erstad, O., Herman, J., Raizen, S., Ripley, M., and Rumble, M. (2010). *Defining 21st Century Skills*. White Paper commissioned for the Assessment and Teaching of 21st Century Skills Project (ATC21S). Available on request from ATC21S: http://atc21s.org/index.php/resources/white-papers/#item1.	• Critical thinking • Problem solving • Decision making • Information literacy (including research on sources, evidence, biases) • Information and communications technology literacy • Creativity/innovation • Personal and social responsibility (including cultural awareness and competence) • Communication • Collaboration
Conley, D.T. (2007). *Redefining College Readiness*. Eugene, OR: Educational Policy Improvement Center. Available: https://www.epiconline.org/files/pdf/RedefiningCollegeReadiness.pdf [October 2011].	• Problem solving • Analysis • Reasoning/argumentation • Interpretation
Finegold, D., and Notabartolo, A.S. (2010). *21st Century Competencies and Their Impact: An Interdisciplinary Literature Review*. Paper commissioned for the NRC Project on Research on 21st Century Competencies: A Planning Process on Behalf of the Hewlett Foundation. Available: http://www7.nationalacademies.org/bota/Finegold_Notabartolo_Impact_Paper.pdf [October 2011].	• Critical thinking • Problem solving • Decision making • Information literacy • Information and communication technology literacy • Creativity/innovation • Flexibility • Communication • Collaboration • Leadership • Responsibility • Initiative • Self-direction • Productivity
Hoyle, R.H., and Davisson, E.K. (2011). *Assessment of Self-Regulation and Related Constructs: Prospects and Challenges*. Paper prepared for the NRC Workshop on Assessment of 21st Century Skills. Available: http://www7.nationalacademies.org/bota/21st_Century_Workshop_Hoyle_Paper.pdf [October 2011].	• Executive function (inhibition, working memory, shifting) • Leadership • Type 1 processes (forethought, performance, self-reflection) • Type 2 processes (self-monitoring, self-evaluation, self-reinforcement)

Report	Skills
Voogt, J., and Pareja Roblin, N. (2010). *21st Century Skills Discussion Paper.* Report prepared for Kennisnet, University of Twente, The Netherlands. Available: http://www.internationalsymposium oneducationalreform.com/storage/21st% 20Century%20Skills.pdf [October 2011].	• Problem solving • ICT literacy • Creativity • Communication • Collaboration

Appendix C

Biographical Sketches of Committee Members

JAMES W. PELLEGRINO (*Chair*) is a liberal arts and sciences distinguished professor and distinguished professor of education at the University of Illinois at Chicago (UIC). He is co-director of UIC's interdisciplinary Learning Sciences Research Institute. Dr. Pellegrino's current work is focused on analyses of complex learning and instructional environments, including those incorporating powerful information technology tools, with the goal of better understanding. A special concern of his research is the incorporation of effective formative assessment practices, assisted by technology, to maximize student learning and understanding. Dr. Pellegrino has served on numerous National Research Council (NRC) boards and committees, including the Board on Testing and Assessment. He co-chaired the NRC committee that authored the report *Knowing What Students Know: The Science and Design of Educational Assessment*. He recently helped the College Board build new frameworks for curriculum, instruction, assessment, and professional development in AP biology, chemistry, physics, and environmental science. Dr. Pellegrino earned his B.A. in psychology from Colgate University in Hamilton, New York, and both his M.A. and Ph.D. from the University of Colorado.

GREG J. DUNCAN is a distinguished professor of education at the University of California, Irvine. He has published extensively on issues of income distribution, child poverty, and welfare dependence. He is co-author with Aletha Huston and Tom Weisner of *Higher Ground: New Hope for the Working Poor and Their Children* (2007) and co-editor with Lindsay Chase Lansdale of *For Better and for Worse: Welfare Reform and the Well-Being* *of Children and Families* (2001). With Jeanne Brooks-Gunn, he co-edited two books on neighborhood poverty and child development. He continues to study neighborhood effects on the development of children and adolescents and other issues involving welfare reform, income distribution, and its consequences for children and adults. Duncan is a member of the interdisciplinary MacArthur Network on the Family and the Economy. He was elected president of the Society for Research in Child Development for 2009-2011. A member of the National Academy of Sciences, Dr. Duncan currently serves on the steering committee for the Board on Testing and Assessment's Workshop on Assessment of 21st Century Skills. He previously served as a member of the Panel to Review the National Children's Study Research Plan, and as co-chair of the Committee on Evaluation of Children's Health. He received his Ph.D. in economics from the University of Michigan.

JOAN L. HERMAN is director of the National Center for Research on Evaluation, Standards, and Student Testing (CRESST) at the University of California, Los Angeles. Her research has explored the effects of testing on schools and the design of assessment systems to support school planning and instructional improvement. Her recent work has focused on the validity and utility of teachers' formative assessment practices in mathematics and science. She also has wide experience as an evaluator of school reform and is noted in bridging research and practice. A former teacher and school board member, Herman also has published extensively in research journals and is a frequent speaker to policy audiences on evaluation and assessment topics. She is past president of the California Educational Research Association, has held a variety of leadership positions in the American Educational Research Association and Knowledge Alliance, is a member of the Joint Committee for the Revision of the Standards for Educational and Psychological Measurement, co-chairs the Board of Education for Para Los Niños, and is current editor of *Educational Assessment*. She served as a member of the National Research Council's Committee on Test Design for K-12 Science Achievement as well as the Roundtable on Education Systems and Accountability and the Committee on Best Practices for State Assessment Systems and is chairing the Board on Testing and Assessment's Workshop on 21st Century Skills. Ms. Herman received her doctorate of education in learning and instruction from the University of California, Los Angeles.

MARGARET A. HONEY joined the New York Hall of Science as president and chief executive officer in November 2008. She is widely recognized for her work using digital technologies to support children's learning across the disciplines of science, mathematics, engineering, and technology. Prior to joining the New York Hall of Science, she was vice president of Wireless

Generation, an education technology company. Earlier, she spent 15 years as vice president of the Education Development Center (EDC) and director of EDC's Center for Children and Technology. There she directed numerous large-scale research projects funded by the National Science Foundation, the Institute for Education Sciences, the Carnegie Corporation, and other organizations. As a member of the Educational Advisory Board of the Partnership for 21st Century Skills, she worked closely with business representatives to define 21st century skills and consider how to teach and assess them. Her activities have included collaborations with public television, investigations of data-driven decision-making tools and practices, and creation of one of the first Internet-based professional development programs in the country. She currently serves on the National Research Council's Board on Science Education and recently chaired the Committee on Learning Science: Computer Games, Simulations, and Education. Earlier, she chaired the steering committee for the workshop on IT Fluency and High School Graduation Outcomes. She received her Ph.D. in developmental psychology from Columbia University.

PATRICK C. KYLLONEN is the director of the Center for New Constructs at Educational Testing Service (ETS), Princeton, New Jersey. Before joining ETS, he was a faculty member at the University of Georgia and director of the Cognitive Performance Division of the Air Force Research Laboratory. He is the recipient of numerous awards, including one from the technical cooperation program for the design, development, and evaluation of the trait-self-description (personality) inventory for use in five countries; has served on the board of several journals; has been a regular reviewer for the National Science Foundation, the Institute of Education Sciences, and other agencies; and is a fellow of Division 15 of the American Psychological Association. Dr. Kyllonen is known for his work on the measurement of human abilities, working memory, learning and skill acquisition, psychomotor abilities, personality assessment, computer-based testing, and psychometrics. Most recently his focus has been on noncognitive assessment. He currently oversees a wide array of research and development projects on measurement of noncognitive abilities at all levels of education, from kindergarten through graduate school. He participated in an expert planning meeting as part of the National Research Council project, Research on 21st Century Competencies: A Planning Process on Behalf of the Hewlett Foundation, and currently serves as a member of the steering committee for the Workshop on Assessment of 21st Century Skills. Dr. Kyllonen received his Ph.D. in educational psychology from Stanford University and his B.A. in experimental psychology from St. John's University.

HENRY M. LEVIN is the William Heard Kilpatrick professor of economics and education at Teachers College, Columbia University, and director of the National Center for the Study of Privatization in Education, a nonprofit, nonpartisan research organization. He is a specialist in the economics of education and human resources, cost-effectiveness analysis, school reform, and educational vouchers. Among his 21 published books are *Readings in the Economics of Education* with C. Belfield (2003) and *Privatizing Educational Choice* with C. Belfield (2005). He has served on several National Research Council committees, including the recent Committee on Strengthening Benefit-Cost Methodology for the Evaluation of Early Childhood Interventions, the Committee on Educational Excellence and Testing Equity (2000-2002), and the Panel on Secondary School Education for the Changing Workplace (early 1980s). He received his bachelor's degree in marketing and economics from New York University and his Ph.D. in economics from Rutgers University.

CHRISTINE MASSEY is the director of research and education at the Institute for Research in Cognitive Science at the University of Pennsylvania. She is also director of PENNlincs, which serves as an outreach arm of the Institute, linking recent theory and research in cognitive science to education efforts in public schools and cultural institutions. She has directed major projects that combine research investigating students' learning and conceptual development in science and math with the development and evaluation of new curriculum materials, learning technology, and educational programs for students and teachers. These projects include development of mathematics learning software that incorporates principles of perceptual learning, creation of the Science for Developing Minds curriculum series, development of a robotics curriculum for the middle grades, and kits and exhibit enhancements to support family learning in zoos and museums. She is an Eisenhower fellow and has also been a fellow in the Spencer Foundation/National Academy of Education's postdoctoral fellowship program. Dr. Massey served as a member of the National Research Council's steering committee for the Workshop on the Intersection of Science Education and 21st Century Skills. She earned her Ph.D. in psychology with a specialization in cognitive development at the University of Pennsylvania.

RICHARD E. MAYER is professor of psychology at the University of California, Santa Barbara, where he has served since 1975. His research interests are in educational and cognitive psychology. His current research involves cognition, instruction, and technology with a special focus on multimedia learning and computer-supported learning. He is past president of Division 15 (Educational Psychology) of the American Psychological Association, past vice president of Division C (Learning and Instruction) of the American

Educational Research Association, and former editor of the *Educational Psychologist*. From the American Psychological Association, he received the E.L. Thorndike Award for career achievement in educational psychology (in 2000) and the Distinguished Contribution of Applications of Psychology to Education and Training Award (in 2008). He has led many research projects funded by the Institute of Education Sciences, the National Science Foundation, and other agencies. He serves on the editorial boards of 14 journals, mainly in educational psychology, and is the author of numerous books and articles, including *Multimedia Learning: Second Edition* (2009), *Applying the Science of Learning* (2010), and the *Handbook of Research on Learning and Instruction* (editor, with P. Alexander, 2011). He served on the National Research Council's Committee on Opportunities in Basic Research in the Behavioral and Social Sciences for the U.S. Military and on the Mathematics Learning Study Committee. He received a Ph.D. in psychology from the University of Michigan in 1973.

C. KENT McGUIRE was recently appointed president and chief executive officer of the Southern Education Foundation. From 2003 to 2010, he served as dean of the College of Education and professor in the Department of Educational Leadership and Policy Studies at Temple University. Previously, he was senior vice president at MDRC, where his responsibilities included leadership of the education, children, and youth division. From 1998 to 2001, Dr. McGuire served in the Clinton administration as assistant secretary of education, focusing on research and development. Earlier, he was an education program officer at the Pew Memorial Trusts and at the Eli Lilly Endowment. Dr. McGuire's current research interests focus on the areas of education administration and policy and organizational change. He has been involved in a number of evaluation research initiatives on comprehensive school reform, education finance, and school improvement. He has written and co-authored various policy reports, monographs, book chapters, articles, and papers in professional journals. He is a member of the National Research Council's Committee on Independent Evaluation of DC Public Schools and previously served as a member of the Center for Education Advisory Board. He received his doctorate in public administration from the University of Colorado at Boulder.

P. DAVID PEARSON is a professor in the programs of language and literacy and cognition and development at the Graduate School of Education at the University of California, Berkeley, where he served as dean from 2001 to 2010. His current research focuses on reading instruction and reading assessment policies and practices. Previously, he was dean of the College of Education at the University of Illinois at Urbana–Champaign. A member of the National Academy of Education, he has served as president of the

National Reading Conference and on the board of directors of both the International Reading Association and the Association of American Colleges of Teacher Education. Among his honors are the William S. Gray Citation of Merit from the International Reading Association, the Oscar Causey Award for Contributions to Reading Research from the National Reading Conference, and the Alan Purves Award from the National Council of Teachers of English. He is the founding editor of the *Handbook of Reading Research*, now in its fourth volume, and has served on the editorial boards of many journals including *Reading Research Quarterly, Science, Journal of Literacy Research, Review of Educational Research, Journal of Educational Psychology,* and *Cognition and Instruction.* He currently serves on the National Research Council's Panel to Review Alternative Data Sources for the Limited-English Proficiency Allocation Formula. Professor Pearson received his B.A. in history from the University of California, Berkeley, after which he taught elementary school in California for several years, and completed his Ph.D. in reading education at the University of Minnesota.

EDWARD A. SILVER is William A. Brownell collegiate professor in education at the University of Michigan and holds a joint appointment in the School of Education and the Department of Mathematics. He is also currently serving as dean of the School of Education at University of Michigan–Dearborn. He was formerly at the University of Pittsburgh, where he was a professor in the School of Education and a senior scientist at the Learning Research and Development Center. His research interests focus on the teaching, learning, and assessment of mathematics, particularly mathematical problem solving. He is also actively involved in efforts to promote high-quality mathematics education for all students, particularly Hispanic and African American students. Dr. Silver's service with the National Research Council includes the Mathematical Sciences Education Board, the Study Group on Guidelines for Mathematics Assessment, the Committee on the Foundations of Assessment, and the Committee on the Study of Teacher Preparation Programs in the United States. He received a B.A. in mathematics from Iona College, an M.S. in mathematics from Columbia University, and an M.A and doctorate in mathematics education from Teachers College of Columbia University.

Index

[Page numbers followed by *b, f, n,* or *t* refer to boxed text, figure captions, notes, or tables, respectively.]

A

Achievement competency, academic performance and, 45–46
Adaptability and flexibility, 25, 55, 64, 89, 93, 138
After-school programs. *See* Informal learning environments
Agreeableness, 24, 29
American Association for the Advancement of Science, 126
Antisocial behavior
cognitive skills to reduce, 22
educational outcomes, 45–47, 94
employment outcomes, 51–52
evidence of linkage to adult outcomes, 4–5, 65
Anxiety, 45, 59
Apprenticeship teaching, 169–170
Argumentation skills, 6
learning goals for mathematics, 123–124
Assertiveness, 24

Assessing 21st century skills
in alignment with Common Core Standards and NRC framework, 13, 190
challenges to, 11–12, 149–150, 189–190
challenges to systemic implementation of interventions for deeper learning, 190–191, 193
classroom systems for, 179
for collaboration, 148, 149
cost of, 12, 189–190
evidence-based approach in, 144
intrapersonal and interpersonal competencies, 12, 148–149, 189
meaningful learning, 83
measurement of typical performance, 149–150
measures of cognitive competence, 22, 145–147
problem-solving skills, 145
to promote deeper learning, 165–166, 176–180, 188–190
psychometric analysis, 25–27, 189
purpose, 176–177
qualities of measures for, 177
recommendations for design and development of instruction, 9, 10, 181, 182

recommendations for development of
Common Core Standards and
science standards, 13, 192
recommendations for research, 12–13,
67, 192
recommendations for systemic
implementation of interventions
to promote 21st century skills,
13–14, 192–193
research needs, 12–13, 67, 189, 191
self-regulation skills, 95
student self-assessment, 178–179
study goals, 2
teacher capacity for, 12, 190
transfer of competencies, 144–145
Assessment, traditional
current approach, 11, 12, 145, 188–189
intelligence testing, 22
retention and recognition tests, 83
study goals, 2, 17–18
transfer tests, 83
See also Assessing 21st century skills
Assessment and Teaching of 21st Century
Skills, 16, 24
ATC21S project, 18, 149
Attention competency
academic performance and, 45–46
educational outcomes, 94
role of, 94
Auditory perception, 28

B

Bar exams, 145–146
Benchmarks for Science Literacy, 126
Bloom, B. S., 21
Board games, for mathematics instruction,
120–121b
Bowling Alone (Putnam), 59

C

Carnegie Corporation, 16–17
Cisco, 16
Civic engagement
definition, 59
determinants of, 60–61
educational attainment as predictive
of, 5, 66
trends, 59, 60

Cognitive competencies
achievement competency and, 45
assessment, 22, 145–147
component skills, 168
components of cognitive architecture,
75–76
deeper learning and, 74, 84–85
development of, to promote capacity
for transfer, 8–9, 180–181
differential psychology, 22–23
domain-general knowledge in problem
solving, 76–77
domain of 21st century skills, 3, 4, 21
employment outcomes and, 49–50
evidence of linkage to adult outcomes,
4, 37, 65–66
goals of Common Core Standards and
NRC framework, 6, 135
health outcomes and, 58
for learning, 98
learning goals for mathematics,
122–125
models of human thinking and
learning, 73–74
noncognitive determinants, 52
practice and feedback in, 79–82
to promote transfer, instructional
design for, 159–173
skill clusters, 4, 32t
stability over time, 23
strategies for coping with complexity,
104
structure of scientific knowledge, 128
successful interventions to promote
deeper learning, 150–159
taxonomy of reflective latent
variables, 27–28
trends in workplace demands, 54–56
types of intelligences, 23
See also Critical thinking skills;
Problem-solving skills
Cognitive load theory, 98
Collaboration. *See* Teamwork and
collaboration
College and career readiness, 1, 17, 35
Common Core State Standards for English
language arts and mathematics
anchor standards for reading,
109–111, 110f
articulation of 21st century
competencies in, 11

assessment frameworks and methods, 13, 190
conceptual approach to English arts instruction, 108–111
evolution of mathematics standards, 113–117
goals for capacity to transfer knowledge, 6, 7, 141
implementation challenges, 189, 191
NRC science framework and, 6
promotion of deeper learning principles in, 6
promotion of intrapersonal and interpersonal competencies in, 6
recommendations for assessment systems, 13
significance of, for future of education, 6, 101, 108
sociocultural perspective in, 74
study goals, 17
21st century skills in context of, 2, 102, 111–112, 114–115*b*, 123–124, 123*f*, 139–141, 189
Common Core State Standards for Mathematics, 117
Communication skills, 4, 16, 17, 24
as component of 21st century skills, 1–2
as element of interpersonal competence, 3, 59
goals of NRC science framework, 139
learning goals for mathematics, 123
trends in workplace demands, 54
Communities of practice, 95–96, 187
Competencies
definition, 3, 23
developmental psychology taxonomy, 45
O*NET content model, 30, 31*t*
psychometric analysis, 25–27, 189
See also Cognitive competencies; Interpersonal competencies; Intrapersonal competencies
Complexity, 104
Conduct disorders, 45
Conflict resolution, 4
Congress
recommendations for, 14
Conscientiousness, 24, 29, 89
in development of expertise, 8
as educational outcome factor, 38–39
employment outcomes, 50–51

evidence of linkage to adult outcomes, 4–5, 65
health outcomes and, 58
Construction of meaning, 104–105
Costs
assessment, 12, 189–190
employer investment in employee training, 155
Council of Chief State School Officers, 2, 17, 101
Creativity, 16, 17
as component of 21st century skills, 2
Critical thinking skills
four resources model of reading, 106–107
importance of, 16, 122–123
societal demand for, 1
study goals, 1–2, 17
See also Cognitive competencies
Crystallized intelligence, 23, 28
Curriculum
developmental considerations in design of, 186
divergent approaches to English arts instruction, 103–104
integrated, 7, 114–115*b*, 134
problem-solving and metacognitive strategies in, 170–171
to promote deeper learning, 7, 186
recommendations for design and development of instruction, 9–10, 181–182
recommendations for systemic implementation of interventions to promote 21st century skills, 13–14, 192–193
research needs, 186, 191
study goals, 2, 17–18
typical mathematics instruction, 113, 118
Curriculum and Evaluation Standards for School Mathematics, 116

D

Decoding texts, 106, 107–108
Deeper learning
assessment, 83, 176–180
case examples of learning environments for, 86–88, 120–121*b,* 136–137*b*
cognitive competencies and, 74, 84–85

components of, 84–86
current understanding of, 82–83,
    160*b*
definition, 1, 2–3, 5, 17, 74, 99
development of 21st century
    competencies and, 8, 19, 70, 74,
    99
early instruction to promote, 161
evidence-based guidelines for
    instruction to promote, 159–161
evidence of successful instructional
    intervention to promote,
    150–159
formative assessment to promote,
    165–166, 188–190
four resources model of reading,
    106–108
goals of Common Core Standards and
    NRC framework, 6, 111–112,
    114–115*b*, 123*f*, 189
guided discovery and feedback to
    promote, 162–164
instructional features for, 7–9, 97–99
interpersonal processes in, 95–97
in mathematics instruction, 119–122
objectives, 5–6, 69–70
practice and feedback in, 79–82
priming student motivation for,
    164–165
questioning techniques to promote,
    162
recommendations for design and
    development of instruction,
    9–10, 181
in science instruction, 131
study goals, 16–18
systemic implementation of
    interventions to promote, 19,
    185–186
teacher preparation for promoting,
    186–188
through problem-based learning,
    166–167
use of examples and cases to promote,
    164
use of multiple and varied
    representations to promote, 9,
    161–162, 163*b*, 181
See also Transfer of knowledge and
    skills
Department of Education, U.S., 13, 190

Depression, 45
Development
    considerations in curriculum design
        for deeper learning, 186
    early academic competencies and later
        academic achievement, 45–47
    intelligence, 23–24
    intrapersonal and interpersonal
        domains, 24
    personality traits, 24, 38
Differential psychology, 22–23
Digital technology
    cognitive demands, 3
    societal demand for 21st century
        skills, 53–54
    study goals, 2
    See also Information and
        communications technology
        literacy
Discourse skills, 6
Disparities in adult outcomes, development
    of 21st century competencies to
    reduce, 13, 190, 192–193
Diversity issues, 136, 138
Domain-general knowledge, 76–77

E

Edison, Thomas Alva, 16
Educational outcomes
    civic engagement and, 60–61
    correlations between competencies
        and behaviors in, 45–47
    development of 21st century
        competencies to reduce
        disparities in, 13–14, 190,
        192–193
    early competencies and later
        achievement, 45–47
    employment outcomes, 47–49
    evidence of linkage to adult outcomes,
        4, 5, 37, 66, 99
    evidence of 21st century skills as
        causal in, 4–5, 40–41*t*, 44*t*,
        65–66
    health outcomes and, 56–57
    international comparison, 15–16
    interpersonal processes in, 96
    personality factors, 38–39, 44*t*
    rates of monetary return, 47–48

significance of 21st century skills in, 2, 18–19
social good, 1, 15
socioeconomic factors, 16
study goals, 17
transfer in the labor market and, 61–64
Education and training of teachers, 186–188
Elementary and Secondary Education Act, 14, 193
Emotional functioning
  instructional design principles for enhancing, 175
  intrapersonal competency in, 3, 21
  stability, 30, 51
  successful interventions to promote competence in, 151–152, 153–154
Engaging Schools: Fostering High School Students' Motivation to Learn, 119
English language arts
  deeper learning goals, Common Core Standards and, 111–112, 114–115*b*
  development of Common Core Standards for, 101–102
  divergent approaches to instruction, 102–106
  four resources model, 106–108
  instructional interventions promoting intrapersonal competencies, 151
  integrated approach to instruction in Common Core Standards, 108–109, 114*b*
  See also Common Core State Standards for English language arts and mathematics; Reading skills
Essential processing, 98–99, 163*b*
Ethics, 2, 17
Examples and cases, instructional use of, 9, 164, 181
Expertise
  current understanding of, 78–79
  development of
  metacognition in, 91–92
  problem-solving strategies and, 77
  self-regulated learning in, 93
  transfer of knowledge and, 82, 85–86, 97–98
Externalizing behaviors, 45

Extraneous processing, 98–99, 163*b*
Extraversion, 26, 30
Extroversion, 29

F

Facebook, 53
Feedback
  in formative assessment, 177–178
  in guided discovery, 162–164
  importance of, in learning, 80–82, 147, 171
  to promote problem solving and metacognition, 10, 182
  self-regulated learning and, 93
Fifth Dimension, 154
Fluid intelligence, 23, 27
Forecasting ability, assessment of, 145
Formative assessment, 10, 165–166, 176, 177–180, 182, 188
Formative latent variable, 26, 27, 30
Four resources model, 106–108, 109–111
Framework for K-12 Science Education, A (NRC science framework), 18
  articulation of 21st century competencies in, 11
  assessment frameworks and methods, 13, 190
  cognitive competency goals in, 135
  Common Core State Standards for English language arts and mathematics, 6
  core disciplinary ideas, 132
  crosscutting concepts, 132–133, 134
  deeper learning goals in, 131
  goals for capacity to transfer knowledge, 6, 7, 141
  goals for science instruction, 130–131
  historical evolution of standards, 126
  implementation challenges, 189, 191
  interpersonal competencies in, 138
  intrapersonal competencies in, 135–137
  key practices, 133, 139
  organization of, 132
  promotion of deeper learning principles in, 6
  promotion of intrapersonal and interpersonal competencies in, 6

recommendations for assessment
systems, 13
significance of, for future of
education, 6, 101
sociocultural perspective in, 74
study goals, 17
21st century skills in context of, 2,
102, 131, 133–134, 135–141,
138f, 189
FrameWorks Institute, 18

G

Generative processing, 89, 98–99, 108,
163b
Gestalt psychology, 72, 82–83
Goal-setting, 21–22
Guided discovery, 162–164

H

Handbook of Educational Psychology,
159–161
Handbook of Reading Research, 105
Health outcomes
cognitive competency and, 58
educational attainment and, 56–57,
66
evidence of 21st century skills as
causal in, 4–5, 43, 65
personality traits and, 58
Hewlett Foundation, 18, 24, 131
Higher order thinking, 1, 17
How Students Learn: History,
Mathematics, and Science in the
Classroom, 121b

I

Individual differences, 22–23
Informal learning environments
exhibit design to promote deeper
learning, 162, 164, 165
priming student motivation in, 165
settings, 2, 17–18, 153
study goals, 2, 17–18
successful interventions to promote
deeper learning, 153–154

Information and communications
technology literacy, societal
demand for, 24, 53–56
Information processing model memory,
75–76, 75f
Initiation, 93
Innovation, 2, 16, 17
Insight, 72
Institute of Education Science, 159–161
Intel, 16
Intellectual openness, 89
Intelligence
developmental stability, 23–24
testing, 22, 168
types of, 23, 27–28
Internalizing behaviors, 45
Internet and social media
utilization trends, 53
See also Information and
communications technology
literacy
Interpersonal competencies
assessment challenges, 12, 149, 189
assessment measures, 22
current assessment practices, 148–149
deeper learning and, 95–97
developmental stability, 23, 24
development of, to promote capacity
for transfer of knowledge, 8,
180–181
domain of 21st century skills, 3, 4,
21, 22
employment outcomes, 55–56
evidence of linkage to adult outcomes,
4–5, 37, 65, 66
in goals of Common Core Standards
and NRC framework, 6,
111–112, 125, 138, 140
instructional design principles,
173–175
learning goals for mathematics, 125
recommendations for design and
development of instruction,
10–11, 182–183
self-regulated learning and, 93, 97
significance of, in learning, 22
skill clusters, 34t, 95
successful interventions to promote,
150–159
teaching practices to support deeper
learning, 7–8

Intrapersonal competencies
    assessment challenges, 12, 149, 189
    assessment measures, 22
    current assessment practices, 148–149
    for deeper learning, 99
    developmental stability, 23, 24
    development of, to promote capacity
        for transfer of knowledge, 8,
        180–181
    domain of 21st century skills, 3, 4,
        21–22
    evidence of linkage to adult outcomes,
        4–5, 37, 65, 66
    in goals of Common Core Standards
        and NRC framework, 6,
        111–112, 125, 135–137, 140
    instructional design principles, 173–175
    learning goals for mathematics, 125
    recommendations for design and
        development of instruction,
        10–11, 182–183
    significance of, in learning, 22
    skill clusters, 4, 33*t*, 88–89
    successful interventions to promote,
        150–159
    teaching practices to support deeper
        learning, 7–8
    See also Motivation; Self-regulation

J

Jangle fallacy, 25
John D. and Catherine T. MacArthur
    Foundation, 16–17

L

Latent variables, 25–27
    formative, 26, 27, 30
    reflective, 26, 27–30
Leadership skills, 4, 95
Learning 21st century skills
    formative assessment to promote, 176
    problem-based approach, 166–167
    role of beliefs and motivation in,
        89–91
    self-regulation in, 92–95
    study goals, 2, 17–18
    See also Deeper learning; Teaching 21st
        century skills and competencies

Learning theory
    memory processes in, 98
    sociocultural perspective, 73–74, 95,
        99
    strong and weak problem-solving
        strategies, 76–77
    of transfer, 70–72
    21st century skills in, 2, 17
    use of schemas, 78–79
Learning to learn, 1–2, 17
Lexical hypothesis, 28
Locus of control, 30, 30*n*
Long-term memory, 76

M

Mathematics
    attention competency and, 94
    case example of environment for
        deeper learning, 86–88, 150–151
    cognitive skills in, 122–125
    deeper learning expectations in,
        119–122
    early academic competencies and
        later academic achievement,
        45–47
    early instruction, 120–121*b*
    evolution of Common Core
        Standards, 113–117
    international comparison of student
        performance, 15–16
    learning goals for intrapersonal and
        interpersonal competency, 125
    recommendations for pedagogical
        reform, 118–119
    research perspectives on teaching for
        understanding, 117–119
    study goals, 17
    typical instructional approach, 113,
        118
    See also Common Core State
        Standards for English language
        arts and mathematics
Memory
    for expertise, 79
    information processing model, 75–76,
        75*f*
    learning theory, 98
    long-term, 76
    in metacognitive skills, 92
    schematic knowledge, 78

taxonomy of cognitive abilities, 28
types of learning outcomes, 83, 83t
working, 75–76
Mental health, academic performance and,
    45–46
Metacognition
    definition, 8, 22, 91, 167
    design principles for teaching,
        168–172, 172b
    function, 167–168
    mathematics instruction to promote,
        122
    recommendations for instruction to
        enhance, 10, 182
    significance of, in learning, 8, 91–92
Microsoft, 16
Model building skills, 145
Modeling, 10, 164, 169, 182
Monitoring and reflecting, 145, 170
Motivation
    in Common Core Standards
        framework, 111–112
    as component of 21st century skills,
        1–2, 17
    as determinant of intelligence, 23–24
    in learning, 89–91, 99
    priming, 10, 164–165, 181
    social dimensions of, 97
Multimedia learning, 98, 161–162, 163b

N

National Council of Bar Examiners,
    145–146
National Council of Teachers of
    Mathematics, 116
National Governors Association, 2, 17,
    101
National Institute of Child Health and
    Human Development, 105
National Science Education Standards,
    126–127, 132
National Science Foundation, 17
Nellie Mae Education Foundation, 17
Neuroticism
    definition, 29
    developmental patterns, 24
    educational outcomes and, 38–39
    employment outcomes and, 51
    health outcomes and, 58

interpersonal relationship success and,
    59
21st century competencies aligned
    with, 89
New basic skills, 1, 17
Next generation learning, 1, 17
Next Generation Science Standards, 13,
    101, 190
No Child Left Behind, 116, 129
Nonverbal communication skills
NRC science framework. See Framework
    for K-12 Science Education, A

O

Occupational Information Network, 25
O*NET content model, 30, 31t, 35–36
Openness to experience, 29, 30, 38–39, 89
Organisation for Economic Co-Operation
    and Development, 15–16, 23
Out-of-school programs. See Informal
    learning environments

P

Packet Tracer, 178
Parenting interventions to promote 21st
    century competencies, 154–155
Partnership for 21st Century Skills, 16, 131
Pearson Foundation, 17
Peer modeling, 165
Persistence, 1–2, 17, 125, 140
Personality theory
    determinants of relationship success,
        59
    determinants of school success,
        38–39, 44t
    developmental stability, 23–24, 38
    in differential psychology, 22–24
    employment outcomes, 50–51
    evidence of linkage to adult outcomes,
        65–66
    Five Factor model, 24, 28–30, 38,
        50–51
    predictors of health outcomes, 58
    taxonomy of reflective latent
        variables, 28–30
Positive Action Program, 153
Power law of practice, 80
Practice, 79–82, 171

Practice-based professional education, 186–187

Preventing Reading Difficulties in Young Children, 105

Priming student motivation, 10, 164–165, 181

Principles and Standards for School Mathematics, 116

Problem-based learning, 166–167

Problem-solving skills
adult outcomes and, 16, 17
assessment, 145
definition, 167
design principles for teaching, 167–172, 172*b*
instructional features of deep learning for, 8–9
learning goals for mathematics, 123–125
recommendations for instruction to enhance, 10, 182
societal demand for, 1
strong methods, 77
weak methods, 76–77
See also Cognitive competencies

Procedural information, 76

Productivity, 62–63, 66

Professional development, teacher
recommendations for systemic implementation of interventions to promote 21st century skills, 13–14, 193
reforms to support instruction for deeper learning, 186–188, 191
study goals, 2, 17–18

Professional Standards for Teaching Mathematics, 118

Programme for International Student Assessment, 15–16, 145, 146, 149

Prompting, in problem-solving instruction, 169

Putnam, Robert, 59

Q

Questioning techniques, 162

R

Raikes Foundation, 17

Reaction time, 28

Reading skills
anchor standards in Common Core Standards, 109–111, 110*f*
attention competency and, 94
divergent approaches to instruction, 102–103
early academic competencies and later academic achievement, 45–47
four resources model, 106–107, 109–111
integrated approach to instruction in Common Core Standards, 108–109
international comparison of student performance, 15–16
study goals, 17
See also Common Core State Standards for English language arts and mathematics; English language arts

Reciprocal teaching, 169–170

Recommendations
for design of instructional practices for deeper learning, 9–10, 181
for development of assessments of 21st century competencies, 12–13, 192
for research into instruction targeted to transferable intrapersonal and interpersonal competencies, 11, 182–183
for research into linkage between 21st century skills and adult outcomes, 5, 66–67
for research into transfer of knowledge and skills, 7, 141

Reflective latent variables
clusters of 21st century competencies, 35
cognitive abilities taxonomy, 27–28
definition, 26
personality taxonomy, 28–30

Representations of concepts and tasks, 9, 98, 128, 134, 161–162, 181

Research needs
    assessment of 21st century
        competencies, 12–13, 189, 191,
        192
    curriculum to develop 21st
        competencies, 186, 191
    instruction targeted to transferable
        intrapersonal and interpersonal
        competencies, 10–11, 182–183
    linkage between 21st century skills
        and adult outcomes, 5, 66–67
    self-regulated learning, 93–94
    self-regulation, 95
    transfer of knowledge within and
        across disciplines, 7, 141
Retrieval ability, 28
Rote learning, 9, 72, 82–83

S

Schematic knowledge, 78–79
Science and engineering instruction
    case example of deeper learning in,
        136–137b
    content and process approaches,
        126–128
    current practice, 129–130
    development of sophisticated scientific
        knowledge in, 128
    evolution of national standards for
        education in, 126
    hands-on activities in, 127
    inquiry in, 127
    in integrated curriculum, 134
    international comparison of student
        performance, 15–16
    science practices goals for, 130–131
    strands of science proficiency, 134
    study goals, 17
    teacher preparation for, 188
    See also Framework for K-12 Science
        Education, A (NRC science
        framework)
Science for All Americans, 126
Scientific method, 127
Secretary's Commission on Achieving
    Necessary Skills, 25, 35
Seeds of Science/Roots of Reading, 114b
Self-affirmation theory, 91
Self-direction, 93

Self-efficacy beliefs, 30, 51, 89–91, 140,
    164–165
Self-esteem, 30, 51
Self-evaluation, 30, 89, 178–179
Self-regulation
    academic and social outcomes
        predicted by, 94–95
    assessment, 95
    defining features of, 21–22, 94
    instructional interventions based on,
        93
    in learning, 92–94, 97, 99
    learning goals for mathematics, 125
    overlap with 21st century skills, 35,
        93, 140
    research needs, 93–94, 95
    social dimensions of, 97
    successful interventions to promote,
        152–153
Semantic information, 76
SimScientists, 146–147, 178
Skill acquisition curves, 80–82, 81f
Social and cultural competency
    determinants of success in personal
        relationships, 58–59
    role of social relationships in learning,
        95–96
    successful interventions to promote,
        151–152, 153–154
    as 21st century competency, 24,
        35
    See also Interpersonal competencies
Sociocultural models of learning, 73–74,
    95, 99
Socioeconomic disparities
    academic performance and, 16
    civic engagement and, 60
State assessments, 11, 111, 189, 191
Stereotype threat, 91
Student centered learning, 1, 17, 103
Study skills, 35
Stupski Foundation, 17
Summative assessment, 176, 188–189
Susan Crown Enchange Fund, 17
Systems thinking, 123

T

Taking Science to School, 129, 134

Teaching 21st century skills and
  competencies
  case example of learning environment
    for, 86–88
  challenges to systemic
    implementation, 190–191, 193
  cognitive competencies to promote
    transfer, instructional design for,
    159–173
  early intervention, 161
  implications of sociocultural model of
    human learning, 73–74
  instructional features for deeper
    learning, 7–9, 97–99
  intrapersonal and interpersonal
    domain, instructional design
    principles for, 173–175
  problem-solving and metacognitive
    strategies, 167–172
  recommendations for design and
    development of instruction,
    9–10, 181–182
  resources for implementation, 7
  role of assessment in, 176–180
  study goals, 2, 17
  successful intervention to promote
    deeper learning, 150–153
  teacher assessment skills for, 12
  teacher preparation for, 186–188
  use of examples and cases, 9, 164,
    181
Team training, 159, 175
Teamwork and collaboration
  assessment, 148, 149
  component skills, 95
  for learning, 95–96
  in mathematics instruction, 118–119
  in science education, 138
  self-regulated learning and, 93
  as 21st century skills, 1–2, 4, 16, 17,
    24
Tools of the Mind, 152
Transfer of knowledge and skills, 19, 143
  assessment challenges, 144–145
  assessment goals, 144
  challenges to systemic implementation
    of interventions to promote,
    190–191, 193
  as characteristic of 21st century skills,
    23, 74

cognitive competencies for,
    instructional design for
    enhancing, 159–173
  current understanding, 70–72, 82, 99
  definition, 15
  delineation of learning goals for
    instruction in, 144
  development of 21st century
    competencies to promote, 8–9,
    180–181
  domain-general knowledge for, 76–77
  domain-specific teaching for, 170,
    172–173
  educational attainment and capacity
    for, 5
  expertise and, 85–86, 97–98
  as goal of Common Core Standards
    and NRC framework, 6, 7, 141
  instructional challenges, 98
  labor market outcomes of educational
    attainment, 61–64
  as product of deeper learning, 5–6, 8,
    69–70, 99
  recommendations for research, 7, 141
  role of beliefs in, 89
  shortcomings of current practice and
    research needs, 7
  specific and general forms, 70–72
  successful instructional interventions
    to promote, 150–159
  types of knowledge and, 84–86
  types of learning and, 83, 83t
  use of schemas, 78
  workplace interventions to promote,
    155–159
  See also Deeper learning
21st century skills and competencies
  alignment with personality factors,
    31–35
  assessment challenges, 11–12
  clusters of component skills, 1–2, 3–4,
    25, 32–34t
  deeper learning for development of,
    5–6, 8, 70, 74, 99
  definition, 1, 2–3, 5, 6, 17, 23, 25,
    35, 67, 74
  degrees of correlation with adult
    outcomes, 37–38
  domains of competence, 3, 21–22, 25

evidence of causality in educational
and adult outcomes, 4–5, 37,
40–44*t*, 64–67
goals of Common Core Standards and
NRC framework and, 111–112,
123*f*, 131, 133–134, 135–141,
138*f*, 189
interactions among, 22
knowledge base, 24–25
parenting interventions to promote,
154–155
recommendations for design and
development of instruction,
9–10, 181
recommendations for research, 5,
66–67
recursive relationship with deeper
learning, 8, 99
resources for implementation in
current instructional practice, 7,
140
self-regulated learning and, 93
societal benefits of promoting, 190
societal demand for, 1, 15, 16, 53–56
study goals, 1–2, 16–18
successful instructional interventions
to promote, 150–159
systemic implementation of
interventions to promote, 13–14,
19, 185–190, 192–193
taxonomy, 35–36
transferable knowledge as
characteristic of, 23, 74
trends in education, 16
See also Teaching 21st century skills
and competencies
Twitter, 53

V

Visual perception, 28

W

William and Flora Hewlett Foundation,
16–17
Work ethic, 89
Working memory, 75–76, 98
Work outcomes
adaptability of firms to technological
change, 62–63
cognitive competency and, 49–50,
54–56
earnings, 47–48, 49, 54, 55, 63–64, 66
educational attainment and, 37,
47–49, 61–64, 66
evidence of 21st century skills as
causal in, 4–5, 37, 42–43*t*,
65–66
interpersonal skills as factor in, 55–56
noncognitive correlations, 51–53
nonmonetary rewards, 48
personality factors in, 50–51
significance of 21st century skills in,
2, 18–19, 70
study goals, 17
team training interventions, 159
transferability of skills across
occupations, 62–64
trends in marketplace demands,
53–56, 70
workplace interventions to promote
transferable competencies,
155–159
Writing skills, 107